# POVERTY ALLEVIATION THROUGH TOURISM DEVELOPMENT

## A Comprehensive and Integrated Approach

# ADVANCES IN HOSPITALITY AND TOURISM BOOK SERIES



## BOOKS IN THE SERIES:

**Food Safety: Researching the Hazard in Hazardous Foods**
Editors: Barbara Almanza, PhD, RD, and Richard Ghiselli, PhD

**Strategic Winery Tourism and Management: Building Competitive Winery Tourism and Winery Management Strategy**
Editor: Kyuho Lee, PhD

**Sustainability, Social Responsibility and Innovations in the Hospitality Industry**
Editor: H. G. Parsa, PhD
Consulting Editor: Vivaja "Vi" Narapareddy, PhD
Associate Editors: SooCheong (Shawn) Jang, PhD, Marival Segarra-Oña, PhD, and Rachel J. C. Chen, PhD, CHE

**Managing Sustainability in the Hospitality and Tourism Industry: Paradigms and Directions for the Future**
Editor: Vinnie Jauhari, PhD

**Management Science in Hospitality and Tourism: Theory, Practice, and Applications**
Editors: Muzaffer Uysal, PhD, Zvi Schwartz, PhD, and Ercan Sirakaya-Turk, PhD

**Tourism in Central Asia: Issues and Challenges**
Editors: Kemal Kantarci, PhD, Muzaffer Uysal, PhD, and Vincent Magnini, PhD

**Poverty Alleviation through Tourism Development: A Comprehensive and Integrated Approach**
Robertico Croes, PhD, and Manuel Rivera, PhD

**Chinese Outbound Tourism 2.0**
Editor: Xiang (Robert) Li, PhD

*Advances in Hospitality and Tourism*

# POVERTY ALLEVIATION THROUGH TOURISM DEVELOPMENT

## A Comprehensive and Integrated Approach

**Robertico Croes, PhD, and Manuel Rivera, PhD**

AAP | APPLE ACADEMI PRESS

Apple Academic Press Inc.
3333 Mistwell Crescent
Oakville, ON L6L 0A2
Canada

Apple Academic Press Inc.
9 Spinnaker Way
Waretown, NJ 08758
USA



*Exclusive worldwide distribution by CRC Press, a member of Taylor & Francis Group*



Printed in the United States of America on acid-free paper

International Standard Book Number-13: 978-1-77188-141-8 (Hardcover)

International Standard Book Number-13: 978-1-4987-3271-0 (eBook)



**Library and Archives Canada Cataloguing in Publication**

Croes, Robertico R., author
Poverty alleviation through tourism development : a comprehensive and integrated approach / Robertico Croes, PhD, and Manuel Rivera, PhD.

(Advances in hospitality and tourism book series)
Includes bibliographical references and index.
Issued in print and electronic formats.
ISBN 978-1-77188-141-8 (hardcover).--ISBN 978-1-4987-3271-0 (pdf)

1. Tourism--Latin America. 2. Poverty--Latin America.
3. Economic development--Latin America. I. Rivera, Manuel (Assistant professor), author II. Title. III. Series: Advances in hospitality and tourism book series

G155.L38C76 2015     338.4'791098     C2015-908023-1     C2015-908024-X

CIP data on file with US Library of Congress

Apple Academic Press also publishes its books in a variety of electronic formats. Some content that appears in print may not be available in electronic format. For information about Apple Academic Press products, visit our website at **www.appleacademicpress.com** and the CRC Press website at **www.crcpress.com**

# DEDICATION

*This book is dedicated to our families. Thanks for your continuous support and unconditional love.*

*We also like to dedicate this book to all the beautiful people that crossed our paths and inspired us to write this book.*

*"Beati pauperes spiritu"*

# ABOUT THE AUTHORS

**Robertico Croes, PhD**

**Robertico Croes, PhD,** currently serves as the Associate Dean, Interim Chair of the Tourism, Events and Attractions Department as well as the Associate Director of the Dick Pope Sr. Institute for Tourism Studies at Rosen College at the University of Central Florida in Orlando, Florida. Dr. Croes has published two recent books, titled *The Small Island Paradox: Tourism Specialization as a Potential Solution and Anatomy of Demand in International Tourism*. Additionally, he is a contributor to several other volumes. Dr. Croes has lectured and made presentations throughout the world, including Armenia, the Netherlands, Venezuela, Colombia, Brazil, Nicaragua, Costa Rica, Aruba, Curacao, the Bahamas, Jamaica, Malta, Ecuador, Barbados, Puerto Rico, and Mexico. His research has also been presented at predominant industry and research conferences around the world.

**Manuel Rivera, PhD**

**Manuel Rivera, PhD,** is an Assistant Professor at the Rosen College of Hospitality Management at the University of Central Florida in Orlando, Florida. Dr. Rivera also serves as the Managing Editor for a tier-one research journal *International Journal of Hospitality Management*. His empirical contributions include reference to important social issues such as poverty reduction through tourism, income inequality, income distribution, economic entrepreneurship opportunities for street vendors, and improving the quality of life for locals residing in tourism destinations in developing countries. He has collaborated with tourism organizations such as the Puerto Rico Convention Bureau, the Puerto Rico Hotel Association, the Cámara de Turismo de Nicaragua, the Consejo Provincial del Guayas in Ecuador, the Curaçao Tourism Bureau, the Aruba Tourism Authority, Coca-Cola's Latin Center Business Unit, and the Kissimmee CVB, among others, in order to assist in determining how to maximize tourism's benefits for host destinations. He has instructed many different courses in subject areas pertinent to hospitality and tourism management, restaurant management, and event management. Dr. Rivera also has experience working with music festivals in the Caribbean, more specifically the Curacao North Sea Jazz Festival, the Aruba Soul Beach Music Festival, and the Aruba Electric Festival. He has 20 years' experience working in the tourism and hospitality industry and has worked with leading national restaurant brands in the United States. He earned his educational degrees from Penn State University, Florida International University, and the University of Central Florida and also holds several certificates from Cornell University.

# CONTENTS

# LIST OF ABBREVIATIONS

| | |
|---|---|
| ADL | autodistributed lag model |
| BDH | Bono de Desarrollo Humano |
| CGE | computable general equilibrium |
| CIO | closed input-output |
| DPA | demand pull approach |
| ECLAC | Economic Commission for Latin America and the Caribbean |
| EDTC | Entrepreneurial Development Training Centre |
| FAO | Food and Agriculture Organization |
| FSI | Failed States Index |
| GDP | gross domestic product |
| GULL | Global University for Lifelong Learning |
| HDI | human development index |
| HDR | Human Development Reports |
| IIED | Institute for Environment and Development |
| ILO | International Labor Organization |
| IMF | International Monetary Fund |
| LAC | Latin America and the Caribbean |
| MDGs | Millennium Development Goals |
| OLS | ordinary least square |
| POP | poverty obliteration paradigm |
| PPP | purchasing power parity |
| PPT | pro-poor tourism |
| SWB | subjective well-being |
| TLG | tourism-led growth |
| TLGH | tourism led growth hypothesis |
| UNDP | United Nations Development Program |
| WTTC | World Travel and Tourism Council |

# PREFACE

The premise of this book is that tourism has the potential to reduce poverty in developing countries. Tourism as a development strategy has gone through cycles of hope and myth for the poor. The cycle has shifted from tourism holding the potential to alleviate poverty to spurring dependency and deterioration of the standard of living for the population in developing countries to, currently, a renewed potential for poverty reduction. Most tourism studies do not contemplate the poverty issue and rely more on trickle-down assumptions.

After more than fifty years of modern tourism, this industry has yet to garner the sufficient consensus and support it needs to be fully utilized as a tool to free the poor from poverty. Part of the problem is that the ability of tourism to deliver to the poor depends on contextual conditions, such as the mix of incentives and organizational capabilities. These conditions define how tourism economies are structured. Recent research indicates that the impact of tourism on the poor hinges more on the structure of tourism economies and less on the types of tourists patronizing destinations.

There are numerous advantages to tourism compared to the export of goods and services. Revenue from tourism may be more stable than revenue from the sale of goods, such as agricultural and mineral commodities. Additionally, tourism products can extract premium prices due to their uniqueness and the inability to export the experience, as well as low transportation and insurance costs. Yet, despite the advantages of tourism revenue, some critics claim that tourism receipts do not reduce poverty, but instead entrench inequality. They also argue that tourism may not automatically relieve poverty. Our research has suggested otherwise.

This book offers a comprehensive and integrated approach to the topic of tourism development and evidence of its contribution to the fight against poverty. The focus of the book is on the world's poorest, and the chapters explore how tourism connects to the poor and unlocks opportunities to escape the poverty trap. The United Nations is at the eve of taking score of its aim of halving the poor in the world, according to the Millennium Development Goals (MDGs) in 2015. It is therefore a fitting moment to assess the realization of the noble goal to alleviate this global scourge, specifically by evaluating the capacity for tourism to play a vital role in poverty reduction.

The MDGs triggered the pro-poor debate on a global scale, a debate that is centered on the notion that for growth to be pro-poor, growth has to go hand in hand with the reduction of inequality. In other words, the growth agenda should be consistent with the equity agenda. Many claim that income inequality is a barrier to poverty reduction, sows growth destruction and threatens democracy. The debate on the nexus poverty–growth–inequality has been strong, extensive, and polarizing over time, pitting those who claim that there is a positive correlation between growth and equality against those who assert that economic growth is irrelevant in reducing poverty when inequality levels remain unchanged. On the other hand, the shift in focus should change if inequality makes growth unsustainable, thereby disrupting poverty reduction strategies. The latter condition rigs the focus of economic development on how to reduce inequality.

Thus far, the tourism literature has not embraced the pro-poor debate in a comprehensive manner. This book is an attempt to do just that. It will assess the impact of tourism development on lifting people from below the poverty level as well as ascertaining if tourism development reduces the gap between the poor and the more affluent within a country. If, however, tourism development raises the income of everybody within a country, more so for the most affluent within that country, then surely tourism development may be efficient from an economic point of view but its impact would be highly inequitable. This means that tourism would help perpetuate an unfavorable development, which in the end will slow growth, thereby making everybody in that country worse off. Assessing the total impact of tourism development on the poor is therefore a rational imperative. From this perspective, the book provides a holistic look at the power of tourism development on the poverty issue in developing countries.

Tourism development is credited to be a powerful source of regional development in developing countries. According to the pro-poor movement, through economic mechanisms such as employment and social and business opportunities, as well as the appropriate distribution of government taxes to the poor, tourism development may reduce poverty. This reduction in poverty occurs in two forms that contribute to economies. The primary form spawns direct effects (e.g., jobs created by hotels and restaurants) emerging from market results and the power relations among owners of factors of production (capital and labor). The secondary form appears as indirect effects spawned by government intervention through regulation, management of macroeconomic conditions (inflation, employment, etc.), and transfer to the poor via social policy. Thus, tourism and its economic contribution are presumed to help the poor.

## WHY FOCUS ON THE POOR?

Poverty is conceived as a situation in which a person cannot meet certain pre-determined consumption requirements or experiences a failure to attain capabilities. The measurement is a head count ratio, a proportion of the population below the common poverty line established by the World Bank. This narrow definition is in contrast with a broader definition that is based on the perception of poverty as a multidimensional construct. The definition of poverty, according to the latter perspective, has shifted from it being perceived as due to unsatisfied material needs or being undernourished. A comprehensive definition would show that poverty also entails powerlessness, inequality, exclusion, vulnerability, relative deprivation, and marginalization.

The literature has attributed the persistence of poverty to issues related to resource endowments and accessibility, disease burden or geographical factors, exclusion, and inequality. Mainstream literature on development economics reveals three important conclusions. First, economic growth in developing countries is not persistent. Typically, per capita incomes do not grow steadily over time. Second, inequality levels in developing countries have persisted over time. And third, reducing inequality is a complex social assignment. Too little inequality may remove the incentives for people to work hard, save, and invest, thereby conflicting with the effective functioning of a market. Too much inequality, on the other hand, could waste talents and lives, be destructive for growth, and affect democracy. However, poverty is not only about motivation and choices; poverty is also about opportunities. Combining motivation and opportunities for the poor is the combustion that poverty programs require. However, mainstream development literature has not met the challenge of designing and delivering a specific pathway or set of pathways to enhance the lives of the poor.

The main premise in the development literature is that the poor should be helped. Reasons range from moral imperatives to the urgency to stop the waste of lives, talents, and capital. The debate lingers around the most effective ways to remedy poverty. For example, freedom seems a powerful concept that defines and shapes choices, aligns private and social interest through the market mechanism, and provides access to private property rights to the poor. The premise that freedom and empowerment may be antecedents for escaping poverty is shared in the literature, albeit under the condition of well-functioning institutions. Other scholars posit that only the poor can decide if they will escape the poverty trap. Thereby, they insist that investigating why the poor make certain choices will enhance the understanding of why some people are poor and remain this way. Others reject the notion that the poor can escape from poverty by themselves, asserting that only foreign aid will make the poor able to escape from poverty. Despite these theories, poverty has persisted.

Poverty has enormous consequences, wasting lives, talents, and the capacity for production. This loss robs millions of people the opportunity to enjoy a better quality of life. Consider this reality: 1.3 billion live in abject poverty (less than US$1.25/d) and one in three persons live with less than US$2.00 a day. About 17% of the population of developing countries is undernourished. And according to UNICEF, every day 22,000 children starve to death.[1] Nearly eight million children die every year before they reach the age of five, and almost 900 million people were chronically lacking food during 2010–2012.[2] The poorest 20% of the world's population accounts for 1.5% of the world's private consumption and the richest 20% consume an astonishing 77% (World Bank, 2009). Within developing countries, the imbalance of the consumption of the rich and the needs of the poor is also appalling. In Brazil, the richest 10% consume 50% of the economy, while the poorest 50% of the country only consume 10% of the economy. Brazil has one of the highest Gini (0.54) coefficients in Latin America.[3]

This abysmal reality of the poor has wasted significant resources in many countries. De Soto estimates that were the poor not excluded from the market and certain social arrangements met, such as private property, the global economy would thrive, producing an increased standard of living for everyone.[4] The exclusion of the poor meant a waste of about US$9 trillion of property, what De Soto termed "dead capital". The poor are thus trapped because they cannot use their assets (savings, houses or business) to generate capital, which they can use to increase their standard of living and free themselves from poverty.

## ARGUMENTS OF THE BOOK

The main premise of this book is that the poor should be helped out of self-interest. Investing in the poor (education, health, nutrition, and infrastructure) means augmenting the productive capacity of the whole economy, thereby increasing the incomes of everybody, including that of the poor. The extension of this premise is that growth is good for the poor and reducing poverty is good for growth. However, the benefits of economic growth cannot be maximized to favor the poor by ignoring the effects of inequality. This means that in order for growth benefits to reach the poor, an assumption must be met that growth is pro-poor. For growth to matter, it has to be inclusive of all players in the market, including the poor. This relationship between growth, poverty, and inequality is shaped by the context of a country's circumstances and choices. There is strong empirical evidence that suggests tourism development may generate facets of economic growth that could change the income configuration for locals.

An important question that should be asked is whether developing countries should continue to spend their scarce resources on tourism development as a means to create "decent" jobs. However, even if the new jobs and income go directly to the poor, it does not mean that they will be wealthier or at an advantage. This is because the relationship between economic growth and equity is not always self-evident in practice. One reason why this relationship fails to materialize in developing countries could be due to the lopsided effects of economic growth on the poor. In times of recession, the poor seem to suffer the most, while in times of prosperity, the poor seem to benefit the least. Therefore, balancing equity with growth becomes a necessity and a policy matter in poverty reduction strategies.

We suggest a new paradigm, *the poverty obliteration paradigm* (*POP*) that provides the theoretical integration of these three elements, although recognizing that these three elements are related in a complex way. *POP* combines opportunities and motivation and takes into account objective as well as subjective elements framing poverty. This paradigm suggests that this complex relationship depends on several intervening variables, such as the pace of poverty reduction, the structure of the economy, macroeconomic policies, health, and educational status. For example, if one of the parents has a job, a child does not have to work till late at night street-vending to squeeze out a living for the family, instead of doing homework and sleeping, or having access to clean water may release time and efforts (typically from small children) that can be used to go to school and study. Having additional resources (incomes) through poverty reduction or economic growth helps. The question is can tourism help in providing these additional resources to enable the poor to enjoy a better life and enhance their capabilities (borrowing from Sen: to lead the life they value)?

This proposition is an empirical question. While the flow of international tourism has increased significantly to developing countries during the past two decades, there appears to be little understanding on the extent to which the flow of money generated by tourism decreases poverty in the developing world. We know that in the past decade several countries have been excluded from the infamous list of "Least Developed Countries" (LDC) as they were helped by tourism development. For example, Cape Verde and the Maldives graduated from the LDC list assisted by tourism. Jobs and small businesses have been created in many underdeveloped regions of the developing world, helping to generate and distribute economic participatory opportunities. However, most studies have not examined the impact of tourism on poor people in a systematic way. The question of whether or not this population benefits from tourism development has remained elusive. In particular, the distributional effects of tourism on poverty reduction is conspicuously lacking in the tourism literature as well as research on subjective well-being of the poor in developing countries.

Therefore, the central question that this books attempts to answer is: can tourism development achieve pro-poor growth? To be exact, does growth from tourism infuse a double effect on poverty reduction, and one that is higher than average? And what choices should governments make? To focus on the poor is one thing, but choices can make things better or worse for the poor. To answer this question, this book builds on the works of Mitchell and Ashley,[5] Scheyvens,[6] and Saarinen et al.,[7] using a central focus on the poor as the unit of analysis.[8] The new book departs from the previous three studies in three fundamental ways: (1) it integrates the debate on the relationship growth-inequality-poverty reduction resonating in the mainstream development economics into tourism studies in a comprehensive way (2) it investigates the conditions that could bring about the twin effects of tourism development on poverty reduction; and (3) it embraces empiricism as its central perspective instead of a normative or ideological perspective.

This book improves our understanding of the dynamic relationship between tourism and poverty reduction in four important ways. First, it explores poverty and its impact upon development at the macro and micro levels. Second, it focuses on tourism development and its effects on growth, inequality, and poverty reduction and how these dynamic relationships affect the most vulnerable groups of the society. Third, it documents whether the poor perceive tourism development as an important vehicle to help them escape from poverty. And fourth, it maps the conditions under which tourism reaches the poor and how the connectedness with tourism capacity defines the opportunities for the poor.

This book is the result of a decade spent studying the effects of tourism development on poverty reduction. Our interest in this topic took us to several countries, particularly to Latin America. Our search for answers also made us study through readings about countries from other continents. When visiting these countries, we would often see poor individuals roaming the streets in search of food, looking confused, weak, and helpless. In some places, people carried out their bare physiological necessities on the streets, defecating in the open by the roadside. Public safety and public health were intertwined with deleterious consequences. The streets were littered, diseases lingered, and areas were covered by a veil of insecurity and fear, instilling a sense of danger and signaling a place off limits.

We saw children aged 6 and 7 years old working late at night as street vendors instead of staying at home doing homework or studying, not aware of the dangers of the street with no future in sight. This picture was very common in the streets of Managua, the Pacific coast of Nicaragua, in the Cerros of Caracas, the Quindio coffee region in Colombia, Puntarenas in Costa Rica, Guayas, Santa Elena, Salinas, Puna, Montañita, Olon in Ecuador, and Colima in Mexico. This view of despair always provoked sadness as well as compelled us to further seek answers and better understand why people are poor, what it takes to free oneself from poverty, and the dynamics of tourism that can pave the road toward freedom from starvation.

Through our experiences, we came to realize ways in which our lives are somewhat parallel. We too strive to live our lives with passion and hopefulness, and seek to view reality with optimism. For the many individuals that we met, poverty is an intricate social phenomenon in which command over resources or commodities seemed a far cognizance when compared to procuring opportunities, respect, and a voice. Throughout our many conversations, any palpable difference between us in terms of sources of income seemed secondary. For the many courageous and magnificent individuals that we came across in some of the poorest communities in

Ecuador, Costa Rica, Nicaragua, Colombia, and Mexico, the inability to exercise choices and freedom and helpless feelings such as powerlessness and lack of attention, was vocalized to a greater extent and took precedence over any discussion about monetary wealth. This book is about these people and how tourism can help them to help themselves and attain freedom from the doldrums of poverty.

## REFERENCES

De Soto, H. *The Mystery of Capital*; Basic Books Perseus Books Group: New York, NY, 2000.

FAO. *The State of Food Insecurity in the World 2012*; FAO: Rome, 2012.

Mitchell, J.; Ashley, C. *Tourism and Poverty Reduction: Pathways to Prosperity*; The Cromwell Press Group: London, UK, 2010.

Saarinen, J.; Rogerson, C.; Manwa, H.; Eds. *Tourism and the Millennium Development Goals*; Routledge: New York, NY, 2013.

Scheyvens, R. *Tourism and Poverty*; Routledge: New York, NY, 2011.

World Bank. *A Break with History: Fifteen Years of Inequality Reduction in Latin America, (LAC Poverty and Labor Brief)*. In *Poverty, Equity and Gender Unit, Latin America and the Caribbean*; the World Bank: Washington, DC, 2011.

World Bank. *World Development Indicators 2009*; The International Bank for Reconstruction and Development/World Bank: Washington DC, 2009.

You, D.; Jones, G.; Wardlaw, T. *Levels and Trends in Child Mortality. Report 2011*; United Nations Children's Fund: New York, NY, 2011.

## ENDNOTES

1 See http://www.globalissues.org/article/26/poverty-facts-and-stats.
2 See You et al. (2011) and FAO (2012).
3 See World Bank (2011).
4 See De Soto (2000).
5 See Mitchell and Ashley (2010).
6 See Scheyvens (2011).
7 See Saarinen et al. (2013).
8 In Latin America there is a large number of people who are not technically poor but are vulnerable to external factors, such as losing a paycheck, an unexpected medical bill, or natural disasters (flooding, droughts and hurricanes) which can put them in the army of the 46 million people struggling to get by under the poverty line in Latin America.

# ACKNOWLEDGMENTS

We owe a great debt to Dr. Alan Fyall, Dr. Richard Teare, Dr. Manuel Vanegas Sr, Dr. Kelly Semrad, Dr. Jorge Bartels, Dr. Carlos Amaya, Dr. Theuns Vivian and Dr. Seung Hyun Lee for their valuable and insightful comments regarding the manuscript.

We are also indebted to our international partners who partook in this incredible journey through Latin America during the past 8 years, specifically Jorge Bartels from the University of Costa Rica; Jorge Machiavello from ECOTEC in Ecuador; Carlos Amaya from the University of Colima, Mexico; Lucy Valenti from Grayline Tours Nicaragua; Fabio Hauagge do Prado from UDC in Foz do Iguazu, Brazil; Alvaro Patino and Jaime Bejarano Alzate from Universidad la Gran Colombia; Rafael Ramirez from Universidad de Colima; and our friend Xavier Ramirez from Combate Beach Resort.

Our gratitude also to our PhD students at the University of Central Florida: Valeriya Shapoval, Ekaterina Sorokina, Abdullah Makki, and Jalayer Khalilzadeh, who worked hard on compiling and sorting out information pertaining to references and endnotes. Finally, we are indebted to Alanna Ritchie for her editing work and Ralph Gerena for his valuable insights.

# CHAPTER 1

# FACES OF THE POOR

## CONTENTS

## INTRODUCTION

There are about 2 billion people living in poverty in the world. This chapter describes how they see themselves as poor, how they feel, and what their aspirations are. They share these common dilemmas: lacking food, feeling abandoned, and living in a state of vulnerability. The chapter also discusses if tourism can provide hope and opportunities for the poor. Finally, the chapter defines the relationship between tourism and poverty reduction as a puzzle, one that may provide resolution to this crisis.

## FACES OF THE POOR

The poor have many faces; the diversity of faces shows the global spread of poverty. Most are sad, humiliated, and embarrassed. They are victims of crime, unable to earn enough to meet their needs, and living with low expectations. The manifestation of the degree of this appalling reality is contextual and relative. Some poor are sadder than others, entertaining lower expectations or completely without expectations. However, what they all have in common is lack of food.

In our conversations with the poor, they gave very detailed and nuanced descriptions of the meaning of being poor. We found the degree of poverty is reverberated when there is lack of food security. Sometimes that ability to secure food is even more difficult for those who depend on subsistence fishing or farming. Their daily scuffle to meet basic needs for foods is affected by their inability to produce or receive aid for their subsistence activities. A fisherman of Punta Arenas community, Costa Rica, mentioned as follows:

> *resources ... I do not have resources ... I sell my catch very cheaply and then have to buy it a double of what I sold it ... there is never enough food*

Concerns over food security are also evident in some of the poorest regions of Africa. This is the case portrayed by Dominic and Patricia in Zambia, who needed to take care of a family of six, including four orphans from Dominic's deceased sisters:

The family lives in two rooms in one of Lusaka's poorer neighborhoods, a shanty town called Garden Compound, about five kilometers outside Lusaka city, and are typical of the millions of Africans who live on less than a dollar a day. Dominic earns 525,000 kwacha a month as his gross pay. After tax and other deductions, he's left with only 300,000 kwacha – roughly $40 – to take home with him. "After paying the rent", she says, "I sometimes have only about 10,000 kwacha ($2) left. That money is only enough for one day. The next morning I have to go and borrow some food or money from my family." Patricia buys her food at a local market stall. She spends half of her remaining money – $1 – on lunch. For six people, she can only afford six teaspoons of rice, three tomatoes, two tablespoons of cooking oil, two onions and some salt. It's hardly a nutritious meal. The rest of the money will be spent on an equally meagre supper. It is all the more important that Patricia and Dominic should have a good diet, because it could actually help prolong their lives – like two million other Zambians they are infected with the HIV virus. Buying drugs of any kind is also out of the question for Dominic and Patricia. Patricia and Dominic's situation is not unique.[1]

The poverty saga includes not only the lack of income but also the inability to secure basic needs. In Zambia, 64% of the 14 million populations live on less than a dollar a day, 14% have HIV, 40% do not have access to clean drinking water, and almost 90% of women in rural areas cannot read. This abysmal reality is shared by 1.3 billion persons who live in abject poverty – subsisting on less than US$1.25/d. Think about how you would live with 99 cents. You cannot buy a Big Mac. You do not have access to information. You cannot buy milk or diapers. You cannot go to the movies, rent DVDs, or download iTunes. You cannot buy medicine to prevent or treat illness. Lastly, you do not have enough to eat or provide food for your children. Even living on US$2.00 a day would be difficult. In another 2.7 billion, one in every three persons lives with less than US$2.00 a day.

A total of 11 million children die every year before they reach the age of 5, and more than 6 million die of preventable diseases like malaria, diarrhea, and pneumonia. More than 1 billion people are lacking food, of which 300 million are children who go to bed hungry. Every day around 21,000 persons die of hunger. More than 2.6 billion people do not have basic sanitation, and more than 1 billion do not have access to healthy drinking water. Women in developing countries walk four miles per day on average to get water for their households.[2] More than 40% of women in Africa do not have basic education.

These bare facts are simply a glance at poverty and do not capture the totality of what it means to be poor. Our multiple conversations with poor people in Latin America uncovered the essence of what it is like living at subsistence level. We recognized an accumulative sense of crisis, propelled by the ever-changing states of sudden joblessness or nearing starvation. The presence of poverty increases with remoteness, far away from paved roads, and a long walking distance to get to drinking water, shops, schools, and health centers.

Living in poverty can mean living in dread, as many lead a life dominated by fear. A person earning US$2 a day, when he/she can find a job, is constantly afraid that when the job is done, his/her children will go hungry. The people we interviewed gave detailed and nuanced descriptions of the meaning of being poor and the feeling of desperation when there is lack of food security. One person in the Montanita Commune in Ecuador said as follows:

> *We are poor ... we are very poor ... our work only ... whatever we make ... simply helps to feed the family day by day ... we subsist day by day.*

Their daily struggle to meet basic needs for food is affected by their inability to produce or receive aid for their subsistence activities. A fisherman in the fishing village of Olon, Ecuador, said as follows:

> *Our community is almost completely fishermen ... we know what is laboring the seas ... unfortunately we lack the resources to know how to get a boat or even a motor.*

The need for food security was evident in many of the poor places that we visited. The hallmark of poor countries is that their people are hungry for food. The United Nations' Food and Agriculture Organization (FAO) estimated that the number of poor people in the world who went hungry between 2010 and 2012 is nearly 870 million. Nearly 98% of these people suffering from chronic undernourishment – that is 852 million people – live in developing countries.[3] Children are the main victims of malnutrition, which leads to almost 1 million child deaths each year. By FAO account, the world has plenty of food to feed everyone on earth according to the nutritional intake requirement of at least 2,720 kcal per person per day.

Poverty is the main cause of hunger, and there is no sign of world hunger abating. The World Bank and other international organizations anticipate that the recent price surge in food crops will worsen the hunger problem. To demonstrate the severity of the situation, the poorest countries in the world are shown in Figure 1.1 according to the United Nations' 2011 Human Development Report.

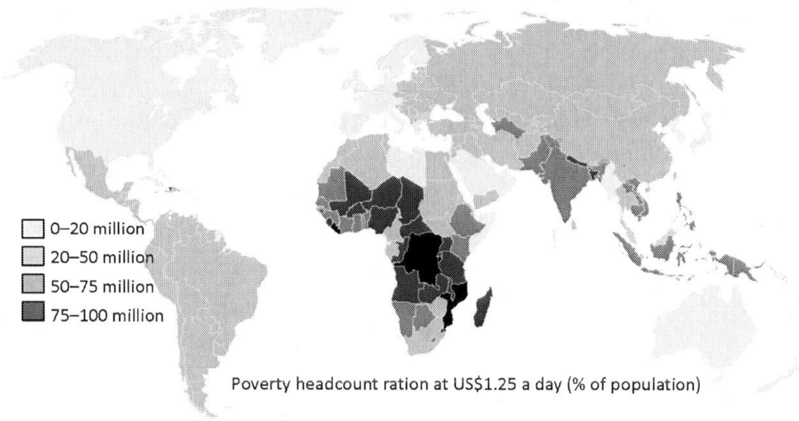


**FIGURE 1.1** Poverty Headcount Map.
(Source: The World Bank (2014) PovcalNet Data Visualizer.)

The story of poverty is not complete if other aspects of the poverty picture are not revealed. Large disparities in education, health, and nutrition are revealed in different wealth levels. These disparities are also present between urban and rural households. United Nations' Development Program (UNDP) (2013) indicates that the likelihood of children living in urban areas completing primary school is 30% higher compared to the children from rural areas. The children are facing challenges not only with education but also with basic survival.

Poor people lack water in their homes, preventing them from bathing and accessing drinking water. In general, rivers are the places for women to bath and do laundry and where their children can brush their teeth. Sometimes they have to walk for hours to get to the river to engage in these activities and gain access to drinking water. The poor have to carry containers for hours to transport water. Imagine living with limited access to water: you cannot grow food, you cannot stay clean, go to school or work clean, or maintain health. Sometimes water that they bath, drink, or carry in containers back to home is unsafe and toxic with disease. That is exactly what happened in Haiti in 2012 when water from the river was infested with cholera, generating a viral epidemic.[4] In Haiti, only 12% of the population had piped, treated water before the earthquake of 2008.

Although poverty is lack of human capital, it also consists of lack in health, labor, and education, thus stopping the opportunities of the poor to lift themselves out of poverty. For the poor, labor and education are considered core components for survival. They understand the limitations of not having an education but at the same time see the importance of becoming productive by working. A poor artisan from the Esmeraldas province in Ecuador echoed this view by criticizing the lack of support and consideration for education that they receive from the municipality as follows:

> *they have no mercy on us, we have the intelligence, we have hands, we have everything to work, unfortunately our parents could not educate us, they could not give us an education that will make us business men, but we can develop we should have opportunities*

Being poor has different contexts when taking age and gender into consideration. The lack of material assets or income poverty was discerned as a major concern among younger men and women. For them, coming out of poverty is only possible by the ability to be productive, and this was their main priority. While dialoguing with a young female farmer in the San Antonio Commune in Ecuador, she indicated as follows:

> *I want to study agronomy ... I already have my own plant nursery ... my goal is to create a garden where people can come and visit and generate money for my family*

A group of single mothers who are needle workers in the communities of Colonche and Manglarito in Ecuador expressed somewhat similar views as follows:

> *imagine ... this group of women here work with nylon, make shoes, blouses, and there are countless beautiful crochet pieces they can make ... but ... when we make a sale we have to pay the intermediaries ... that puts us in jeopardy ... our goal is to have our own microenterprise*

However, the opportunities of the poor are being thwarted by slim health opportunities for their children. While child mortality has subsided over time in developing countries, many children are still victims of premature deaths. Figure 1.2 reveals this sad reality of child mortality in developing countries.

Residential place has a bearing about the opportunities to live a longer live. Rural child mortality is even higher compared to the mortality rate in the urban areas. For example, the rural–urban gap in child mortality is the largest in Latin America and the Caribbean, where the gap between the two areas is 34% higher in rural areas. Similarly, the gap in rural–urban child nutrition is the most prominent in Latin America and the Caribbean.

Residential place seems to impact the level of education, health, and nutrition in developing countries.

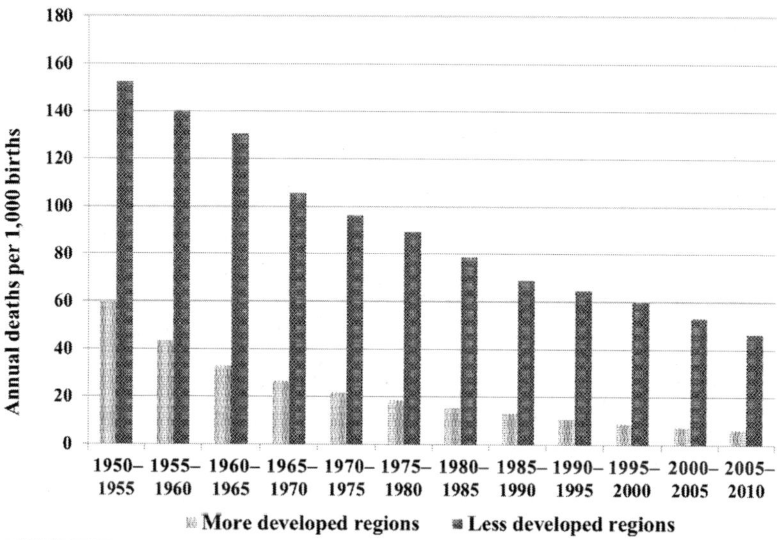


**FIGURE 1.2** Infant Mortality Rates in Developed Regions and Less Developed Regions. (From: http://esa.un.org/unpd/wpp/Excel-Data/mortality.him.)

Economic inequality is appalling in the world and is of central global importance. The World Economic Forum in its 2014 report considers the widening income disparity as the most worrisome global trend in 2014. The statistics are alarming. For example, the poorest 20% of the world's population accounts for 1.5% of the world's private consumption and the richest 20% consume an astonishing 77%, in other words, 65 times the total wealth of the bottom half of the world's population. The top 100 billionaires earned an additional US$240 billion in 2012 – four times the amount needed to end global poverty. The Brookings Institution documented that it would need US$66 billion a year to end global poverty.[5]

Within developing countries, the imbalance of the consumption of the rich and poor is also appalling. The income share held by the countries under top 10% compared to the rest of the world is in an imbalanced state, especially in a number of developing countries. The income shares held by the countries under top 10% are as follows (income share in parentheses): Comoros (55.19), Namibia (54.75), Seychelles (60.16), South Africa

(51.69), Angola (44.74), Bolivia (43.28), Brazil (42.93), Central African Republic (46.13), Chile (42.77), Guatemala (44.92), Haiti (47.67), Honduras (42.4), Paraguay (41.11), Swaziland (40.11), and Zambia (43.15).

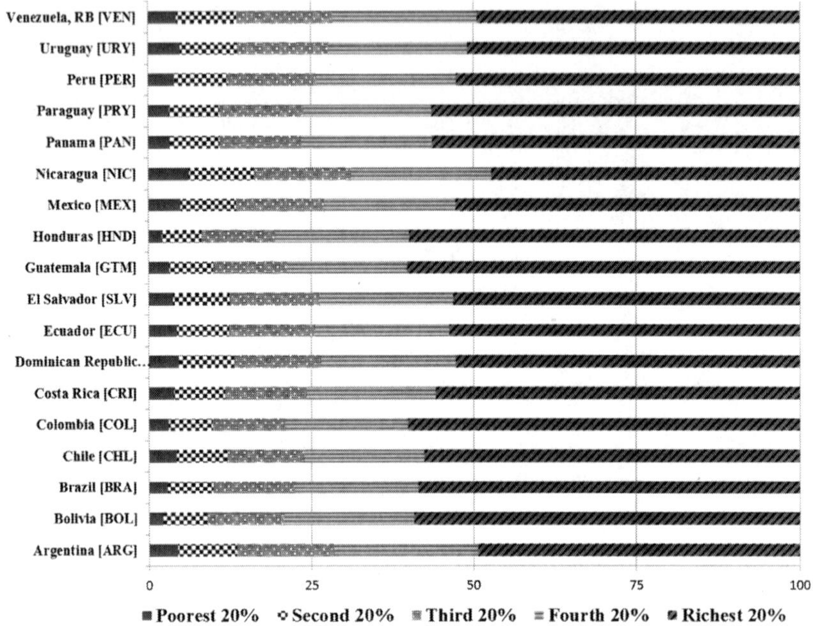


**FIGURE 1.3** Income Shares by Quintile Latin America.
(Source: The World Bank (2014) PovcalNet Data Visualizer.)

The 10% of the population at the top of the economic ladder control the highest share of national income compared to the rest of the world. In Haiti, the poorest country in the Western hemisphere, where more than 50% of the population live under the poverty line, the top 10% earns more than half of the country's wealth. Figure 1.3 reveals the degree of inequality in Latin America.

## POVERTY CAUSES FEAR AND VULNERABILITY

These people live in constant fear of something happening beyond their control that can push them back below the poverty line. They feel vulnerable. Any disease, natural disaster, or even government action or market condition may signal the loss of a job or even dead. Let us contemplate what happened in Haiti in 2010. It was struck by an epidemic of cholera that was brutal. It decimated a large portion of the population. The *New York Times* describes one such case of cholera death as follows[6]:

On Oct. 16, 2010, Mr. Pelette, 38 woke at dawn in his solitary room behind a bric-a-brac shop off the town square. As was his habit, he loped down the hill to the Latem River for his bath, passing the beauty shop, the pharmacy and the funeral home where his body would soon be prepared for burial. The river would have been busy that morning, with bathers, laundresses and schoolchildren brushing their teeth. Nobody thought of its flowing waters … as toxic. When Mr. Pelette was found lying by the bank a few hours later, he was so weak from a sudden, violent stomach illness that he had to be carried back to his room … by 4 that afternoon … [he] was dead.[7]

While considering also the natural disasters that strike poor countries, poor people are usually their main victims. In 2009, a powerful storm hit Bangladesh destroying the homes of thousands of people, causing hardship, and obliterating the lives of hardworking families. The *New York Times* describes one such situation during the storm as follows:

When Aila hit, Ms. Khatun was home with her husband, parents and four children. A nearby berm collapsed, and their mud and bamboo hut washed away in minutes. Unable to save her belongings, Ms. Khatun put her youngest child on her back, and with her husband, fought through surging waters to a high road. Her parents were swept away.

Khatun lost her modest shack, her parents, and her husband who died sometime later after the storm where she became a destitute:

Ms. Khatun now lives in a bamboo shack … about 50 yards from a sagging berm. She spends her days collecting cow dung for fuel and struggling to grow vegetables in soil poisoned by salt water.

Compound vulnerability and fear with nutritional deficiency and the potential for disastrous choices increases. Poverty imposes mental strain that blurs clarity in making good choices.[8] This state of living in crisis, because of the lack of food and job insecurity, makes the poor extremely vulnerable. The poor's perspective of the future is marred by constant insecurity, which may harm any effort to break away from poverty. Why invest in education and health and commit hope to the future, if the prospects of sustaining these efforts are beyond one's control?

## SHIFTING PERSPECTIVES: POVERTY AS A BLOT ON SOCIETY

The world has made impressive strides in global poverty reduction. Between 1981 and 2010, about half a billion people were hauled out of poverty (see Figure 1.4). Thus, the international community has achieved ahead of time its Millennium Development Goal of halving global poverty by 2015, i.e., 5 years ahead of time.[9]

Still, there are about 2 billion people living in poverty, of which 870 million are estimated to be undernourished. One in every five persons in the developing world earns less than US$1.25/d (World Bank, 2013). A report issued by the International Labour Organization in 2011 complained about the slow pace of development and its impact of poverty reduction.[10]

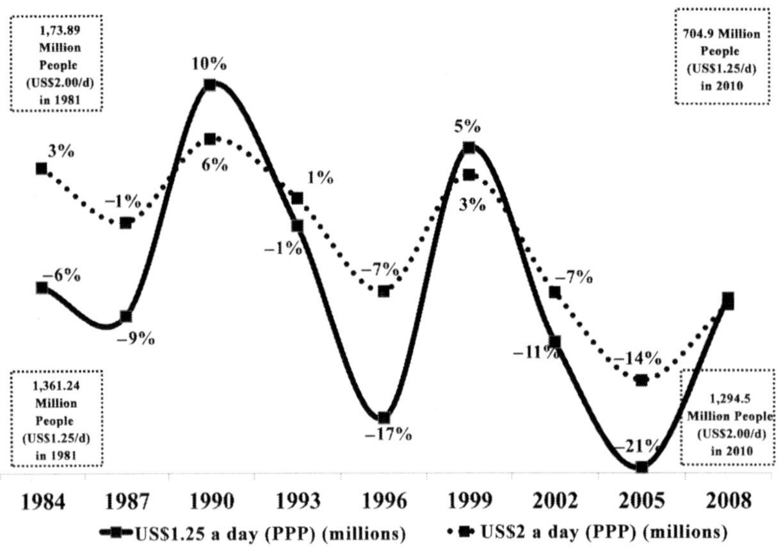


**FIGURE 1.4** Changes of Poverty Headcount from 1981 to 2010 (US$1.25/d and US$2.00/d).

There are still too many people, for example, in Latin America who remain poor and suffer from hunger, which deprives them from engaging in economic and social opportunities. There are 164 million people, or 28%, of the total Latin American population living as poor; 68 million, or 12%, of the Latin American population are living as extremely poor in Latin America. When poverty is broadly measured, including the fulfillment of basic needs and peoples' capabilities to lead the life that they want, the number of poor people soars to greater heights. Additionally, poor people remain vulnerable, and poverty reduction strategies in Latin America remain tenuous as revealed by the recent economic recession.

The premise of society's debate is that the poor are no different than other human beings. Many believe that the poor would like to lead lives that are similar to any other human being. The poor want to lead a pleasant life instead of a boring one, which may be one of the reasons for not having the main priority to buy more food when they receive additional money.[11] Banerjee and Duflo claim that the poor are interested in things that make life less boring and more pleasant. In India, they found that "the poor do not eat any more or any better when their income goes up ...."[12] This finding is also confirmed by a recent study conducted by the UNDP suggesting that the level of income does not impact nutrition outcomes.[13]

In our visits to multiple countries in Latin America, we have observed something similar. The poor seem to want the same opportunities as everybody else to indulge in a good life. They do not care about definitions and discussions. They want to free themselves from indigence, lead a decent life, and provide food and safety for their children.

When uttering their experiences about being poor, men and women articulate a sense of marginalization, hopelessness, and even humiliation. These feelings are grounded in their daily exchanges and contact with other individuals, government agencies, and the private sector. The responses and treatment they receive from these groups further sway them to feel powerless and without a voice. While the participants were met in a church in the Venus de Valdivia Commune, they were suspicious and reluctant to talk to us, and even outright hostile. Only after explaining the purpose of our visit, the attendees were more at ease and keen to participate. One of the "cabildos" (council man), very motivative and emotional, indicated as follows:

> *the importance of having you here is the project potential .... these people are simple, people definitely want to progress ... thank you and excuse us ... you're here at home, you can get to any of our homes ... any them .... and you will be greeted with great affection, we are a big family*

Immediately, the "presidente" (the highest authority in the commune) of the Manglarito Commune declared how important it was that they were included in the meeting and given a voice that could help them as follows:

*all our people have inspiration and want our projects to become a reality ... we want to dazzle everyone ... excuse me my friend but .... we are tired of projects, and hopefully with you ... dear friends ... .our words do not remain in your heart but in projects, thank you very much.*

These words show their lack of voice and power. But they also speak with a certain amount of hope, optimism, and anticipation. A "comunero" from Manglarito who works as a mason by trade said very emotionally as follows:

*I hope you take something of what you hear here today and let people in the United States know ... hopefully with time we will have something, hopefully God can pay handsomely. Thank you.*

In one of our multiple conversations with the residents of Cerro Santa Ana in Guayaquil, we noted a common desire to lead a good life, have a decent job, and garner respect. This was in an area that was an urban dump in the middle of the city of Guayaquil. The city began a regeneration project in the year 2000 to enhance the quality of life of the poor residents living in that area. By the time the project was completed, Cerro Santa Ana became a tourist attraction in the middle of the city. Residents were proud of their new dwellings and actively engaged in upkeep activities and neighborhood watch to keep the place safe. The place changed the quality of life of the residents in significant ways by providing freedom of mobility and encouraging social participation in activities due to its enhanced safety. One resident from Cerro Santa Ana described the importance of safety for their children as follows:

*On being outside ... they can be outside playing until whatever time they want ... I am not worried, there is no danger. The kids have great relationships and friendships, they are always at ease. In the past, we had some fear and were always suspicious ... suddenly (out of nowhere) "el patan" [slob] appeared around the corner, since our kids were little we conceal them to avoid the rubbing with them. Nowadays ... no more ... they are wandering through the afternoon and we feel calm.*

Having the opportunity to live a decent and pleasant life is crucial for the well-being of the individual, and this condition has important ramifications for society. Many claim that happy people are motivated, and hence, more productive. Poor people, on the other hand, reveal apathy and lethargy because they are defined by scarcity, and scarcity spawns stress and anxiety. Deprivation and scarcity make people anxious and stressed.

The poor do not have enough time to focus; they work on the farm, must cook, attend to the sick, get drinking water, tend to animals, and do a host of activities. Parents do not have time to take care of their children, take them to school, or take their children to health centers.

The behavior of poor people shown in the choices that they make is puzzling. Banerjee and Duflo describe how poor people reject inexpensive effective sanitation, the demand for immunization is low, and visits to healthcare centers are infrequent, despite spending a large portion of their meager budget on healthcare.[14] The reason, according to Banerjee and Duflo, is that the poor procrastinate and underestimate the benefits of preventative care and medicine.

Mullainathan and Shafir found that stress and anxiety due to scarcity induce cognitive deficiencies that affect the choices of poor.[15] A person living under the condition of scarcity will make poor decisions and choices because that person is completely focused on what is lacking and not on how to enhance his well-being. In this particular case, according to Mullainathan and Shafir, the extreme poor would be solely focused on food. The longing for food overwhelms their mind, and the short term becomes the overriding reality of their existence. In other words, the strong need to satisfy their immediate present clouds the poor mind to think and act on behalf of the future, preventing them to think about benefits that will be accrued in the future. Everything that we take for granted in our daily life, such as clean drinking water, sewage water going on its own, easy accessibility to utilities, compulsory children immunization, and food on the table, are daily struggles for the poor. These difficult thought processes under the condition of scarcity impairs good choices. Context matters.

## THE CONTEXT OF POVERTY

The consequences of poverty are enormous. The poor feel frustrated and forgotten. They are undernourished, without job prospects, and in unsafe neighborhoods and, consequently, they are incurring high human and social costs. Human costs refer to the loss of well-being, dignity, and self-esteem for those who are poor, and poverty also spawns social costs to society, such as healthcare, education, and crime.

In Latin America alone, there are more than 100,000 homicides registered per year, compelling the poor to seek protection on their own.

The state is failing them by not providing enough protection, while the poor continue to become victims of violence. By the account of the World Health Organization, the crime level afflicting the poor is reaching epidemic levels.[16] The danger leads to insecurity that wastes lives, talents, and productivity. The fear of violence limits capabilities, like their freedom to participate in social arrangements and know how to organize themselves. People are scared to participate in leisure activities or to venture out into the streets – to participate in any social activity. We already referred to how more safety has improved the quality of life of the poor in Cerro Santa Ana in Ecuador. Without security, millions are robbed of the opportunity to enjoy a better quality of life.

The abysmal reality of the poverty consumes resources as well as the lives of many. One way poverty manifests itself is through infections that kill many people. Dengue fever and malaria are endemic in many poor countries and have devastating effects on countries and families. The recent cholera epidemic in Haiti killed nearly 8,000 Haitians and sickened nearly 500,000, or 5%, of the Haitian population.

Even when they have good health, the poor are beset with challenges. They are denied access to institutions stifling their opportunities in life. De Soto, for example, estimated that if the poor were not excluded from the market and certain social arrangements, such as private property, the global economy would have been more thriving and would have enhanced significantly the standard of living for everyone. The exclusion of the poor meant a waste of about US$9 trillion of property to the global, what De Soto termed "dead capital".

The lack of voice and power of the poor is more apparent when the poor try to communicate their ideas and find possible financing for growing their farms or small businesses. A farmer from the Santa Elena Commune in Ecuador expressed his frustration by recounting his experiences with various financial institutions. While revealing his challenges, he mentioned as follows:

> *The bank manager is someone who doesn't even like the "comuneros" ... any documentation we provide he literally throws in the garbage ... they cannot help us because we are "cholitos" [slur to depict indigenous people] ... but yes ... we are intelligent ... we know what we are doing ... what happens is that Ecuador politics is like that ... the big society and the people on the top only need to pick up the phone and get whatever ... and us ... we can't even get a five hundred dollar "quirografario" [Unsecured loan]*

The exclusion of the poor in developing countries is mainly ascribed to the high disparity in wealth and access to education and health. As we mentioned before, inequality can stifle growth and ruin opportunities for the poor. Where inequality is high, rent-seeking is common along with social tensions and political instability.[17] The 2006 World Development Report refers to the tragic consequences of inequality, and a study from Bourguignon and colleagues described the persistence of inequality as follows:

> *[P]ersistent differences in power, wealth, and status between socioeconomic groups that are sustained over time by economic, political, socio-cultural mechanisms and institutions [...] lead to suboptimal development outcomes of 'inequality of opportunities' (p. 236).*[18]

The majority of the poor also live in fragile countries. Fragile countries are defined as those countries that cannot deliver reasonable public services and provide protection from corruption and criminal behavior. Some other attributes are identified as the inability to collect taxes, sharp economic decline, group-based inequality, and widespread persecution and discrimination.[19] According to the Failed States Index (FSI) from the Fund for Peace, the amount of poor living in failed countries has increased steadily.[20] The Fund's estimate of poor living in these countries was 41% in 2005, and it is expected that by 2015, the proportion of poor living in failed countries will reach 63%. The top 10 countries in the ranking of the FSI are all African countries, with the exception of Afghanistan and Haiti.

Acemoglu and Robinson attribute the failure of countries to exclusion in economic as well political sense.[21] When large portions of the populations do not have the opportunity to participate in productive occupations, countries may be doomed to fail and bestow poverty on large sections of their population. By diminishing the opportunities of participation in productive operations and activities of a country, the most valuable asset, i.e., human capital, is not possibly used in the most productive way. Surely, a context permeated by exclusion will make poverty reduction within these countries unsustainable.

## CAN TOURISM HELP THE POOR?

Tourism development is credited to be a powerful source of economic progression in developing countries. In these areas, tourism has significantly expanded over time. Developing countries saw their share of global tourism increase by 46% in 2011, amounting to 465 million arrivals. The trend toward a more diversified global distribution of international tourism revealed the steady and higher growth rates of international tourist arrivals in developing countries during 2005 and 2012. In those periods, the share of international tourism toward developing countries increased by 4.8%, compared to 2.6% in advanced countries. In 2012, Latin America, Asia, and sub-Saharan Africa were in the top regions with the fastest growth rates in international tourism arrivals.

The expansion of international tourism in developing countries was particularly pronounced in the least developing countries (LDCs). Table 1.1 reveals the presence of tourism in the LDCs, as it has evolved from 1995 to 2011. International arrivals increased the annual average by 11%, from 4,074,465 in 1995 to 20,827,119 in 2011. Similarly, international receipts increased, at a higher pace, from US$2,716,245,933 in 1995 to US$15,509,678,642 in 2011. The annual average growth rate was 12%.[22]

Table 1.1 reveals the tourism's prominence in the LDCs over time. Tourism has become a major player in the economy of these countries. The expansion of tourism may unlock opportunities to power the needed transformation in developing countries by providing more steady jobs, access to healthcare, education, and growth that is inclusive. Inclusive growth means that the distribution of the growth matters for poverty reduction.[23] This is evidenced by the facts that 80% of the 56 countries with a poverty reduction poverty strategy identify tourism as the vehicle to reduce poverty, create jobs, and spur economic growth.[24]

Tourism may trigger development through a number of channels, like expanding the domestic market by tourists with higher disposable income. One of the challenges of poor countries is the lack of a domestic market with sufficient buying power. Tourism may also give a country the means to diversify its economy, thereby mitigating the volatility of traditional export revenues. Compared to agriculture, mining, and manufacturing, tourism seems more stable and resilient as an export earner that can withstand external shock. Finally, tourism may democratize the dollar by including the poor in the benefits from tourism through steady jobs and income.[25]

Tourism may provide the poor with more opportunities than any other economic sector. The tourist must go to a place because the tourist product is not portable. When the tourist gets to a place, the tourist roams around and may therefore easily make contact with poor people. Poor people seem to concentrate at important heritage junctures. For example, in Bolivian Amazon, the inscription of the Ichapekene Piesta Moxos onto the 2012 UNESCO Representative List of the Intangible Cultural Heritage of Humanity has prompted opportunities for the poor and the tourists to mingle.[26] That interaction can bring jobs and income to this very poor region of the country.

**TABLE 1.1** Evolution of International Tourism Arrivals and Receipts in LDCs (1995–2011)

| Year | Arrivals | Change (%) | Receipts | Change (%) |
|---|---|---|---|---|
| 1995 | 4,074,465 | – | US$2,716,245,933 | – |
| 1996 | 4,860,462 | 19 | US$2,948,238,777 | 9 |
| 1997 | 5,267,309 | 8 | US$2,766,847,735 | –6 |
| 1998 | 5,385,207 | 2 | US$3,029,023,450 | 9 |
| 1999 | 5,595,011 | 4 | US$3,329,293,938 | 10 |
| 2000 | 5,729,424 | 2 | US$3,403,858,192 | 2 |
| 2001 | 5,972,901 | 4 | US$3,816,739,880 | 12 |
| 2002 | 6,731,651 | 13 | US$4,148,948,957 | 9 |
| 2003 | 6,926,447 | 3 | US$4,504,396,804 | 9 |
| 2004 | 8,766,369 | 27 | US$5,588,126,147 | 24 |
| 2005 | 10,331,582 | 18 | US$6,436,386,071 | 15 |
| 2006 | 13,188,891 | 28 | US$7,313,649,025 | 14 |
| 2007 | 15,178,548 | 15 | US$9,630,429,301 | 32 |
| 2008 | 16,464,119 | 8 | US$12,133,993,055 | 26 |
| 2009 | 16,517,139 | 0.3 | US$11,975,691,390 | –1 |
| 2010 | 18,431,055 | 12 | US$13,269,030,585 | 11 |
| 2011 | 20,827,119 | 13 | US$15,509,678,642 | 17 |

The pro-poor movement claims that tourism and its economic contribution are presumed to help the poor. According to the pro-poor movement, through economic mechanisms, such as employment, social, and business opportunities as well as the appropriate distribution of government taxes to the poor, tourism development may reduce poverty. Tourism feeds the following three channels provoking development and poverty reduction: (1) direct effects, (2) secondary effects, and (3) dynamic effects. Reduction in poverty occurs in two forms that contribute to economies. The primary form provokes direct effects (e.g., jobs created by hotels and restaurants). The secondary form appears as indirect effects (e.g., cleaning services and IT services rendered to hotels and restaurants).

The dynamic effects are related to the overall impact of tourism on the economy, going beyond the tourism sector. For example, as already alluded to, tourism may expand domestic demand, may spur diversification, and may mitigate macroeconomic volatility due to external shocks. Revenues from tourism seem more stable as a source of revenues than from the sale of goods, such as agricultural and mineral commodities. Additionally, tourism products can extract premium prices due to their uniqueness that cannot be exported and have lower transportation and insurance costs. Thus, there are numerous advantages to tourism compared to the export of goods and services.

## THE PUZZLE BETWEEN POVERTY REDUCTION AND TOURISM DEVELOPMENT

Unfortunately, these transmission channels of tourism do not appear to work effectively in all circumstances, contexts, and countries. The aggregate numbers mask some important differences within the group of developing countries. For example, international tourist arrivals in the LDCs increased from 0.7% in 1995 as a proportion of the world, compared to 2% in 2011. While the proportion of global tourism arrivals to the LDCs has increased, it is clear that the LDCs remain in a marginal position within global tourism (see Table 1.2).

There are a number of reasons for various results. Tourism development has been uneven with some regions having a longer history of tourism development than others. Some countries have also been more successful in attracting tourists than others. For example, the Caribbean islands have been more successful in tourism development than the countries in Central America. The populations in the Caribbean countries also enjoy a higher quality of life than the populations in Central America based on the human development index. The World Economic Forum provides the ranking of countries in terms of their tourism performance.

All the 20 top ranked countries belong to the most affluent countries, while the 20 bottom ranked countries are some of the poorest countries in the world. This may be an indication that development within a country may play an important role in shaping the performance of the industry.[27]

While countries may be endowed with abundant natural and cultural resources, these resources by themselves do not necessarily make a destination more attractive, with the ability to prompt increased demand and enhanced quality of life. Mediating factors, such as market distortions, inequality, and institutional weaknesses, can weaken the ability of countries to better the quality of life of residents and tourists alike. Arguably, these challenges affecting the ability of countries to promote and sustain development are more pronounced in developing countries.[28] For example, in developing countries, sustained high economic growth does not necessarily lead to more and better quality schooling. Institutional barriers may stifle progress and creativity. For example, creative destruction did not get a foothold in developing countries because unpredictable government policies got in the way, negatively affecting investments and innovation.[29] In other words, not every developing country does well in tourism development.

Despite the advantages of tourism revenues, some critics claim that tourism revenues do not reduce poverty but instead entrench inequality. Despite efforts, tourism may not automatically relieve poverty. The dynamic effects of tourism could be either positive (lifting the poor outside the tourism sector) or straddling the poor by negative externalities, such as inflation, exchange rate, deterioration of the environment, or displacement. The benefits of tourism development in developing countries are at best ambiguous. For example, studies conducted in Central America reveal that the effects of tourism expansion on poverty reduction are uneven. Poverty elasticities vary among the countries in Central America. For example, tourism has strong effects in Costa Rica, Guatemala, and Nicaragua, and modest-to-weak effects in Salvador and Honduras.

**TABLE 1.2** Tourism Development and Poverty in Less Developed Countries

| Region/Country | Poverty Headcounts in % (US$1 a day) | Tourism Receipts as % Exports | Tourism Receipts as % GDP | Year Poverty Data |
|---|---|---|---|---|
| Africa[a] | | | | |
| Burkina Faso | 56.54 | 9.6 | 0.9 | 2003 |
| Ethiopia | 39.04 | 24.5 | 4.3 | 2005 |
| Madagascar | 67.83 | 8.6 | 1.4 | 2005 |
| Malawi | 73.86 | 9.4 | 2.5 | 2004 |
| Mali | 51.43 | 10.1 | 3.1 | 2006 |
| Uganda | 51.53 | 25.8 | 3.5 | 2005 |
| United Republic of Tanzania | 88.52 | 28.1 | 4.5 | 2000 |
| Zambia | 64.29 | 11.2 | 3.4 | 2004 |
| Latin America[b] | | | | |
| Haiti | 54.90 | | | 2001 |
| Nicaragua | 45.06 | 11.9 | 3.8 | 2001 |
| Bolivia | 19.62 | 9.4 | 2.2 | 2005 |
| El Salvador | 20.44 | 12.9 | 3.5 | 2002 |
| Guatemala | 13.97 | 15.7 | 2.6 | 2002 |
| Honduras | 14.05 | 12.8 | 4.9 | 2003 |
| Paraguay | 16.37 | 2.8 | 1.3 | 2002 |
| Peru | 12.83 | 9.0 | 1.6 | 2002 |
| Costa Rica[c] | 2.37 | 16.9 | 7.3 | 2005 |
| Dominican Repub-lic[c] | 3.96 | 37.7 | 17.1 | 2006 |
| Others[d] | | | | |
| Bangladesh | 36.03 | 0.7 | 0.1 | 2000 |
| Lao | 27.37 | 18.4 | 5.9 | 2002 |
| Nepal | 25.27 | 21.8 | 4.0 | 2003 |

Source: Croes (2014)

[a]This table includes countries with a poverty headcount of >20% and with data availability from 2000 to the present.

[b]Countries included are those with a poverty headcount >10% and data availability from 2000 to the present.

[c]These two countries are included as a matter of comparison.

[d]Countries included are those with a headcount of 20% of more and data availability from 2000 to the present.

Part of the problem is that the ability of tourism to deliver to the poor depends on contextual conditions, such as the mix of incentives and organizational capabilities. This mix of incentives and organizational capabilities define how tourism economies are structured. Recent research indicates that the impact of tourism on the poor hinges more on the structure of tourism economies and less on the types of tourists patronizing destinations.[30] For example, the lack of collaboration so necessary in delivering the tourism experience seems rampant in Latin America.[31] These imperfections stem from the lack of trust and the free-riding practice so pervasive in the creation of the tourist experience. Common pool resource challenges combined with coordination problems, induced by the complementary nature of the delivery process of tourist experience, shape and compromise the level and degree of collaboration among stakeholders. In addition, market conditions seem to reward competition above cooperation. Thus, the relationship between tourism development and poverty reduction is not self-evident.

The role of tourism in poverty alleviation seems inconclusive. If we assume that economic growth will lift people from below the poverty line, then one obvious conclusion would be that tourism should prompt economic growth.[32] But does tourism really provoke economic growth? The direct link between tourism and economic growth is not obvious; tourism may have a positive impact or diminishing returns on economic growth. The vast tourism literature on the topic of the direct link between tourism and economic growth is still without a clear answer.[33] If the answer is still inconclusive regarding the route tourism–economic growth–poverty, then perhaps tourism may directly impact poverty reduction. Here again, unfortunately, our knowledge is hindered by the lack of empirical evidence.

While our observations of a direct link between tourism and economic improvement are inclusive, our research provides significant insights into the poverty dilemma. We found that mainstream development theory attributes the persistence of poverty to three empirical findings. First, economic growth in developing countries is not persistent. Typically, per capita incomes do not grow steadily over time. Second, inequality levels in developing countries have persisted over time. Thus, inequality seems to be a poverty reduction barrier limiting the effectiveness of growth. And third, reducing inequality is a complex social assignment.

Too much inequality could slow down economic growth and the poverty reduction process, and too little inequality could slow down economic growth and the poverty reduction process too. The magnitude of inequality determines the degree of political stability and social opportunities in a country, either by excluding large portions of the population in productive activities or by providing few incentives to take up risks and to innovate the economy. Evidently, the poor are not only hungry for food but also yearn for opportunities. The situation remains dire for millions of people. The next chapter will explore the conceptualization of poverty and its causes.

## REFERENCES

Acemoglu, D.; Robinson, J. *Why Nations Fail. The Origins of Power, Prosperity, and Poverty*; Crown Publishing: New York, NY, 2012.

Balakrishnan, R.; Steinberg, C.; Syed, M. *The Elusive Quest for Inclusive Growth" Growth, Poverty and Inequality*; World Bank: Washington, DC, 2013.

Banerjee, A.; Duflo, E. *Poor Economics. A Radical Rethinking of the Way to Fight Global Poverty*; Public Affairs: New York, NY, 2011.

Bourguignon, F.; Ferreira, F. H.; Walton, M. Equity, efficiency and inequality traps: a research agenda. *J. Econ. Inequal.* 2007, 5(2), 235–256.

Chandy, L.; Gertz, G. *Poverty in Numbers: the Changing State of Global Poverty from 2005–2015*; Brookings Institution: Washington, DC, 2011.

Croes, R. A paradigm shift to a new strategy for small island economies: embracing demand side economics for value enhancement and long term economic stability. *Tourism Manage.* 2006, 27(3), 453–465.

Croes, R. The role of tourism in poverty reduction: an empirical assessment. *Tourism Econ.* 2014, 20(2), 207–226.

Dollar, D.; Kraay, A. Growth is good for the poor. *J. Econ. Growth.* 2002, 7(3), 195–225.

Easterly, W. *The Elusive Quest for Growth: Economists' Adventures and Misadventures in the Tropics*; MIT Press: Cambridge, MA, 2002.

Hawkins, D. E.; Mann, S. The World Bank's role in tourism development. *Ann. Tourism Res.* 2007, 9(1), 115–132.

Lall, S. Competitiveness indices and developing countries: an economic evaluation of the global competitiveness report. *World Dev.* 2001, 29(9), 1501–1525.

Lejárraga, I.; Walkenhorst, P. Diversification by deepening linkages through tourism; 2007. Retrieved from http://siteresources.worldbank.org/INTEXPCOMNET/Resources/Lejarraja_Diversification_by_Deepening_Linkages_with_Tourism.pdf.

Mani, A.; Mullainathan, S.; Shafir, A.; Zhao, J. Poverty impedes cognitive function. *Science.* 2013, 341(6149), 976–980.

Mitchell, J.; Ashley, C. *Tourism and Poverty Reduction: Pathways to Prosperity*; Earthscan: London, 2010.

Mullainathan, S.; Shafir, A. *Scarcity, Why having too Little Means so Much*; Henry Holt: New York, NY, 2013.

Nissanke, M.; Thorbecke, E. Channels and policy debate in the globalization-inequality-poverty nexus. *World Dev.* 2006, 34(8), 1338–1360.

Olavarria-Gambi, M. Poverty reduction in Chile: has economic growth been enough? *J. Hum. Dev.* 2003, 4(1), 103–123.

Ridderstaat, J.; Croes, R.; Nijkamp, P. Modelling tourism development and long-run economic growth in Aruba. *Int. J. Tourism Res.* 2012, 16(5), 472-487.

Sachs, J. *The End of Poverty: Economic Possibilities for Our Time*; Penguin Press: New York, NY, 2005.

UNDP. *Regional Human Development Report 2013-2014. Evidence and Proposals for Latin America*; UNDP: New York, NY, 2013.

Winters, P.; Corral, L.; Mora, A. Assessing the role of tourism in poverty alleviation: a research agenda. *Dev. Policy Rev.* 2013, 31(2), 177–202.

World Bank. World Bank Poverty Data; 2013. http://www.worldbank.org/en/topic/poverty/overview (retrieved February 21, 2014).

World Economic Forum. *The Travel and Tourism Competitiveness Report 2013, Reducing Barriers to Economic Growth and Job Creation*; 2013. http://www3.weforum.org/docs/WEF_TT_Competitiveness_Report_2013.pdf (retrieved March 12, 2014).

## ENDNOTES

[1]See BBC News January 18, 2005, http://news.bbc.co.uk/2/hi/africa/4181939.stm.

[2]See http://www.waterinfo.org/resources/water-facts, retrieved March 29, 2014. South African women walk long distances to supply their households with water. South African women together walk a trip to the moon and back 16 times a day. See, UNWomen Retrieved March 13, 2014, from http://www.unifem.org/gender_issues/women_poverty_economics/facts_figures.html.

[3]See FAO (2012) at http://www.worldhunger.org/articles/Learn/world%20hunger%20facts%202002.htm.

[4]See Sontag (2012, April 1). Global failures on a Haitian epidemic. *The New York Times*, p. 1.

[5]See Chandy and Gertz (2011).

[6]See Harris (2014, March 29). As seas rise, millions cling to borrowed time and dying land. *The New York Times*, p. 1.

[7]See Sontag (2012, April 1). Global failures on a Haitian epidemic. *The New York Times*, p. 1.

[8]See, for example, Mani et al. (2013).

[9]Between 1980 and 2010, about one billion people were lifted from poverty. The United Nations indicates that one of its main missions is to halve poverty by 2015, using 1990 as its baseline. By 2010, this goal was accomplished. See the World Bank (2014). Global Monitor-

ing Report 2013, Monitoring the MDGs. Retrieved April 5, 2014, from http://econ.worldbank.org/WBSITE/EXTERNAL/EXTDEC/EXTDECPROSPECTS/0,,contentMDK:23391146~pagePK:64165401~piPK:64165026~theSitePK:476883,00.html.

[10]See ILO (2011). *Growth, employment and decent work in the least developed countries*. Geneva: ILO.

[11]Banerjee and Duflo (2011) make this point in a study conducted in 18 countries, observing how the poor spent their money and why they are spending proportionally less on food with additional money; "The basic human need for a pleasant life might explain why food spending has been declining in India" (p. 37).

[12]See Banerjee and Duflo (2011), p. 39.

[13]See UNDP (2013).

[14]See Banerjee and Duflo (2011).

[15]See Mullainathan and Shafir (2013).

[16]See UNDP (2013).

[17]See, for example, Nissanle and Thorbecke (2006).

[18]See Bourguignon et al. (2007).

[19]Visit the Failed States Index FAQ, retrieved on March 19, 2014 at http://ffp.statesindex.org/faq#12.

[20]See http://ffp.statesindex.org/.

[21]See Acemoglu and Robinson (2012).

[22]These figures were derived from the World Bank's World Development Indicators.

[23]There is an extensive debate regarding the impact of economic growth on poverty reduction. For example, Dollar and Kraay (2002) posit that growth is good for the poor. Olavarria-Gambi (2003), on the other hand, challenged the previous assertion in the case of Chile that was able to reduce poverty through a combination of growth and human capital accumulation. Balakrishnan et al. (2013) also claim that the recent growth period has been less inclusive and pro-poor.

[24]See, for example, Hawkins and Mann (2007).

[25]See, for example, Croes (2006), Lejárraga and Walkenhorst (2007), Mitchell and Ashley (2010), and Winters et al. (2013).

[26]See http://www.unesco.org/culture/ich/?pg=00173.

[27]See the World Economic Forum (2013).

[28]See, for example, Lall (2001), Easterly (2002), and Acemoglu and Robinson (2012).

[29]Creative destruction refers to Schumpeter's claim in 1942 that innovation is an incessant and restricting process, whereby new products and processes replace outdated ones and, in so doing, affect macroeconomic performance, factor allocation, economic fluctuation, functioning of markets, and economic growth in the long run. Steady innovation spawns economic growth and prosperity according to Acemoglu and Robinson (2012), Sachs (2005), and others.

[30]See, for example, Mitchell and Ashley (2010).

[31]The delivery of the tourist experience depends on the nature of the interaction among multiple stakeholders at a destination.

[32]Development economics is inconclusive on whether economic growth by itself reduces poverty. For an interesting debate, see, for example, Olavarria-Gambi (2003).

[33]See, for example, Ridderstaat et al. (2012).

## CHAPTER 2

# THE POVERTY OBLITERATION PARADIGM

## CONTENTS

## INTRODUCTION

The complexity of the concept of poverty is revealed through multiple channels in politics, media, associations, and the international community. Different views and positions are adopted with regard to the meaning, causes, and approaches to poverty. This diversity in definitions poses enormous hurdles for realizing the perennial objective of reducing poverty by modern society. Varying conceptualizations of poverty make measurements controversial, affecting estimates of the magnitude of poverty and subsequent actions to be undertaken. Conflicting notions of poverty can leave poor people without the necessary attention to policies and actions. This chapter explores the meanings and measurements of poverty and their implications. This exploration is directed by the question: how do we make sense of the helplessness of the faces discussed in the previous chapter? Finally, the chapter introduces a new paradigm assessing poverty, the poverty obliteration paradigm (POP).

## WHAT IS POVERTY?

Despite the poor sharing similar needs and aspirations, the concept of poverty remains difficult to comprehend. Poverty is a complex construct. It has multiple conceptualizations and measurements colored by ideologies and research traditions and reinforced by institutions and organizations that are interested, committed, and shaped by this notion.

Poverty is perceived as a situation in which a person cannot meet certain predetermined consumption requirements or fails to meet capabilities. The conceptualization of poverty has shifted from physical existence (subsistence poverty) to include people who fail to achieve a certain standard of living, and therefore are excluded from participation in social arrangements. Thus, eligibility for participation in social arrangements requires more than food, shelter, and clothing. It requires education, health, and opportunities to lead the life that one desires. Poverty is not only a question of lack of money; it is also concerned with the capacity to enjoy a fulfilling and desirable life.[1]

For centuries, the discussion regarding poverty has been attributed to the nature of man. Man's nature is perceived by some as immutable, while others perceive man's nature as flexible. The difference in conceptions of man's nature has various consequences for how to approach the social processes. While the immutable version of mankind focuses on processes and trade-offs, the flexible version of mankind centers on results and consequences. The former version considers causes of prosperity and wealth, while the latter investigates the causes of poverty.[2] These two visions permeated the subsequent discussion regarding poverty that was elicited after the Second World War. They are revealed in four paradigms that investigate poverty: the income poverty paradigm, the basic needs approach, the capabilities poverty paradigm, and the subjective poverty paradigm. The income poverty paradigm explains poverty in terms of the command of resources and sees poverty as a situation that falls below a minimum amount of income needed for consumption. The basic needs approach refers to poverty as a situation wherein a person lacks adequate calories intake, housing, healthcare, education, clothes, and to access in basic public services. The capabilities approach is a human condition wherein a person lacks in many dimensions of human life (deprivation of opportunities), and is specifically reflected in the human development reports (HDRs) in four key areas: education, health, command over resources, and participation. Lastly, the subjective well-bcing (SWB) paradigm defines poverty as a self-reported condition of being poor. Figure 2.1 provides a snapshot of the different meanings of poverty stemming from the four paradigms that we will discuss.

| | Paradigms | | | |
|---|---|---|---|---|
| | Income paradigm | Basic needs | Capabilities | Subjective well–being |
| Evaluative criterion | Deprivation of income | Deprivation of consumption | Command resources | Deprivation of happiness |
| Metrics | Income | Basic needs | Human development index | Satisfaction with life |
| Unit of analysis | Individual | Individual and society | Society | Individual and society |
| Focus of analysis | Externally determined (objective) | Externally determined (objective) | Externally determined (objective) | Subjective |

**FIGURE 2.1** Poverty Through the Lens of Four Paradigms.

## THE INCOME POVERTY PARADIGM

Income effects have been associated with deaths of children in Africa in places such as Burundi, Madagascar, and Uganda; with oppression in India through some form of debt bondage; with forbidding child labor; and violence against women.[3] On the other hand, income effects have also been associated with reduced poverty when there is a situation of economic growth. For example, in 1991, India experienced a take-off in its economic growth with significant poverty reduction effects. Similarly, Brazil witnessed some impressive poverty reduction effects due to economic growth.[4]

The relationship income (growth) and poverty are intertwined through the income poverty paradigm. This paradigm presumes that individual consumers use their income to buy marketed goods and combine these goods with time, knowledge, and nonmarket goods to provide a more preferable quality of life. It infers, therefore, that the value that consumers place on a product (marginal value) can be identified by observing their actual consumption of the product without having to discuss the reasons or motives behind their choice (Samuelson's revealed preference approach). The evaluative criterion of welfare is income and consumption. The observed behavior in the market is the unit of social valuation. How does this paradigm define the poor? Or, in other words, how does this paradigm separate the poor from the nonpoor?

This paradigm defines poverty in terms of the level of command of resources. The level of command of resources is measured as the total consumption enjoyed and is proxied either by expenditure or by income. Poverty, thus, is a situation wherein a person's resources falls below a certain minimum level of expenditure or income, termed the poverty line. A poor person is defined as someone whose resources fall under a particular level or threshold, a so-called "poverty line".[5] This line may be defined in absolute terms, such as the US$1 or US$2 a day per person used by international organizations. For example, the millennium development goals (MDGs) define poverty as people living under US$1/d (extreme poor) and US$2/d (poor).[6] Poverty from this perspective is viewed as an inferior state of life than wealth, the latter being defined as abundance of material resources.

The poverty income definition was pioneered in England by the work of Booth and Rowntree.[7] Their works prompted a practice that focused on three elements that are still valid today from the perspective of this paradigm: (1) the individual is the central focus of inquiry; (2) the inquiry is objective, being defined by its objective properties such as conditions and resources, which are independent from a person's awareness, thereby suggesting some scientific properties to the inquiry; and (3) the inquiry is external to the poor, meaning that the inquiry does not take the opinions, feelings, or emotions of the poor into account.

The unit for analysis of this paradigm is the individual. Individuals are seen as rational actors who are defined by self-interest in pursuit of maximizing their benefits or welfare. The focus of this paradigm is explaining the efficient alignment of preferences and utility. Preferences were centered in the pursuit of gaining the maximum amount of commodities and services; and utility was founded on the realization of these preferences. Individuals were considered homogenous with equal chances to participate in this material pursuit; and the ultimate objective of economic life is to procure more income and consumption.

If the individual is the focus of analysis and the information space required to define a person as poor is derived from a minimum level of resources, then the shortfall from the poverty line is related to the individual motivation and efforts. Based on this line of thinking, several causes have been associated with this shortfall, which is equated with poverty. One such approach has been to "blame" the poor.[8] This approach is based on the notion that the poor are different and entertain particular personal attributes that are shaping their "negative" behavior. This "negative" behavior is revealed in lack of motivation, bad choices, habits, values, and belief systems.

Throughout history, three main approaches have stressed this individual shortfall or deficiency, namely, the neoclassical economics approach, the attribution theory, and the culture of poverty framework. The neoclassical approach blames the poor for bad choices shaped by their short-sightedness and low-payoff returns. For example, by foregoing education and training, they are foregoing job opportunities.[9] The attribution theory posits that the poor should blame themselves for accomplishing the least in society. This low accomplishment, according to this theory, is due to their personal traits, such as having big families, dropping out from school, being lazy, not saving more, and simply apathy.[10] One of the main roots of blaming the poor is the "culture of poverty" approach.[11] This approach posits that the poor hang out with other people who shape their beliefs, attitudes, and behavior, and that over time, these influences are internalized and become their way of life. This way of life, according to this approach, is detrimental to any social mobility, productive work, and social responsibility.

Based on these approaches, there are several policy implications using interventions that target individual behavior focusing on how to make the poor more productive, more socially responsible, and more invested in the future. One overriding concern is the impact of economic growth on behavior. Economic growth has the potential of generating opportunities through, for example, jobs that will positively change the aspirations of the poor, provoking investments into the future, such as education for their children. However, absolute income is not the main factor influencing the poor. Some studies posit that relative income is also important in determining poverty and addresses the question of who benefits from growth and posits that growth is pro-poor only if the growth rate of the income of the poor is greater than the nonpoor.[12] In other words, growth benefits the poor if inequality is reduced. This strand within the literature considers inequality as a breakpoint for poverty reduction. For example, Lopez and Serven found that growth explains a much smaller proportion of poverty reduction in richer countries than poorer countries.[13] Inequality under this condition functions as a filter in between economic growth and poverty reduction.

The income poverty approach is based on five main tenets: (1) subsistence level defines poverty; (2) the poor are different from the nonpoor; (3) individuals are completely responsible for their situation; (4) the separation of the poor and the nonpoor is based on the level of command of resources as cut-off point; and (5) economic growth can lift the poor out of poverty. These tenets, however, do not provide a complete picture of the poverty dimension. There is more to poverty than simply blaming the poor or the embracing trickle-down approach.

The idea of subsistence to define poverty can be challenged because poverty is not only a question of suffering from hunger; social needs are as important as physical needs. Similarly, in the previous chapter, we already discussed and questioned whether the poor are different from the nonpoor. We disregarded this claim on the ground that context makes a huge difference on people's choices.[14] Hunger, disease, and predatory and criminal violence are not endemic to everyone; they are endemic only to poor people.[15]

The information space stemming from a unidimensional concept of poverty based on command of resources is also questionable because there are other aspects in life such as subsistence, protection, affection, respect, and connections that define individual opportunities besides income or consumption. Finally, it is not clear if economic growth can solve issues related to poverty. Empirical evidence suggests that economic growth provokes positive influence of poverty reduction. However, this influence is not strong in all circumstances. Mediating factors are coloring the relationship between economic growth and poverty reduction.

## THE BASIC NEEDS APPROACH AND POVERTY

By the seventies, the notion that poverty is defined by physical needs, like hunger, was considered inadequate. The basic needs approach moved the focus to minimizing poverty. Before, increasing private incomes as a policy implication of the goods-centered focus was not working as global poverty significantly increased. The notion that economic growth through trickle-down economics will reach the poor, lifting them out of poverty was clearly not working. Not only were the poor not receiving the incomes stemming from economic growth but they were also denied access to essential public services and facilities. Consequently, the claim was made to expand the notion of command of resources to access of a bundle of basic consumption.[16]

The basic needs approach thus eschewed the poverty notion that poor people can be identified by looking at the total consumption of their household. Instead, the basic needs approach defines the poor as those lacking in adequate calories intake, housing, healthcare, education, clothes, and access to basic public services. By extending the information space of poverty, the basic needs approach shifted the meaning of poverty from attention to output maximization to minimization of poverty.

The central tenet of the basic needs approach, however, remains essentially materialistic. It claims that individuals should have a guaranteed subsistence in order to have well-being. Thus, poverty is viewed as a situation of consumption deprivation. To determine poverty, the approach invokes a procedure that identifies a minimum bundle of basic consumption and assesses whether the population has access to the minimum bundle. Two informational requirements were considered relevant in separating the poor from the nonpoor. First, shelter, clothing, and certain household furniture and equipment were considered along with nutritional requirements. And second, the lack of certain public goods, and the provision thereof, was integrated in the definition of poor, such as safe water, sanitation, public transportation, and facilities and services for healthcare and education for the whole community. The approach was widely advocated, particularly by international organizations such as the International Labor Organization. Community development became the cornerstone of this perspective.

This new information space, however, faced two challenges: first, the lack of a single indicator, which made it difficult to identify the poor; and second, the determination of adequate level of basic needs was subjectively based. Because the bundle of basic goods was imposed without consideration of the opinion of the poor, this approach was considered paternalistic as well as not revealing consumers' preferences. Additionally, the basic needs approach is very much focused on the material deprivation without considering values and aspirations of the poor.

The basic needs approach was contested by the income paradigm of poverty. The main contest stems from the perspective that basic needs would divert scarce resources away from productive sectors, thereby affecting economic growth. The trade-off with economic growth would ultimately hurt the poor and put poverty reduction programs in jeopardy. Critics argue that the poor would be better off by increasing private incomes that will enhance their basic needs satisfaction than through increasing consumption levels directly.[17]

## THE CAPABILITIES APPROACH AND POVERTY

Sen claims that the end game of economic life is not the command of resources; instead it is what these resources do to people.[18] Sen investigated the effects of resources on the individual and created the capabilities approach, claiming that poverty is a multidimensional concept. Income is not an adequate metric to define well-being or the lack thereof; instead freedom to lead a valued and fulfilling life is what should define well-being. Poverty, thus, is not the inability to command sufficient or adequate income, or meet basic human needs. A person may have good health and live a productive life, but still could become unemployed due to circumstances beyond his/her control. When the person is unemployed, he/she loses his/her income, and thereby the ability to meet basic needs. Rather, poverty from Sen's perspective is lack of opportunities.

Two aspects of freedom are crucial in Sen's perspective: capabilities and functionings. Capabilities refer to the range of opportunities present for an individual to pursue the lifestyle that he/she values and determine the range of achievements (functionings) possible for the individual, such as a good job. Thus, Sen makes the connection between capabilities (inputs) such as years of schooling, financial resources, protection of freedom of thoughts and property rights, and functionings (outputs) such as life expectancy, morbidity, literacy, and nutritional levels. The scope of choice hinges upon individual characteristics (for example, being disabled) and external conditions affecting the conversion process of capability into achievement.

Sen considers equity a crucial factor in the pursuit of social optimality and argues to distinguish the notion of efficiency from equity: an action that might improve everyone's well-being may enhance some people's welfare more than others. If those who benefited from this efficiency are the richest, then improved efficiency might be entirely consistent with more inequality. This would be unacceptable in light of the persisting poverty in the world. Sen rejects the notion that all individuals have the same capability to convert resources into functionings (valued achievements), implying that individuals would require different levels of resources.

The information space shifts from resources or income to indicators of freedom, or from a "goods-centered" to a "people-centered" focus. Sen shifts the pendulum from lower levels of human needs (basic needs) to integrating factors of higher human needs such as freedom and opportunities.[19] The main contribution of the capability approach to the understanding of poverty is the focus on the context of the lives people live and the freedoms they enjoy. The income focus is substituted by a human focus and defines poverty as a multidimensional construct aiming at a higher quality of life and well-being.[20] This shift in focus has significant implications regarding how to separate the poor from the nonpoor. Questions posed to decipher who is poor shift from, for example, the early conceptualization that would assess reading and writing by asking: how much money is allocated to primary education? Sen's approach would prompt the question: can people read or write?

One could infer based on the previous analysis that a person's achievements (functionings) are dependent on the resources that he commands and the ability to use the available resources. The relationship between achievements and resources can be construed as a production process where resources are considered inputs, while functionings or achievements will be considered as outputs. Inputs are defined as resources that matter in association with benefits realized in the process of economic growth. For example, the only commodity a majority of people possess is their labor power. The ability to find a job and the wage the person is able to extract is crucial in determining the choices and opportunities one has in life.

The lack of this ability impairs a person's well-being by removing the opportunity to earn income to buy food, to own property, to enjoy social reputation, and to prevent discrimination. Poverty, therefore, is not only a result of lack of income. The problem is multidimensional. The ability of the poor to influence decisions that affect their daily lives, vulnerability or resilience to shocks, access to services and assets, and strength or disruption of social networks, are all important factors to consider in assessing poverty.

On the other hand, enlargement of capabilities is an important contributor to the expansion of resources (e.g., incomes). However, this ability or capabilities (qualities of a person) to achieve functionings cannot be observed directly. It is assumed that capabilities are a mediating force in the conversion of resources into functionings. The capability approach employs revealed achievements (literacy rate, life expectancy, incomes), following standard economics, to gauge a person's well-being. Figure 2.2 depicts the relationships among the elements configuring the capability framework.

The United Nations and the international community have adopted the capability perspective, as revealed in the MDGs and diffused through the United Nations' Development Program (UNDP) HDRs. The refocusing of poverty as a human condition lacking in many dimensions of human life (deprivation of opportunities) is specifically reflected in the HDRs in four key areas: education, health, command over resources, and participation.

However, this framework for poverty analysis is not without challenges. One of these main challenges is the identification of a list of basic capabilities.[21] Sen rejected the notion of a universal list of basic capabilities, because capabilities are associated with personal characteristics and context. Nussbaum suggests a list of ten "central human functional capabilities" but Sen seems willing to compromise with a basic list of capabilities to undertake pressing social problems, such as extreme poverty.[22]

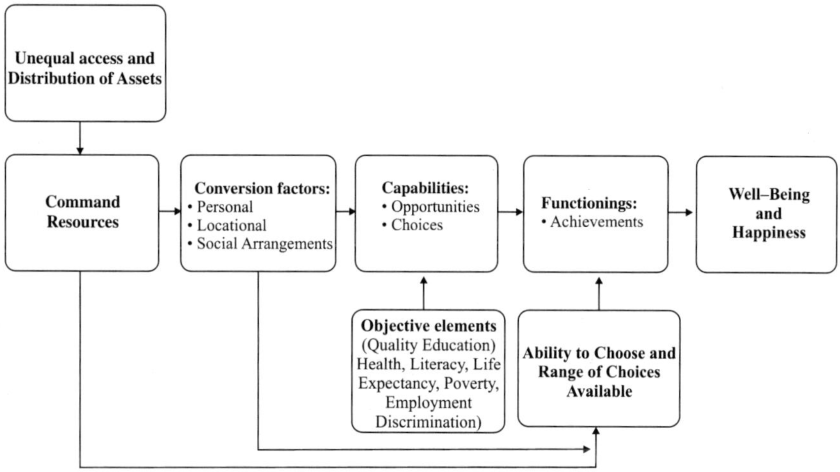


**FIGURE 2.2** The Capability Approach.
(Source: Croes (2012).)

Sen contends that "in dealing with extreme poverty in developing economies, we may be able to go a fairly long distance in terms of a relatively small number of centrally important functionings (and the corresponding basic capabilities, e.g., the ability to be well-nourished, the capability of escaping avoidable morbidity and premature mortality, and so forth)."[23] The other major challenge is the issue of measurement. Thorbecke claims that "the difficulties inherent in measuring a broadly based, multidimensional concept of poverty impose severe restrictions on the number and type of attributes that constitute poverty."[24]

The capability approach reveals an important hidden assumption that more is correlated with well-being; in other words, more income, more education, health, and participation imply that people would be happier. Rojas found in Mexico that the overwhelming majority (90%) of respondents were happy, while 55% of respondents were poor by UNDP standards based on the capability approach. This study questions whether objective standards stemming from the income paradigm, the basic needs approach, and the capability approach can separate poor from nonpoor. In separate studies, Rojas claims that by not integrating the opinions of the poor into the equation of the meaning of poverty, previous approaches may have compromised the determination of who is a poor person.[25]

## SWB AND POVERTY

While the capability approach underscores the multidimensionality of poverty, it remains silent on the question of the feelings and emotions of the poor about their own situation. Objective indicators may suggest that individuals are poor, while they consider themselves not poor. Rojas illustrates this condition in the case of Mexico.[26] Also, the objective indicator may suggest somebody as not being poor, while that somebody feels poor. The cause of this discrepancy is that in poor countries a large portion of consumption happens outside of the marketplace and is based more on home production and barter (exchange in kind). For example, the informal sector of the economy is large and prominent in Latin America.[27] The SWB approach, therefore, considers poverty not as an objectively defined status of deprivation, but views poverty as an individual feeling. Poverty is defined here as a status below a certain degree of life satisfaction.

Intuitively one would think that an individual would like to prevent being in a situation of extreme poverty, and therefore pursue higher income. Thus, higher incomes rather than lower incomes are associated with positive appraisals of well-being, according to this "objective" definition of poverty. Income is assumed to be the most important asset to provoke a positive feeling about life. Assuming that the poor themselves can reveal their true life satisfaction better than any objective indicator, economic and noneconomic aspects of well-being can be traced. Thus, expressed preferences are gauged in lieu of revealed preferences. This strand of thought uses surveys in order to gauge how the poor feel about a number of life aspects, such as income, reference group consumption, institutional quality, social trust, mobility, health, safety from crime, education, employment.

Respondents in general are asked, all things being equal on a scale of one to ten, "On the whole, how satisfied are you with your life?" Several studies found that some conditions that increase income do not increase happiness, or may even lower happiness.[28] In other words, the influence of some conditions on income appears to be substantially different from the ways they affect happiness. Graham and Pettinato found that relative income and social consumption matter in the case of Latin American countries and Rojas found that Mexico has a large presence of "happy poor".[29] Schimmels found some interesting discrepancies in country ranking comparing the human development index (HDI) ranking and Happiness ranking. For example, Colombia together with Switzerland is second on the happiness ranking (8.1 happiness average), while Colombia's standing is much lower in the HDI ranking. Schimmels argues that either people do not assess their situation in a discrete manner (poverty vs. wealth) or they consider other dimensions in assessing their situation. Kingdon and Knight found similar indications of a weak relationship between income and well-being poverty in the case of South Africa.[30]

People may have a different notion of poverty, eschewing the popular assumption that poverty can be viewed objectively. Rojas claims that experienced poverty is not strongly related to income poverty. He explains this discrepancy by looking at how respondents in Mexico interpret the notion of happy life. His findings suggest that there is no universal conceptualization of a happy life. The reverse of this finding is that if there is heterogeneity of happiness, then it is possible that poverty does not enjoy a universal conceptualization. Holden also points to the possible lack of a universal conceptualization of poverty, documenting this claim with the case of the *Adivasi* people from the Nilgiri Mountains of Tamil Nadu in India.[31]

*Voices of the poor*, a study conducted by the World Bank in 1999, and which reveals the voices of 40,000 people covered in 23 countries, also suggest the significance of relativity in conceptualizing poverty.[32] This work provides a rich tapestry of differences and similarities facing the poor around the world, and reveals the multidimensional and interlocking nature of poverty. While the voices clearly indicate that poverty integrates multiple life aspects such as the lack of resources, income, access to health services, and education opportunities, the voices also underscore the feelings of being excluded socially. The experience of being poor is related to wealth and living in stressful conditions. Accordingly, "it is not only wealth that matters, it's peace of mind too."[33] However, some caution is in order because feelings and emotions are a mental appraisal of an objective condition, but not the condition itself. An individual is able to socially adapt to its situation thereby engage in self-denial in terms of the deprivation. This is Sen's main concern with SWB.[34]

In conclusion, the meaning and measurement of poverty has shifted through time from *output maximization* to *poverty minimization*, from *potential and opportunities* to *ability to achieve happiness*.

## POVERTY IN TOURISM STUDIES

Tourism studies that address poverty issues reflect poorly the discussion in the mainstream development studies regarding poverty paradigms. These paradigms are connected in expanding the informational basis to better our understanding of the complexity and multidimensionality of poverty. Income, basic needs, freedom, and happiness are important dimensions in shaping the opportunities, choices and the quality of life of the poor. But why have tourism studies not focused on poverty in a systematic way?

**TABLE 2.1** Tourism and Poverty

| Authors | Country | Empirical Method | Main Findings |
|---|---|---|---|
| Sharpley and Naidoo (2010) | Republic of Mauritius | N/A | Tourism might provide short-term benefits to the poor; however, these benefits could diminish in a long-term |
| Jiang et al. (2011) | Asia-Pacific, Caribbean and Africa | Correlations | Tourism contributed to poverty alleviation and improved human development in small island developing states |
| Zapata et al. (2011) | Nicaragua | Survey data analysis | The results of the study suggested that donors and policy-makers should provide stronger support to local markets |
| Kwaramba et al. (2012) | South Africa | Survey data analysis | Women who provided the home-stays scored low in terms of self-management, social skills, self, and also social awareness. |
| Lacher and Oh (2012) | USA | Estimation and margining | Tourism expenditures resulted in a lower income distribution compared to the general income distribution |

**TABLE 2.1** *(Continued)*

| Authors | Country | Empirical Method | Main Findings |
|---|---|---|---|
| Snyman (2012) | Botswana, Malawi and Namibia | Survey data analysis | Ecotourism employment enhanced financial security and social welfare for people in the remote rural areas |
| Scheyvens (2011) | Fiji | N/A | The article identified a number of issues that posed a threat to the PPT initiatives |
| Tucker and Boonabaana (2012) | Turkey and Uganda | N/A | Authors found a number of socio-cultural factors that both limited and facilitated men and women's participation in tourism |
| Adiyia et al. (2014) | Uganda | N/A | Tourism provided a diversification of livelihood for the locals. Those who relied on the employment in the accommodations sector had the lowest income |
| Truong et al. (2014) | Vietnam | N/A | The poor perceived benefits to be unequal |
| Zeng et al. (2014) | China | Survey data analysis | The locals were found to benefit financially from the tourism development. Could not increase those benefits due to a lack of the investment resources |

For the longest time, tourism studies have centered their attention on the trickle-down theory to propel growth and private incomes. Tourism has relied on this framework instead of proving its link to poverty reduction. Most studies assume that the benefits from tourism will just spread to the poor. The trickle-down effect suggests that the poor would reap the benefits of such growth through various benefits of tourism spending at the destination. The studies focus mainly on efficiency and economic growth, while equity or the distribution of benefits reaching the poor directly remained under-researched. A list of previous research about tourism and poverty is presented in Table 2.1.

Studies were more concerned with tourism's potential rather than evidence of tourism's impact on poverty reduction. It was not until the second half of the twentieth century that tourism studies began focusing on the direct impact of tourism on poverty. These studies eschewed the trickle-down theory and are mainly empirically grounded.[35] Only recently have frameworks other than the trickle-down approach begun to be applied in tourism studies. For example, Sen's capabilities approach and the SWB were integrated in assessing the role of tourism in poverty reduction in countries such as Costa Rica, Nicaragua, Ecuador, and South Africa, and in areas such as global fisheries. A review of these studies is provided in Table 2.2.

Tourism studies investigating the link between tourism and poverty reduction have been relatively restrained in integrating the conceptual discussion about the construct of poverty. Only a few studies venture in the discussion regarding the interpretation of poverty. Of those studies that discuss the meaning of poverty, the construct is conceived by implicitly borrowing a number of components stemming from the frameworks discussed previously.[36] The conceptualization of poverty as a multidimensional and complex construct is common in these studies.

For example, Holden borrows from all the frameworks, such as income paradigm, basic needs, capabilities, and SWB. According to his perspective, the meaning of poverty should be directly derived from the experience of the poor while taking into account freedom and social norms as well as the possession of resources and the level of participation or marginalization from society. Zhao and Ritchie also stress the multidimensional aspect of poverty. However, although they pose the question "what is poverty and who are the poor?" as one of the three basic questions of their proposed framework, they remain silent about providing an answer.[37]

Similarly, Scheyvens integrates ideas from capabilities, empowerment, sustainable livelihoods, and human rights defining poverty as the lack of material resources, satisfaction of basic needs, and freedom to choose. According to Scheyvens, this conceptualization of poverty also incorporates peoples' assessment of their own condition. Coulthard, Johnson, and McGregor combine the objective and subjective dimensions of well-being within a relational context, and define a poor person as one who is undernourished, is in physiological decline while being happy, and lacking relational experience. Croes perceives poverty as not only the inability to consume a bundle of goods but also as the lack of opportunities to pursue a life that is valued. Both Holden and Croes underscore the objective perspective regarding the meaning poverty, while Scheyvens mentions the subjective approach to poverty in passing. Only Croes has empirically assessed the relationship between tourism and poverty reduction by applying the income paradigm lens and the capabilities approach filter.[38]

## TOWARD A FIFTH PARADIGM: THE POP

A comprehensive view would now inspect and address poverty by linking several elements from the four paradigms discussed earlier. Our view on poverty relates to a fifth paradigm anchored in a lack of economic resources as the defining element of poverty. Lack of resources is associated with scarcity, and scarcity impacts the degree of satisfaction of the absolute and relative needs of individuals. The degree of satisfaction of these needs is connected to social arrangements and rules. This connection ultimately defines the objective and SWB of the individual. To reverse the abject situation of poverty, the poor should have access to economic resources either through jobs or government transfers towards health, education, and other needs. Only economic growth seems to provide the opportunity to pull out people from the condition of lack of resources, and hence, poverty.

The previous discussion regarding poverty reveals that the four mainstream paradigms have perceived poverty as lacking, deficient, or as an opposite version of well-being, affluent, and happy. Poverty is related to ill-being in terms of lack of resources, assets, nutrients, shelter, clothes, opportunities, choices, freedom and happiness, marginalization from society, powerlessness, and inferiority compared to other groups in benefits and responsibility sharing in society. The conceptualization of poverty stemming from the four frameworks suggests an incremental build-up of relevant aspects that shape the face of the poor. Resources, basic needs, freedom, and voices are all integrated in the conceptualization of the poor.

However, defining poverty solely in terms of deprivation would compromise the conceptual distinction between poverty and well-being. Sen, for example, considers freedom as the heart of well-being. He makes this point by claiming that the difference between fasting and starving is in the free choice of fasting, while starving is the consequence of lack of access to food. One could make the point, however, that a tyrant can take away your freedom of choice, but this is certainly not poverty. While restricting opportunities to pursue someone's well-being, the defining feature of poverty seems to be the failure to achieve certain basic capabilities.

While Sen does not identify these basic capabilities, one could argue that these basic capabilities lie in the realm of economic resources. For one thing, poverty perceived as a social problem has over time gained a social meaning that is narrow and is related to lack of economic resources. Lack of economic resources prompt "failure of basic capabilities" to support adequate well-being. In other words, lack of economic resources is part of the causal chain leading to a low level of well-being. Resources in this context include income, access to health, education, social networks, and so on.

This lack of command of economic resources has an absolute and relative meaning. In an absolute sense, poverty means that resources are not adequate to satisfy basic needs. Basic needs were perceived as physical needs, needs that are related to the physical human conditions such as food, shelter, and clothes. These needs were perceived as basic, absolute needs. Satiating these needs was essential in Adam Smith's thought process; in his words, "... necessaries ... which are indispensably necessary for the support of life ...". The focus on basic human needs was later underscored by Keynes in his 1930 essay "Economic Possibilities for Our Grandchildren". In this essay Keynes underscored the relevance of basic needs.[39]

**TABLE 2.2** Tourism and Well-Being

| Authors | Focus | Empirical/ Conceptual | Unit of Analysis | Major Findings |
|---|---|---|---|---|
| Hall and Brown (2006) | Tourists | Conceptual | Welfare | Integration of pro-poor tourism (PPT) initiatives with higher level development programs was necessary |
| Andereck and Nyaupane (2010) | Residents | Empirical | Quality of life | Benefits from tourism mediated the effect of the economic aspects of quality of life |
| McCabe et al. (2010) | Tourist | Empirical | Well-being and quality of life | Participation in tourism enhanced quality of life of low-income families |

**TABLE 2.2** *(Continued)*

| Authors | Focus | Empirical/ Conceptual | Unit of Analysis | Major Findings |
|---|---|---|---|---|
| Nawijn and Mitas (2011) | Residents | Empirical | Well-being | Tourism impacts were found to affect the cognitive component (i.e., life satisfaction) of residents' subjective well-being (SWB). The effect of tourism on the affective component of SWB was not confirmed |
| Fyall et al. (2013) | Tourists and residents | Conceptual | Well-being and quality of life | Well-being and quality of life of both tourists and residents should play the central role in the tourism agendas |
| Kim et al. (2013) | Residents | Empirical | Life satisfaction | Authors confirmed the link between residents' perceptions of tourism impact with residents' life satisfaction |
| McCabe and Johnson (2013) | Tourists | Empirical | Well-being | Tourism enhanced well-being of social tourists |
| Pagán (2013) | Tourists | Empirical | Satisfaction | People with disabilities had higher levels of life satisfaction after taking holiday trips compared to people without disabilities |
| Smith and Reisinger (2013) | Tourist | Conceptual | Quality of life | Author advocated for the wellness tourism, which could help to find authentic selves, enhance peoples' emotional and spiritual well-beings |

Yet, basic needs do not comport to the total universe of human needs. Prompting productive efforts to satiate our basic needs also provokes social exchange, which in turn, prods social needs together with physical needs. Social needs color our perceptions regarding poverty. Smith refers to the relevance of these social needs in human exchange. In comparing the situation between Scots and Englishmen, Smith claims that poverty should be defined by the ability of someone to engage socially without embarrassment.[40] Social comparison stemming from the pursuit of superiority or status was subsequently endorsed by Keynes and Veblen. Keynes in his 1930 essay made the relevant distinction between our basic (absolute) needs in isolation from others, and our relative needs, which is related to our feeling of superiority regarding others. Veblen also alluded to the importance of positional lifestyle and goods that infer social status to an individual. Veblen mentioned this competition as conspicuous consumption consisting of high social value that eventually will become insatiable.[41]

The end result of the pursuit of insatiable needs exacerbates the context of scarcity. Combining physical and social scarcity is a social combustion that propels inequality and poverty. In this context, whatever we produce due to our work to increase wealth tends to raise inequality and prolong poverty. The race for status breeds inequality, and inequality in turn decreases opportunities, slows wealth creation (growth) and may unravel the social fabric and institutions, destabilizing society.[42] Higher levels of income growth and faster economic growth do not necessarily result in lower inequality, in more access to education, health and nutrition outcomes. For example, education is claimed to be an important capability to improve one's standard of living and is correlated with higher levels of growth.[43] However, years of more schooling and improvement in education levels in Africa has not correlated with economic growth.[44] Inequality has erased most of the effects of growth in that continent due to education. The reason is that inequality distorts incentives, discourages motivation, and consequently, discounts the future for many, blocking social mobility.

Inequality also prolongs poverty through perpetuating poverty triggering secular poverty. Poverty is not only a result of social arrangements and rules but also of bad choices made by individuals. These bad choices are mainly the consequence of scarcity, thereby completing the full circle. In other words, poverty propels low levels of human capital that breeds on itself. For example, under-nutrition may reduce school attendance or poor performance of these children at school, or may reduce effective use of education in life. On the other hand, public health programs may be less successful in a context of illiteracy. Thus, forms of human capital are interconnected, a failure or lack in one form may lead to a lack of investment in others.

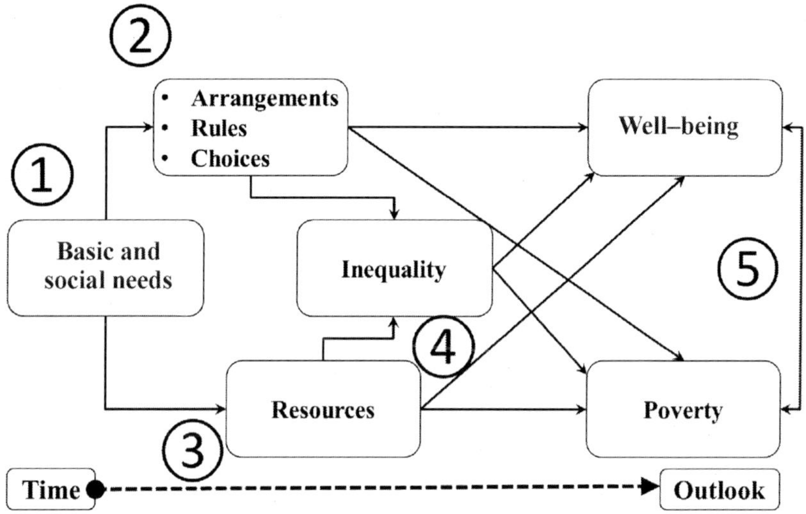


**FIGURE 2.3** The Poverty Obliteration Paradigm.

A recent study in South Africa found that females with low income are not able to gauge the benefits from development programs, and therefore do not engage in these programs.[45] In other words, scarcity is a product of insatiable needs, which engenders inequality; inequality slows growth, generating and prolonging poverty, poverty feeds on itself through more scarcity, and consequently spawns secular poverty. Viewing poverty through the filter of scarcity means that poverty is a multidimensional as well as a contextual concept that refers to the possession of a few goods and accessibility to services (health and education) as well as part of a social status (social exclusion). The poor see themselves deprived from most resources and assets, and the social constraints that restrict their access to these resources.[46] This definition integrates both income and nonincome aspects of poverty and allows for the identification of the poor and the determination of the scale of poverty in a country as well as the identification of the determinants of poverty. The question is, however, whether absolute needs and relative needs enjoy the same weight in defining poverty.

We saw evidence that indicates that poverty is intertwined with the daily activities and choices that people make. From this perspective, poverty seems a relative concept that is related to a lack of socially perceived necessities. The answer to our needs seems to depend on place and time, and poverty, from this perspective, is not a situation of free will, but a forced situation. While this reasoning is intuitively appealing, studies have identified a set of life domains (employment, health, education, social relations) that are perceived as being crucial for the well-being of a vast majority of people. Studies in Mexico, Bangladesh, Guatemala, and in Calcutta, India, indicate a large number of "happy poor" despite living in deprived situations.[47] This finding suggests that not everything is relative, and there are some needs that are fundamental to human life such as subsistence, protection, and affection. Consequently, we argue that these life domains require priority in our poverty framework. Figure 2.3 depicts the *POP* framework.

The *POP* framework indicates that satisfaction of needs depend on individual motivation, opportunities, social arrangements, rules, and resources. Motivation is shaped by individual achievement, recognition, responsibility, advancement, self-esteem, and optimism, and defines choices. Choices are also influenced by opportunities triggered by social arrangements and rules, and by past experiences and future expectations. Objective conditions and how these conditions are perceived define the degree of satisfaction of needs. How these needs are satisfied may lead to well-being or poverty. Experienced poverty may be different than income poverty from this perspective. The path to well-being or poverty is shaped by some intervening factors such as inequality and opportunities.

The POP framework also contemplates that poverty is not a static situation, but may reveal a fluid situation; a person can experience poverty at different points in time, escaping poverty, being trapped in poverty, or returning to poverty. These fluid situations (or multiple equilibria) reveal conditions of insecurity, risk, vulnerability, lack of assets, and social exclusion. In the next chapter, we will discuss the relationship between tourism development and the *POP* framework.

## REFERENCES

Adiyia, B.; Vanneste, D.; Van Rompaey, A.; Ahebwa, W. M. Spatial analysis of tourism income distribution in the accommodation sector in western Uganda. *Tourism Hospitality Res.* 2014, 14(1–2), 8–26.

Alkire, S. The missing dimensions of poverty data: introduction to the special issue. *Oxford Dev. Stud.* 2007, 35(4), 347–359.

Andereck, K. L.; Nyaupane, G. P. Exploring the nature of tourism and quality of life perceptions among residents. *J. Travel Res.* 2010, 50(3), 248–260.

Banerjee, A.; Duflo, E. *Poor Economics. A radical rethinking of the way to fight global poverty*; Public Affairs: New York, NY, 2011.

Bhagwati, J.; Panagariya, A. *Why Growth Matters*; Public Affairs: New York, NY, 2013.

Biswas-Diener, R.; Diener, E. Making the best of a bad situation: Satisfaction in the slums of Calcutta. *Soc. Indic. Res*. 2001, 55, 329–352.

Booth, C. The inhabitants of Tower Hamlets (School Board Division), their condition and occupations. *J. R. Stat. Soc*. 1887, 50, 326–340.

Bradshaw, T. *Competing Theories of Poverty and Anti-poverty Programs in Community Development (Working Paper Series No.06-05)*; Rural Poverty Research Center: Columbia, MO, 2006.

Brock, K. "It's Not Only Wealth that Matters – It's Peace of Mind Too": A Review of Participatory Work on Poverty and Illbeing. Prepared for the Global Synthesis Workshop, Consultations with the Poor, World Bank: Washington, DC, 1999.

Camfield, L.; Choudhury, K.; Devine, J. *Relationships, Happiness and Wellbeing: Insights from Bangladesh*; Economic & Social Research Council, University of Bath: UK, 2006.

Clark, D. Sen's capability approach and the many spaces of human well-being. *J. Dev. Stud.* 2005, 41(8), 1339–1368.

Coulthard, S.; Johnson, D.; McGregor, J. Poverty, sustainability and human wellbeing: a social wellbeing approach to the global fisheries crisis. *Global Environ. Change*. 2011, 21, 453–463.

Croes, R. Assessing tourism development from Sen's capability approach. *J. Travel Res*. 2012, 51(5), 542–554.

Croes, R. The role of tourism in poverty reduction: an empirical assessment. *Tourism Econ.* 2014, 20(2), 207–226.

Croes, R.; Vanegas, M. Tourism and poverty alleviation: a co-integration analysis. *J. Travel Res*. 2008, 47(1), 94–103.

Easterly, W. *The Elusive Quest for Growth: Economists' Adventures and Misadventures in the Tropics*; MIT Press: Cambridge, MA, 2002.

Frank, R. H. Should public policy respond to positional externalities? *J. Public Econ*. 2008, 92(8–9), 1777–1786.

Fyall, A.; Hartwell, H.; Hemingway, A. Public health, wellbeing & tourism: opportunities for the branding of tourism destinations. *Tourism Trib*. 2013, 28(2), 16–19.

Graham, C.; Pettinato, S. Happiness, markets, and democracy: Latin America in comparative perspective. *J. Happiness Stud*. 2001, 2, 237–268.

Guardiola, J.; Garcia-Muñoz, T. Fulfillment of basic needs from a subjective point of view in rural Guatemala. *J. Soc. Welfare*. 2011, 20, 393–403.

Hall, D. R.; Brown, F. *Tourism and Welfare: Ethics, Responsibility and Sustained Well-being*; CABI: Wallingford, UK, 2006.

Haugen, G. *The Locust Effect. Why the End of Poverty Requires the End of Violence*; Oxford University Press: Oxford, UK, 2014.

Hicks, N. Growth vs. basic needs: is there a trade-off? *World Dev*. 1979, 7, 985–994.

Holden, A. *Tourism, Poverty and Development*; Routledge: New York, NY, 2013.

Jiang, M.; DeLacy, T.; Mkiramweni, N. P.; Harrison, D. Some evidence for tourism alleviating poverty. *Ann. Tourism Res*. 2011, 38(3), 1181–1184.

Kakwami, N.; Pernia, E. What is pro-poor growth? *Asian Dev. Rev*. 2000, 18(1), 1–16.

Kenny, C. Does development make you happy? Subjective wellbeing and economic growth in developing countries. *Soc. Indic. Res.* 2005, 73, 199–219.

Keynes, J. *Economic Possibilities for Our Grandchildren.* In *Essays in Persuasion*; Keynes, J. (1963); W.W. Norton & Co: New York, NY, 1930, p 358–373.

Kim, K.; Uysal, M.; Sirgy, M. J. How does tourism in a community impact the quality of life of community residents? *Tourism Manage.* 2013, 36, 527–540.

Kingdon, G.; Knight, J. Subjective well-being poverty vs. income poverty and capabilities poverty? *J. Dev. Stud.* 2006, 42(7), 1199–1224.

Kwaramba, H. M.; Lovett, J. C.; Louw, L.; Chipumuro, J. Emotional confidence levels and success of tourism development for poverty reduction: the South African Kwam eMakana home-stay project. *Tourism Manage.* 2012, 33(4), 885–894.

Lacher, R. G.; Oh, C.-O. Is tourism a low-income industry? Evidence from three coastal regions. *J. Travel Res.* 2012, 51(4), 464–472.

Layard, R.; Nickell, S.; Mayraz, G. The marginal utility of income. *J. Public Econ.* 2008, 92(8–9), 1846–1857.

Lewis, O. *Five Families: Mexican Case Studies in the Culture of Poverty*; Basic Books, Inc: New York, NY, 1959.

Lopez, H.; Servén, L. *The Mechanics of Growth-Poverty-Inequality Relationship*; Mimeo, World Bank: Washington, DC, 2004.

McCabe, S.; Johnson, S. The happiness factor in tourism: subjective well-being and social tourism. *Ann. Tourism Res.* 2013, 41, 42–65.

McCabe, S.; Joldersma, T.; Li, C. Understanding the benefits of social tourism: linking participation to subjective well-being and quality of life. *Int. J. Tourism Res.* 2010, 12(6), 761–773.

Mitchell, J.; Ashley, C. *Tourism and Poverty Reduction, Pathways to Prosperity*; Earthscan: London, UK, 2010.

Moynihan, D.P. The Negro Family: The Case for National Action, 1965. http://library.drmasonsclasses.com/wp-content/uploads/2013/12/Moynihan_The-Negro-Family-The-Case-for-National-Action2.pdf (retrieved April 20, 2014).

Mullainathan, S.; Shafir, A. *Scarcity, Why Having Too Little Means So Much*; Henry Holt: New York, NY, 2013.

Narayan, D.; Chambers, R.; Shah, M.; Petesch, P. *Global Synthesis. Prepared for the Global Synthesis Workshop: Consultations with the Poor*; World Bank: Washington, DC, 1999.

Nawijn, J.; Mitas, O. Resident attitudes to tourism and their effect on subjective well-being: the case of Palma De Mallorca. *J. Travel Res.* 2011, 51(5), 531–541.

Nussbaum , M. *Poverty and Human Functioning: Capabilities as Fundamental Entitlements.* In *Poverty and Inequality*; Grusky, D. B., Kanbur, R., Eds.; Stanford University Press: Stanford, CA, 2006; pp 47–75.

Nussbaum, M. *Women and Human Development: A Study in Human Capabilities*; Cambridge University Press: Cambridge, UK, 2000.

Pagán, R. (2015). The contribution of holiday trips to life satisfaction: the case of people with disabilities. *Current Issues in Tourism, 18*(6), 524-538.

Ravallion, M. *Poverty Lines in Theory and Practice, Living Standards Measurement Study. (Working Paper No. 133)*; World Bank: Washington, DC, 1998.

Ravallion, M.; Chen, S. Measuring pro-poor growth. *Econ. Lett.* 2003, 78, 93–99.

Robeyns, I. The Capability approach: a theoretical survey. *J. Hum. Dev.* 2005, 6(1), 93–114.

Rodrik, D. *In Search of Prosperity, Analytic Narratives on Economic Growth*; Princeton University Press: Princeton, NJ, 2003.

Rojas, M. Experienced poverty and income poverty in Mexico: a subjective well-being approach. *World Dev*. 2008, 6, 1078–1093.

Rojas, M. Well-being and the complexity of well-being-A subjective well-being approach. UNU-WIDER, United Nations University, No. 2004/29, 2004. http://www.rrojasdatabank.info/unurp04/rp2004-029_1.pdf (retrieved April 20, 2014).

Rowntree, B. S. *Poverty, a Study of Town Life*; MacMillan and Co: London, UK, 1902.

Scheyvens, R. *Tourism and Poverty*; Routledge: New York, NY, 2011.

Schimmel, J. *Development as Happiness and UNDP's Analysis of Poverty, Wealth and Development*. In *The Exploration of Happiness*; Della Fave, A., Ed.; Springer: Dordrecht, the Netherlands, 2013; pp 281–302.

Schneider, F.; Buehn, A.; Montenegro, C. New estimates for the shadow economies all over the world. *Int. Econ. J*. 2010, 24(4), 443–461.

Sen, A. *Commodities and Capabilities*; Elsevier Science: New York, NY, 1985.

Sen, A. *Development as Freedom*; Anchor Books: New York, NY, 1999.

Sen, A. *Inequality Reexamined*; Clarendon Press: Oxford, UK, 1992.

Sen, A. *On Economic Inequality*; Clarendon Press: Oxford, UK, 1997.

Sen, A. *Poverty and Famines: An Essay on Entitlements and Deprivation*; Clarendon Press: Oxford, UK, 1982.

Sharpley, R.; Naidoo, P. Tourism and poverty reduction: the case of Mauritius. *Tourism Hospitality Plann. Dev*. 2010, 7(2), 145–162.

Smith, M.; Reisinger, Y. *5 Transforming Quality of Life Through Wellness Tourism*. In *Transformational Tourism: Tourist Perspectives*; Reisinger, Y., Ed.; CABI Publishing: Wallingford, 2013; pp 55–67.

Snyman, S. L. The role of tourism employment in poverty reduction and community perceptions of conservation and tourism in southern Africa. *J. Sustainable Tourism*. 2012, 20(3), 395–416.

Sowell, T. *A Conflict of Visions. Ideological Origins of Political Struggles*; Basic Books: New York, NY, 2007.

Stiglitz, J. *The Price of Inequality*; W.W. Norton: New York, NY, 2012.

Streeten, P. Basic needs: premises and promises. *J. Policy Modell*. 1979, 1, 136–146.

Thorbecke, E. Multi-dimensional Poverty: Conceptual and Measurement Issues. Paper presented at the Many Dimensions of Poverty International Conference, UNDP International Poverty Center, Brasilia, 2005, August 29–31.

Truong, V. D., Hall, C. M., & Garry, T. (2014). Tourism and poverty alleviation: perceptions and experiences of poor people in Sapa, Vietnam. *Journal of Sustainable Tourism*, *22*(7), 1071-1089.

Tucker, H.; Boonabaana, B. A critical analysis of tourism, gender and poverty reduction. *J. Sustainable Tourism*. 2012, 20(3), 437–455.

Veblen, T. *The Theory of the Leisure Class*; Penguin: New York, NY, 1987.

Verspoor, A. Educational development: priorities for the nineties. *Finance Dev*. 1990, 27, 20–23.

White, H.; Anderson, A. Growth vs. Redistribution: Does the Pattern of Growth Matter? DFID white paper on Eliminating World Poverty: Making Globalization Work for the Poor. Retrieved April 20, 2014 from Eliminating World Poverty: Making Globalization Work for the Poor, 2000. http://www.hivpolicy.org/Library/HPP000152.pdf.

Zapata, M. J.; Hall, C. M.; Lindo, P.; Vanderschaeghe, M. Can community-based tourism contribute to development and poverty alleviation? Lessons from Nicaragua. *Curr. Issues Tourism*. 2011, 14(8), 725–749.

Zeng, B., Ryan, C., Cui, X., & Chen, H. (2015). Tourism-generated Income Distribution in a Poor Rural Community: A Case Study from Shaanxi, China.*Journal of China Tourism Research, 11*(1), 85-104.

Zhao, W.; Ritchie, J. Tourism and poverty alleviation: an integrative research framework. *Curr. Issues Tourism*. 2007, 10(2&3), 119–143.

## ENDNOTES

[1]See, for example, Sen (1999).

[2]See, for example, Sowell (2007).

[3]See, for example, Easterly (2002) and Rodrik (2003).

+See, for example, Bhagwati and Panagariya (2013).

[5]See Ravallion (1998).

[6]See http://www.un.org/millenniumgoals/.

[7]See Booth (1887) and Rowntree (1902).

[8]For a discussion on blaming the poor, see, for example, Bradshaw (2006).

[9]See, for example, Bradshaw (2006).

[10]In Mozambique people are grouped as *Ovelavela* and *Wihacha*, or undeserving of help. The former refers to people who are ostracized by their family due to their own actions, and the latter refers to lazy young men, divorced, and addicted to alcohol and drugs. See Holden (2013).

[11]See, for example, Lewis (1959), and Moynihan (1965).

[12]For examples see Ravallion and Chen, 2003White and Anderson (2000), and Kakwami and Pernia (2000).

[13]See Lopez and Serven (2004).

[14]See, for example, Sen (1982), Mullainathan and Shafir (2013) and Banerjee and Duflo (2011).

[15]Haugen refers to the predatory and criminal violence destroying everything for poor people as the "locust effect" (see Haugen, 2014).

[16]See, for example, Streeten (1979).

[17]For a discussion on this topic, see, for example, Hicks (1979).

[18]See Sen (1985, 1999).

[19]See Sen (1999).

[20]Sen distinguishes income inequality from economic inequality by expanding the information requirements to perform social evaluations. See Sen (1997).

[21]See Clark (2005), Robeyns (2005), and Alkire (2007).

[22]See Nussbaum (2000, 2006).

[23]See Sen (1992, pp. 44–45).

[24]See Thorbecke (2005, p. 4).

[25]See Rojas (2004, 2008) and Schimmel (2013).

[26]See Rojas (2008).

[27]See, for example, Schneider et al. (2010).

[28]See, for example, Layard et al. (2008) claim that marginal utility of income decreases with higher incomes. Similarly, Frank (2008) argues that after some wealth threshold social consumption becomes relevant in social interaction.

[29]See Graham and Pettinato (2001) and Rojas (2008).

[30]See Kingdon and Knight (2006). The scant attention regarding happiness in developing countries is remarkable and surprising. Poverty has been a subject of study and attention since World War II; however, only a handful of studies have focused on the expressed preferences of the poor.

[31]See Holden (2013) and Rojas (2008).

[32]See Brock (1999) and Narayan et al. (1999).

[33]See Brock (1999) at http://siteresources.worldbank.org/INTPOVERTY/Resources/335642-1124115102975/1555199-1124138742310/ngorev.pdf, retrieved April 18, 2014.

[34]According to Sen (1985, pp. 308–309), "The most blatant forms of inequalities and exploitations survive in the world through making allies out of the deprived and exploited. The underdog learns to bear the burden so well that he or she overlooks the burden itself. Discontent is replaced by acceptance … suffering and anger by cheerful endurance. As people learn to adjust … the horrors look less terrible in the metric of utilities."

[35]Only a few studies attempted to empirically demonstrate this link. Croes and Vanegas (2008) found that tourism reduces poverty in the case of Nicaragua, but Croes (2012, 2014) found mixed results regarding the impact of tourism on poverty reduction in the cases of Nicaragua and Costa Rica.

[36]See, for example, Croes (2014), Holden (2013), and Scheyvens (2011). On the other hand, Mitchell and Ashley (2010) neglect the discussion altogether in their research regarding the channels through which tourism impacts poverty reduction.

[37]See Holden (2013) and Zhao and Ritchie (2007).

[38]For more details see Coulthard et al. (2011), Croes (2012, 2014), and Scheyvens (2011).

[39]"Those needs which are absolute in the sense that we feel them whatever the situation of our fellow human beings may be … the absolute needs- a point may soon be reached, much sooner perhaps than we are all of us aware of, when these needs are satisfied in the sense that we prefer to devote our further energies to non-economic purposes." Sen (1992, p. 109) also underscores the meaning of poverty as "the failure of basic capabilities to reach certain minimally acceptable levels."

[40]For a discussion on Smith's views on the relevance of social comparison, see, for example, Kenny (2005).

[41]See Keynes (1930) and Veblen (1987). Veblen states that "… a satiation of the average or general desire for wealth is out of the question … no general increase of community's wealth

can make any approach to satiating this need, the ground of which is the desire of everyone to excel everyone else in the accumulation of goods."

[42]See, for example, the discussion by Stiglitz (2012).

[43]See, for example, Verspoor (1990).

[44]For a discussion on the relationship between education and growth, see, for example, Easterly (2002) and Stiglitz (2012).

[45]For a discussion, see Kwaramba et al. (2012).

[46]See Brock (1999).

[47]For a discussion on the case of Mexico, see Rojas (2004, 2008); the case of Bangladesh, see Camfield et al. (2006); for the case of India, see Biswas-Diener and Diener (2001); and for the case of Guatemala, see Guardiola and Garcia-Muñoz (2011).

## CHAPTER 3

# THE POTENTIAL DOUBLE IMPACT OF TOURISM DEVELOPMENT AND POVERTY REDUCTION

## CONTENTS

## INTRODUCTION

Tourism development is credited to be a powerful source of economic progression in developing countries. In these areas, tourism has significantly expanded over time. Developing countries saw their share of global tourism increase to 46% in 2011, amounting to 465 million arrivals. The steady and higher growth rates of international tourist arrivals in developing countries during 2005 and 2012 demonstrate the trend of a more diversified global distribution of international tourism. In those periods, international tourism in developing countries increased by 4.8% compared to 2.6% in advanced countries. In 2012, Latin America, Asia, and sub-Saharan Africa were in the top regions with the fastest growth rates in international tourism arrivals.

Tourism has become an important economic activity for many developing countries in their search to lessen poverty and increase economic growth. The tourism-led growth (TLG) strategy remains the main reason for developing countries to allocate resources to tourism. The TLG asserts that tourism creates jobs and income, leads to positive balance of payments, prompts business opportunities, and results in increased economic activity. Many developing countries have already adopted tourism as an important development tool in their strategies to lessen poverty.[1] For example, Mitchell and Ashley assert that 80% of poverty reduction documents in Africa reference tourism.

As a whole, mitigating factors as well as the low amount of studies dedicated to this solution makes it difficult to clearly recognize the link and its possible benefits. Empirical evidence showing poverty reduction directly linked to tourism development is lacking or weak. However, unlike other economic stimuli previously suggested for the least developing countries, the tourism development strategy aimed at poverty reduction has unique advantages.

Tourism development may indirectly offer the following benefits:

- higher stable employment,
- increased access to healthcare,
- increased access to education,
- stable export revenue,
- opportunity in remote areas,
- economic diversity,
- tangible and location-specific commodity value.

Without delving into the link between tourism and poverty reduction and its potential to fight poverty, developing countries run the risk of squandering scarce resources and missing alternative opportunities. Tourism could bring food to the table while simultaneously providing opportunities to live a fulfilling and meaningful life. This chapter analyzes the relationship of tourism development to poverty reduction, utilizing the poverty framework discussed in the previous chapter.

## THE EXPANSION OF INTERNATIONAL TOURISM IN DEVELOPING COUNTRIES

When tourism is used as a growth engine to assist in poverty reduction, there may be several advantages over other forms of economic stimuli. Tourism may provide the poor with more opportunities than any other economic sector. The tourist must go to a place because the tourist product is not portable. When the tourist gets to a place, the tourist roams around, and may therefore easily make contact with poor people. The direct tie to tourists is the source why there is widespread belief that tourism can reduce poverty.[2] This is because the tourist consumes a bundle of services and nontraded goods locally from more than one supplier. Thus, many different service suppliers participate in creating a tourism experience. This creates the opportunity for poor, marginal, and remote areas to benefit from the advantages (increased employment opportunities, higher income levels, and a trickle-down effect) that tourism spending may bring to a destination.

Poor people seem to concentrate at important heritage junctures that exercise a large appeal to tourists. For example, in the Bolivian Amazon, the inscription of the Ichapekene Piesta Moxos onto the 2012 United Nations Educational, Scientific, and Cultural Organization (UNESCO) Representative List of the Intangible Cultural Heritage of Humanity has prompted opportunities for the poor and the tourists to mingle.[3] Being on this list may increase the appeal of the attraction or site, as poor countries in general are blessed with rich cultural and natural assets. Nature, culture, and heritage are some of the main motivations for people to engage in international travel, and this segment has steadily grown over time. Of the 48 least developed countries, more than half have world heritage sites within their borders. Actually, close to half of the world heritage sites are located outside the European and North American regions.[4] The potential for cultural tourism to contribute to their development is considerable. This interaction can bring jobs and income to this very poor region of the country.[5]

International organizations embrace tourism because of this interaction.[6] The potential of tourism to reduce poverty has exercised powerful influence on development programs of these organizations. For example, the 7th session of the United Nations Commission on Sustainable Development (CSD7) in 1997 reviewed the important relationship between tourism and sustainable tourism. This review was continued in the Canary Island Declaration on Tourism in the Least Development Countries (LDCs) in March 2001, the World Summit on Sustainable Development held in Johannesburg in 2002, and the establishment of joint project between the UNCTAD and the WTO, called Sustainable Tourism – Eliminating Poverty (STEP).

STEP has as its main purpose the promotion of development and the creation of jobs for people living on less than US$1/d through tourism. WTO issued a report in 2002 stating that tourism should be used as a tool to fight poverty.[7] The WTO report on page 17 states that "the power of tourism – one of the most dynamic economic activities of our time –can be more effectively harnessed to address the problems of poverty more directly." This report departs from the notion that tourism as a development strategy may alleviate poverty. This notion is contrary to the view revealed in De Kadt's (1979) report, which questioned the usefulness of tourism for developing countries. The new WTO report asserts that not only has tourism become more important in the development of these poor countries (in 11 of the 12 economies of the poorest countries tourism plays a "significant" role), but tourism has also become almost the only hope for a quick reduction of poverty in these countries.[8]

## THE PUZZLE BETWEEN TOURISM DEVELOPMENT AND POVERTY REDUCTION

Despite the advantages of tourism revenues, some critics claim that tourism revenues do not reduce poverty, but instead entrench inequality. They claim that despite efforts, tourism may not automatically relieve poverty. The dynamic effects of tourism could be either positive (lifting the poor outside the tourism sector) or straddling the poor by negative externalities such as inflation, exchange rate, or deterioration of the environment. From their empirical viewpoint, the benefits of tourism development to developing countries are at best ambiguous. For example, studies conducted in Central America reveal that the effects of tourism expansion on poverty reduction are uneven. Poverty elasticities vary among the countries in Central America. For example, tourism has strong effects in Costa Rica, Guatemala, and Nicaragua, and modest-to-weak effects in Salvador and Honduras.[9]

Part of the problem is that the ability of tourism to deliver to the poor depends on contextual conditions, such as the mix of incentives and organizational capabilities. This mix of incentives and organizational capabilities define how tourism economies are structured. Recent research indicates that the impact of tourism on the poor hinges more on the structure of tourism economies and less on the types of tourists patronizing destinations.[10] For example, the lack of collaboration so necessary in delivering the tourism experience seems rampant in Latin America. Two studies conducted in Puntarenas in Costa Rica suggest that backward linkages are not occurring in the tourism sector, and poor governance structure and human, social, and institutional capacities are excluding the participation of many communities in the tourism market.[11]

Heritage projects in the Bolivian Amazon, such as the inscription of the Ichapeken Piesta Moxos onto the 2012 UNESCO Representative List of Intangible Cultural Heritage of Humanity and the Museo Yacuma have not brought the expected benefits to the communities. Similarly, the expected benefits from heritage projects in the North Coast of Peru seem elusive due to lack of trust and contention between local and central government officials.[12] The Economic Commission for Latin America and the Caribbean documents the level of distrust in Latin American institutions. This low level of trust in institutions is also extended to societal rules and fellow citizens.[13] This level of distrust of the poor is caused by their accumulated experience with displacement at heritage sites and their endured official violence that often goes with impunity.[14]

Human capital also seems to play a role in mitigating evidence of the expected benefits in poor communities. For example, lack of knowledge and knowhow in the designing, packaging, and on-time delivery of the tourism product have prevented 23 of the 24 small-scale initiatives comprising a pro-poor project in Costa Rica from rendering the expected positive impact on poor communities.[15] The low performance of these initiatives suggests the difficulties surrounding these pro-poor projects in developing countries. Thus, the relationship between tourism development and poverty reduction is not self-evident.

## TOURISM, ECONOMIC GROWTH, AND COMPARATIVE ADVANTAGE

Tourism can impact poverty indirectly through economic growth. For a long time, mainstream economics claimed that growth prompts poverty reduction. Recent empirical studies indicate that growth is the best strategy for the poor.[16] Boosted by these empirical studies, a large group of advocates, including the World Bank and the International Monetary Fund, are looking at tourism as a strategy for getting out of the poverty trap. Implicit in the propositions of the international organizations is that growth reduces poverty and that since tourism generates growth, tourism therefore can alleviate poverty. Tourism, therefore, offers the best development opportunity in terms of growth, job creation, and foreign exchange. If we assume that economic growth will lift people from below the poverty line, then tourism clearly prompts economic growth.

There is strong empirical evidence in the tourism literature that tourism growth leads to economic growth. Pablo-Romero and Molina examined a sample of 87 studies covering several countries (developed and developing), regions, time periods, and methods and found that only four in the sample did not identify any relationship between tourism growth and economic growth.[17] The sample of studies examined is anchored in the TLG hypothesis (TLGH), which claims that the channel through which tourism can spawn economic growth is a comparative advantage. Comparative advantage is grounded on supply-side factors, which are considered the main trade drivers among nations. Productive efficiency through technology (Ricardian perspective) or factors abundance (Heckscher-Ohlin perspective) drive price differentials that determine what countries produce and with whom they should exchange.

Exchanging based on comparative advantage (price differentials) will improve countries economically, according to the comparative advantage perspective. In other words, openness through exports has a positive impact on the economic output of a country. This theory maintains that exports promote growth through several channels, such as economies of scale, the potential of positive externalities in nonexport sectors, the encouragement of efficient allocation of resources through increasing competition, the stimulation in R&D investment and human capital, and the loosening of foreign exchange constraints.[18] International trade can provide countries the opportunity to attain the desired increasing returns to scale. Thus, trade has the advantage of increasing choices and lowering prices.

Since a destination's success with tourism depends on natural resources and its comparative advantage, a country's specialization in the context of global demand is directly linked to the abundance of resources needed to create and maintain the tourism product. For example, the Caribbean islands, with their abundant sun, sand, and sea (SSS) product, align their resources to the tastes, preferences, and demand of tourists.

Theories of factor endowment can be applied to tourism, such as mainstream trade theory.[19] Several studies have examined the importance of supply-side factors in tourism development, such as infrastructure, the environment, resources, quality, and destination life cycle. Theoretical justification, however, is lacking in most of these studies, even though each of these factors as well as combination of factors has been found to be statistically significant in explaining tourism flows. Several tourism studies posit that the availability of natural resources is the main source of comparative advantage.[20] Additionally, Zhang and Jensen propose that existing trade theories may explain tourism flows, and the authors showcased three key supply factors that explain the drivers of competitive advantage of tourism: natural resources, technology, and infrastructure.[21]

Discussions why some countries perform better in tourism compared to other countries has been at the heart of discussions regarding comparative advantage of a destination. Both traditional and newer trade theories have given astute explanations of tourism flows. Literature has shown that factors that provide a destination's comparative advantage include price competition (Ricardian comparative advantage), natural resources (e.g., SSS product, H–O theorem), multinational hotel chains, tourism clusters (agglomeration), cultural resources and heritage, natural endowments, branding, and reputation.

However, Gray suggests that the H–O model may only partially explain tourism flows. This is because of the unique nature of tourism that is riddled by imperfect competition and differentiated products and services, which violates the strict assumptions of mainstream trade theory.

Additionally, measuring factor quality and abundance is difficult to gage, and comparisons between natural endowments in the global marketplace can be challenging. This could be because several of the tourism products and goods are not exchanged on a public market. Rather, they are enjoyed collectively as combined goods. Thus, a consequence of this condition is that goods may rise to overuse since they may be offered for use at a zero price. This results in demand that is excessive with regards to the capacity for consumption.

The TLG studies have a number of common traits. They do not focus specifically on the poor, but their unit of analysis is the economic system and structure. The studies are more interested in tourism potential and do not measure the direct link between tourism and poverty. They assume that the economic benefits from tourism will automatically spread to the poor (trickle-down). The topic of interest is mainly efficiency and economic growth and how tourism can generate more income. And, finally, they tend to consider only the linear aspects of the relationship tourism and economic growth. Most of the studies investigating the link between tourism and economic growth found a positive relationship. Only a handful of studies found a negative or no significant relationship between tourism and economic growth.

The mixed experience of applying the TLG strategies to developing countries suggests serious gaps in the existing research. We already alluded to the potential intervening factors that may impact the relationship tourism and growth. A more serious problem may be that the nature of tourism development does not sustain increasing returns. Although tourism development may under certain conditions trigger positive returns, tourism development may contain aspects of diminishing returns. That is exactly what the studies of Adamou and Clerides and Ridderstaat et al. suggested in the cases of Cyprus and Aruba. Both studies suggest that tourism may not sustain a linearity relationship, but after some time the relationship may become nonlinear in nature.[22] The implications of this thought are that the sign of the relationship between tourism and growth varies over time, and the value of the elasticity is not constant. Surely, this nonlinearity aspect affects tourism demand projections in the future, potentially impacting economic growth.

## TOURISM, ECONOMIC GROWTH, AND THE ROLE OF DEMAND

As alluded to earlier, trade-growth theory seems incomplete in explaining the link between tourism and growth because the theory is mainly involved with ascertaining the efficient allocation of resources. This theory skews the tourism development evidence on two grounds. First, more inputs do not explain more outputs. In other words, performance in tourism does not depend on inputs; rather, tourism performance depends on demand. Second, trade theory does not consider the distributional effects of the allocation of resources. Traditionally, tourism as an engine of growth was measured based on its efficiency aspects. These aspects were further stressed through tourism economic impacts studies. The latter gaged how tourism reverberates through the economy by identifying this impact through several channels, such as jobs, taxes, income, and backward or forward linkages.[23] The main criticism is that trade based on comparative advantage is grounded in factor inputs and technological progress, which are exogenously determined and not linked to demand.

The demand perspective is an alternative view to comparative advantage in explaining tourism flows.[24] The demand approach suggests that differences in the levels of factor endowments between countries did not always reflect international exchange. Kaldor claims that foreign demand triggers economic growth because it enables countries to extend their markets. Countries should shift their resources that enjoyed high income elasticities of demand for exports away from sectors that command high elasticities of demand for imports. In other words, growth lies in the terms-of-trade that a country can command.[25] Kaldor's focus on demand also found empathy with Linder's demand side model in which the pattern or trade is derived from "overlapping demand". This means that countries create goods for the domestic market and then export the surplus. The assumption is that countries that acquire the supplies would have demand patterns that are similar to those of the exporting countries.

One can predict international tourism flows based on Linder's recommendations. For example, Linder assumed that the gross domestic product (GDP) provides a reasonable proxy to measure tastes. Buyers in higher income per capita of countries tend to demand higher quality goods, whereas those in lower income per capita countries tend to demand lower quality goods. Consequently, the likelihood of trade is greater between countries that have similar demands for products supplied by different countries.

This is evidenced in the fact that 63% of US international tourism payments went to higher income per capita countries like France, the Netherlands, and the UK. As a result, a clear association between domestic tourism and the level of GDP should exist.

Some researchers offer theoretical considerations focusing on demand instead of supply. First, the demand level of consumers depends on some minimal level of income. Once lower-level needs and wants are satisfied, consumers seek out "something different", which is an outward manifestation of the marginal utility concept. Travel has become an important source of additional marginal utility for consumers. Second, tourism supply is highly elastic with regards to the total costs of a vacation. The most important factors of the tourism product are nonsubstitutable goods (i.e., a beautiful beach) or nonrival goods (i.e., the nice weather at the beach), quality of the product, and marketing. The beautiful beach in this example cannot be replicated or substituted as the beach is a unique product.

Conversely, the nice weather, in this example, does not necessarily mean that the resource is wasted, since other tourists can enjoy the weather at the same time. The demand is determined by nonrival goods and nonsubstitutable goods, although the supply does not necessarily respond to prices. Instead, inputs of tourism adjust to any demand level without having a large effect on price, such as accommodations, restaurants, and entertainment. Croes, in his study, found this about tourism competitiveness in small islands that nonprice characteristics of the tourism goods are the most important factors in determining tourism performance.[26]

And third, income elasticity of tourism products is high, suggesting that an increase in the quantity of tourism products will rise more than the percentage increase of income. Thus, price elasticity of demand seems to matter less than what is expected. The combination of these two elasticity phenomena adds to stable export earnings of tourism products compared to commodity groups spawning benefits from terms of trade of destinations that specialize in tourism. Studies done by Vanegas and Croes indicated that tourism receipts are more stable over time than other economic sectors, such as agriculture and mining. Demand characteristics of products seem to define economic growth, and therefore what a country exports matters.[27]

Studies about demand have dominated the tourism literature in explaining growth and flows of tourism. Factors of demand such as income growth, as well as changes in tourists' preferences, have been found to be associated strongly with tourism growth.[28] And tourism growth has been found to be strongly correlated with economic growth. For example, Benković and Mejia found a strong correlation between tourism growth and economic growth in Colombia.[29] They conclude that the impact of the "tourism economy" on the economy as a whole has been relevant in all aspects (jobs, GDP, and expenditures by government). Therefore, if tourism growth causes economic growth and economic growth alleviates and reduces poverty, tourism development is an important catalyst in reducing poverty in developing countries. However, it is not clear that the direct link between tourism and economic growth is sustainable; tourism may have a positive impact or diminishing returns on economic growth.

The vast tourism literature on the topic of the direct link between tourism and economic growth is still without a clear answer on this important question of increasing or diminishing returns of tourism on growth. The lack of a clear answer to this question makes a positive correlation of the role of tourism and its long-term impact on poverty reduction murky.

## THE MISSING LINK

While so many developing countries have tourism development as a leading vehicle to alleviate poverty challenges, few empirical studies have been conducted showing the link between tourism development and poverty alleviation. Previously, we alluded to the strong tradition of tourism studies anchored in the trickle-down premise that has prevented the formulation of clear theoretical thinking and empirical analysis. Winters et al. found the link between tourism and poverty reduction to be "an insufficiently interesting question", and consequently many researchers do not consider it in depth.[30] Mitchell and Ashley embrace three main channels (i.e., direct, secondary and dynamic effects) through which tourism impacts poverty without providing empirical evidence of the link.[31] The previous study skipped the link question and jumped into finding "pathways" to make the link stronger. Similarly, the research agenda assessing the role of tourism influencing poverty reduction by Winters et al. stressed conditions to make the link stronger without considering if the link exists in all countries.

A small number of studies test the specific empirical relationship between tourism and poverty reduction. All other studies assume that growth will trickle down to the poor. Croes and Vanegas applied a vector autoregressive approach in assessing the role of tourism in poverty reduction in Nicaragua.[32] They found a significant positive relationship between the two variables. Blake et al. used a computable general equilibrium (CGE) model to assess the contribution of tourism on poverty reduction in Brazil. They found that tourism benefits the lowest income households, albeit to a lesser extent than higher income groups.[33] Wattankuljarus and Coxhead also employed a CGE framework to analyze the case of Thailand and conclude that high income groups benefited the most from tourism expansion.[34]

Croes found mixed results regarding the impact of tourism on poverty reduction in the cases of Nicaragua and Costa Rica. The mixed results suggest that the link is not automatic and warrants a closer examination of the conditions, such as the export structure and inequality that may be effectively replicated (or avoided) elsewhere. A recent study by Vanegas found poverty elasticities induced by tourism development vary among the countries in Central America. For example, tourism has strong effects in Costa Rica, Guatemala, and Nicaragua, and modest-to-weak effects in Salvador and Honduras.[35]

The tourism literature addressing the relationship of tourism development and poverty reduction thus reveals mixed results, and a discrepancy in explaining why tourism has failed to reduce poverty in all developing countries. Can we find a theoretical link that can explain whether tourism development reduces poverty? Our research thus far (as alluded to in the previous chapter) suggests that mainstream development theory attributes the persistence of poverty to three empirical findings. First, economic growth in developing countries is not persistent.[36] Typically, per capita incomes do not grow steadily over time. Second, inequality levels in developing countries have persisted over time. Thus, inequality seems a barrier to poverty reduction, limiting the effectiveness of growth. And third, reducing inequality is a complex social assignment.

## TOWARD A NEW THEORETICAL LINK BETWEEN TOURISM DEVELOPMENT AND POVERTY

Copeland was one of the first observers to pinpoint that tourist expenditures might have different distributional effects on different social groups despite the fact that aggregate welfare gains may be significant. Growth through tourism is attributed to increasing terms-of-trade. Terms-of-trade is an important channel through which tourism expansion can spawn economic growth.[37] The taste and preferences of consumers reveal that the marginal utility of nontourism products is less compared to tourism products. This means that a desire for travel has become a valuable source of additional utility for the consumer.

Since tourism production is lagging in technological inputs compared to other economic sectors, tourism production may run the risk of becoming an economic laggard in productivity output, thereby imperiling economic growth. This "productivity gap", which was revealed in the study of Smeral, is manifested in the so-called Baumol's disease.[38] This disease refers to the fact that productivity in tourism is lower than other industries, but wages in the former sector increase as fast as wages in other industries. Cutting labor in the tourism sector may be difficult or even self-defeating because labor input is a crucial part of the production and consumption of the tourist experience.

Therefore, the only way to survive is to increase price in real terms in order to cover steady increases in labor costs. While Baumol's disease may be incurable, it is survivable if attended correctly. Small island destinations are an example of surviving this disease. Small island destinations specializing in tourism have enjoyed fast and high growth rates, and were able to stretch their small market by integrating the international tourism market. Extension of the market through tourism means integrating non-traded goods, such as beaches and landscape, into the world market. If a country is able to shift toward superior demand characteristics of goods, a country may enhance and sustain its quality of life.

One of the main challenges that developing countries face is demand constraints. Tourism development grounded in international demand can alleviate those constraints and impart economic growth. A survey of studies conducted in developing countries show unidirectional causality supporting a TLG relationship. Table 3.1 lists a selected sample of these studies. These studies focus on countries or regional groupings, and they employ several techniques, such as error correction co-integration techniques with Granger causality tests for individual countries, or panel regressions in the case of developed (OECD countries; Organization for Economic Co-operation and Development countries) and developing economies. The commonality among these studies is the unreserved support of the expansion of tourism and development strategy.

Nevertheless, very few studies have found a unidirectional causality supporting the economics-driven tourism growth, meaning that tourism growth is a product of economic growth and not vice versa. For example, Oh found that in Korea, any expansion in tourism does not result in tourism-driven economic growth.[39] Since Korea is considered a highly industrialized country, the author recommends that policy makers support for the expansion of tourism should consider policies that sustain the demand created by business-related travelers. Similarly, in the case of the USA, the expansion of economic sectors such as airlines, restaurants, casinos, and hotels is also a product of economic growth.[40] In this particular case, the use of aggregate data does not allow the isolation of the long-term effect of international travelers. Nevertheless, the implications for policy makers are to support and allocate more resources to the lodging and airline sector, as the performance of other sectors is dependent on their success to grow.

Additional research, mostly in Europe and Asia, has found bidirectional causality between tourism and growth by also applying a co-integration error correction methodology. The existence of a mutual influence in which higher levels of economic growth lead to higher levels of tourism development and vice versa deserves a different policy set and will result in more complex implications in terms of sustainability and long-run impacts. For example, in the case of Greece and Taiwan, economic policy should support and justify the need for government intervention in fostering tourism supply, while at the same time promoting and increasing the demand for tourism products.[41]

**TABLE 3.1** Tourism and Economic Growth Nexus in Developing Countries

| Authors | Country | Empirical Methods | Granger direction |
|---|---|---|---|
| Ghali (1976) | Hawaii | Ordinary least square | Tourism → economic growth |
| Balaguer and Cantavella-Jorda (2002) | Spain | Unit root, Vector Auto regression (VAR), and Granger causality | Tourism → economic growth |
| Lanza et al. (2003) | 13 OECD countries | Almost ideal demand system | Tourism → economic growth |
| Durbarry (2004) | Mauritius | Vector Error Correction Model (VECM) and Granger causality | Tourism → economic growth |

**TABLE 3.1** *(Continued)*

| Authors | Country | Empirical Methods | Granger direction |
|---|---|---|---|
| Gunduz and Hatemi (2005) | Turkey | Granger causality | Tourism → economic growth |
| Oh (2005) | Korea | Unit root, co-integration, VAR, and Granger causality | Tourism ← economic growth |
| Skerritt and Huybers (2005) | 37 developing economies | Panel | Tourism → economic growth |
| Nowak et al. (2007) | Spain | Unit root, co-integration, VECM, and Granger causality | Tourism → economic growth |
| Brida et al. (2008a) | Mexico | Unit root, co-integration, VECM, and Granger causality | Tourism → economic growth |
| Brida et al. (20b10) | Uruguay | Unit root, co-integration, VECM, and Granger causality | Tourism → economic growth |
| Lee and Chang (2008) | 23 OECD countries | Panels (heterogeneous panel with co-integration and causality tests) | Tourism → economic growth |
| Chen and Chiou-Wei (2009) | Taiwan | Unit root, co-integration, VECM, and Granger causality | Tourism → economic growth |
| Tang and Jang (2009) | USA | Unit root and Granger causality | Tourism ← economic growth |
| Zortuk (2009) | Turkey | VECM and Granger causality | Tourism → economic growth |

The mixed results from the studies discussed above make it impossible to, a priori, estimate the potential or direction of the impact of an increase in tourism receipts on economic growth. Despite the fact that some scholars have made use of mathematical modeling to investigate whether or not the expansion of the tourism sector improves welfare, the use of aggregate measures of economic growth does not allow identifying the beneficiaries. So far, the results from mathematical simulations are mixed. For example, Hazari and Ng show that under monopolistic conditions, tourism reduces welfare. Meanwhile, Hazari and Sgro posited that tourism always improves welfare. The above arguments suggest that, despite certain positive signs of growth, the benefits from tourism could either disappear as leakages or only benefit certain social groups. This suggests that a gap in the literature exists, and understanding whether or not the benefits from tourism "trickle down" deserves more attention.[42]

## THE MARKET STRUCTURE AND DISTRIBUTIONAL EFFECTS

The benefits of tourism reaching the poor as a special group could be thwarted by the structure of the market. The presence of market imperfections and moral hazard issues in the production and consumption of tourism could increase transaction costs as well as exclude individuals from the production process of tourism. The latter could affect the quality of the product because the tourism industries need the support of the local communities as tourism activities are influenced and affect the entire community.

In particular, distributional effects of tourism may affect the well-being of the entire community. We already alluded to some unequal effects from tourism benefits, and if tourism is not able to promote efficiency as well as equity, then tourism by being consistent with more inequality would be unacceptable in light of the large presence of poverty in the world.[43] The concept of inequality seems at the core of the poverty fight. Inequality refers to a social process that nurtures differences in results, such as opportunities and treatment among individuals. The debate regarding inequality in tourism embraced the pro-poor movement. This movement claims that tourism and its economic contribution are presumed to help the poor.

There is debate on the extent to which inequalities are merited: some argue that inequality is onus for societal prosperity, while others consider inequality as premonition for society's well-being. Inequality in the former view is an unintended and innocuous innocent side effect of how society is organized based on self-interest and competition; the latter perspective considers inequality to lead to a divided society, thereby endangering the future. If inequality is all pervasive, it has the capacity to break democracy and prosperity; on the other hand, if talents and hard work are not rewarded, incentives will be lacking for individuals to exhume their talents to the maximum. In other words, too much inequality could slow down economic growth and the poverty reduction process, and too little inequality could slow down economic growth and the poverty reduction process too. The magnitude of inequality determines the degree of political stability and social opportunities in a country, either by excluding large portions of the population in productive activities or by providing few incentives to take up risks and innovate the economy.

Evidently, the poor are not only hungry for food but also yearn for opportunities. Opportunities are transformed through economic mechanisms such as employment and social and business opportunities as well as the appropriate distribution of government taxes to the poor; tourism development may reduce poverty, according to the pro-poor movement. As indicated previously, tourism feeds three channels provoking development and poverty reduction: (1) direct effects, (2) secondary effects, and (3) dynamic effects. Reduction in poverty occurs in two forms that contribute to economies. The dynamic effects are related to the overall impact of tourism on the economy, going beyond the tourism sector. For example, as already alluded to, tourism may expand domestic demand, may spur diversification, and may mitigate macroeconomic volatility due to external shocks. Tourism seem more stable as a source of revenues than the sale of goods, such as agricultural and mineral commodities. Additionally, tourism products can extract premium prices due to their uniqueness, which cannot be exported, and have lower transportation and insurance costs. Thus, there are numerous advantages to tourism compared to the export of goods and services.

## THE POVERTY OBLITERATION PARADIGM

The theoretical reasoning for including poverty in the three-way relationship tourism development–economic growth–poverty reduction is derived from the social equity construct, one of the basic tenets of sustainable tourism development. Tourism industries need support and accession from the local communities, as tourism activities impinge their lives. This means that the new development strategy should focus on social equity, and thus poverty reduction. Tourism and sustainability were initially linked through the economic management of scarcity of resources as inputs "upstream" in the value chain and the amelioration of impacts "downstream".[44]

As mentioned before, poverty is a multidimensional concept and is the negation of the concept of well-being. The well-being diagram is grounded on two main premises: (1) tourism connects directly to the poor and (2) tourism through economic growth benefits the poor. However, reducing poverty or improving well-being can be subjected to mediation or moderation. Any direct contributions from either tourism or economic growth toward poverty obliteration could be easily shattered by the abatement of basic needs, opportunities, resources, and inequality. These could partially or fully mediate or moderate the potential links from tourism and growth.

We propose a tourism–growth poverty obliteration paradigm (POP), which claims that tourism can have a direct or indirect impact (via economic growth) on the level of poverty. The theoretical reasoning underscoring these effects (direct or indirect) is grounded in terms-of-trade opportunities. The tourism and the *POP* diagram in Figure 3.1 captures the multiple and complex relationship among tourism, economic growth, well-being, and poverty.

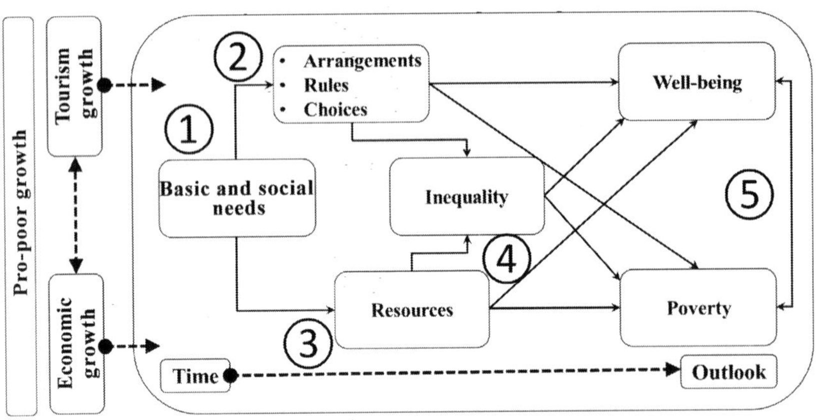


**FIGURE 3.1** Tourism and the Poverty Obliteration Paradigm Diagram.

As previously discussed, tourism and economic growth may entertain feedback effects, which mean that economic growth may also benefit tourism growth through higher marketing efforts and investments in the tourism infrastructure. Both tourism growth and economic growth enter the well-being system of residents through income effects, which are revealed either through jobs or transfers from the government. Again, the impact of these income effects is contingent on the market situation (structure, distortions, etc.) and power relations. The market situation and power relations, in their turn, determine the degree to which individual basic and social needs are satisfied.

The provision of basic and social needs must be seen as the first step in developing pro-poor growth. These are the foundations or first pillars to move people away from poverty. For example, Sen indicates that "Some functionings are very elementary, such as being adequately nourished, being in good health, etc., and these may be strongly valued by all, for obvious reasons."[45] In a similar vein, Rawls see these as primary goods related to things people are presumed to need regardless of their different conceptions of the good. This includes the idea of enabling conditions, or prerequisites to ensure sustenance and functioning.

The satisfaction of these needs can then invigorate societies' interest and influence existing social arrangements, rules, and choices. Once basic needs are fulfilled, individuals are more capable of controlling or influencing various social arrangements. This in turn stabilizes the power relations by including them in the development of rules and choice selections. This is observed by gaining power and voice. The provision of basic needs can bestow additional resources to the poor. Surely, inequality, a hallmark in most developing countries, constrains the voice and influence of the poor to muster additional resources for their well-being.

Institutional rearrangements and reconfigurations should take place in order to mitigate against inequality and to ensure that the poor would be lifted out of poverty through greater accessibility of basic needs and resources. The scope of choices and the allocation of resources result from power relations reflected in the degree of inequality. The importance of basic needs and resources, from a pro-poor perspective, must be directed to ensure that no harm is caused to the individuals.

The benefits from tourism or growth can be considered pro-poor only when their effects consider the inequality context of the poor. If tourism growth leaves the amount of those living in absolute poverty intact or if it is immiserizing, then tourism is not benefiting the poor. In other words, an increase in tourism activities will go hand in hand with a fall of real living standards. Being poor is dependent on two factors mainly: the average level of income and the extent of inequality in income distribution. Although an increase in average income reduces poverty, any increase in inequality will intensify it. Nowadays, the impression is that poverty in many developing countries has remained at higher levels or practically unchanged due to increases in income inequality. Despite the importance of incomes, tourism and the POP also considers well-being as the second important element that should enhance the life of the poor.

The individual's well-being covers a whole spectrum of life situations, including income, freedom, and happiness. The individual's well-being is grounded in three well established conceptualizations found in the literature: quality of life, social relations, and sustainability. Together, these three concepts form the vision of a world without poverty, or at least with minimum poverty. Quality of life covers both objective and subjective well-being; social relations address the issues pertaining to inequality, exclusion, and opportunities; and sustainability relates to human and natural capital. Indicators related to these domains measure the state of well-being in developing countries and reveal the dynamics of social change in these countries. Our study claims that the relationship among these three domains is a dynamic one, shaping the direction between tourism and the *POP*. We posit that the direction between tourism and *POP* is also dynamic, moving not only from tourism to *POP* but also from *POP* to tourism.

In the next chapters, the *POP* will be applied to several developing countries, and we will discuss the results according to the two standards of pro-poor, namely, reduction of the number of absolute poverty and enhancement of the quality of life of the poor.

## REFERENCES

Adamou, A.; Clerides, S. Prospects and limits of tourism-led growth: the international evidence. *Rev. Econ. Anal.* 2010, 3, 287–303.

Archer, B. *The impact of Domestic Tourism. Occasional Paper in Economics, No. 2*; University of Wales Press: Bangor, 1973.

Arezki, R.; Cherif, R.; Piotrowski, J. *Tourism Specialization and Economic Development: Evidence From the UNESCO World Heritage List*; IMF: Washington, DC, 2009. [Working Paper].

Balaguer, J.; Cantavella-Jordá, M. Tourism as a long-run economic growth factor: the Spanish case. Appl. Econ. 2002, 34(7), 877–884.

Balakrishnan, R.; Steinberg, C.; Syed, M. *The Elusive Quest for Inclusive Growth: Growth, Poverty, and Inequality*; IMF: Washington, DC, 2013. [Working Paper WP/13/152].

Benkovic, A.; Mejia, J. Tourism as a Driver of Economic Development: The COLOMBIAN Experience. 2008. https://www.uni-hohenheim.de/wi- theorie/globalisierung/dokumente/26_2008.pdf (September 2, 2014). [Nr.26/2008].

Blake, A.; Arbache, J.; Sinclair, M.; Teles, V. Tourism and poverty relief. *Ann. Tour. Res.* 2008, 35(1), 106–127.

Brida, J., Sanchez-Carrera, E. and Risso, W. Tourism's Impact on Long-Run Mexican Growth. Economic Bulletin. 2008. http://papers.ssrn.com/sol3/papers.cfm?abstract_id=1076225.

Brida, J., Lanzilotta, B., Lionetti, S. and Risso, W. The Tourism-led-growth Hypothesis for Uruguay. 2010. http://papers.ssrn.com/sol3/papers.cfm?abstract_id=1333102.

Chen, C. F.; Chiou-Wei, S. Z. Tourism expansion, tourism uncertainty and economic growth: new evidence from Taiwan and Korea. Tour. Manage. 2009, 30(6), 812–818.

Copeland, B. Tourism, welfare and de-industrialization in a small open economy. *Economica.* 1991, 58, 515–529.

Croes, R. A paradigm shift to a new strategy for small island economies: embracing demand side economics for value enhancement and long term economic stability. *Tour. Manage.* 2006, 27(3), 453–465.

Croes, R. Measuring and explaining competitiveness in the context of small island destinations. *J. Travel Res.* 2011, 50(4), 431–442.

Croes, R. Assessing tourism development from Sen's capability approach. *J. Travel Res.* 2012, 51(5), 542–554.

Croes, R. The role of tourism in poverty reduction: an empirical assessment. *Tour. Econ.* 2014, 20(2), 207–226.

Croes, R.; Vanegas, M. Sr. Cointegration and causality between tourism and poverty reduction. *J. Travel Res.* 2008, 47(1), 94–103.

De Kadt, E.; Ed. *Tourism: Passport to Development?*; Oxford University Press: Oxford, UK, 1979.

Dollar, D.; Kraay, A. *Growth is Good for the Poor*; Development Research Group, The World Bank: Washington, DC, 2000.

Dritsakis, N. Tourism as a long-run economic growth factor: an empirical investigation for Greece using causality analysis. *Tour. Econ.* 2004, 10(3), 305–316.

Durbarry, R. Tourism and Economic Growth: The Case of Mauritius. Tourism Economics 2004, 10, 389-401.

Easterly, W. *The Elusive Quest For Growth*; MIT Press: Cambridge, MA, 2002.

Ferroni, M.; Mateo, M.; Payne, M. *Development Under Conditions of Inequality and Distrust. Social Cohesion in Latin America*; International Food Policy Research Institute: Washington, DC, 2008.

Ghali, Moheb A.. Tourism and Economic Growth; An Empirical Study. Economic Development and Cultural Change. 1976. 24 (3): 527-38.

Gray, H. *International Travel-International Trade*; Heath Lexington Books: Lexington, KY, 1970.

Gray, H. The demand for international travel by United States and Canada. *Int. Econ. Rev.* 1982, 7, 83–92.

Gunduz, L.; Hatemi-J, A. Is the tourism-led growth hypothesis valid for Turkey? Appl. Econ. Lett. 2005, 12(8), 499–504.

Hawkins, D.; Mann, S. The World Bank's role in tourism development. *Ann. Tour. Res.* 2007, 34(2), 348–363.

Hazari, R.; Ng, A. An analysis of tourist's consumption of non-traded goods and services on the welfare of the domestic consumers. *Int. Rev. Econ. Finance.* 1993, 2, 43–58.

Hazari, R.; Sgro, P. Tourism and growth in a dynamic model of trade. *J. Int. Trade Econ. Dev.* 1995, 4, 243–252.

Jin, J. On the relationship between openness and growth in China: evidence from provincial time series. *World Econ.* 2004, 27(10), 1571–1582.

Kaldor, N. *Strategic Factors in Economic Development*; Cornell University Press: Ithaca, NY, 1967.

Kaldor, N. The case for regional policies. *Scott. J. Polit. Econ.* 1970, 17(3), 337–348.

Lanza A., Temple P., Urga G. The implications of tourism specialisation in the long run : an econometric analysis for 13 OECD economies. Tourism Management, 2003. 24, 315-321.

Lee, C.; Chang, C. Tourism development and economic growth: a closer look at panels. *Tour. Manage.* 2008, 29(1), 180–192.

Lejarraja, I.; Walkenhorst, P. *Diversification by Deepening Linkages with Tourism*; World Bank: Washington, DC, 2007.

Mak, J. *Tourism and the Economy: Understanding the Economics of Tourism*; University of Hawaii Press: Honolulu, HI, 2003.

Mathieson, A.; Wall, G. *Tourism. Economic, Physical and Social Impacts*; Addison Wesley Longman Limited: Essex, UK, 1992.

Mazzanti, M. Cultural heritage as a multi-dimensional, multi-value and multi-attribute economic resource. *J. Socio Econ.* 2002, 31(5), 1–31.

Mihalic, T. *Tourism and economic development issues*. In *Tourism and Development, Concepts and Issues*; Sharpley, R., Telfer, D., Eds.; Channel View Publications: Clevedon, UK, 2002; pp 81–111.

Mitchell, J.; Ashley, C. *Tourism and Poverty Reduction: Pathways to Prosperity*; The Cromwell Press Group: London, UK, 2010.

Nowak, J.J., M. Sahli, and I. Cortés-Jiménez, Tourism, Capital Good Imports and Economic Growth, Theory and Evidence for Spain, *Tourism Economics.* 2007 13 (4), 515–536.Oh, C. The contribution of tourism development to economic growth in the Korean economy, Tourism Management, 2005. 26 (1), 39–44.

Olavarria-Gambi, M. Poverty reduction in Chile: has economic growth been enough? *J. Human Dev.* 2003, 4(1), 103–123.

Pablo-Romero, M.; Molina, J. Tourism and economic growth: a review of empirical literature. *Tour. Manage. Perspect.* 2013, 8, 28–41.

Ridderstaat, J.; Croes, R.; Nijkamp, P. Modelling tourism development and long-run economic growth in Aruba. *Int. J. Tour. Res.* 2012, 16, 472–487.

Sachs, J. D. *Investing in Development: A Practical Plan to Achieve the Millennium Development Goals: Overview*; UNDP/Communications Development: New York, NY, 2005.

Sahli, M.; Nowak, J. Does inbound tourism benefit developing countries? A trade theoretic approach. *J. Travel Res.* 2007, 45, 426–434.

Semrad, K.; Bartels, J. An inward look using backward economic linkages in a developing country: the case of Puntarenas, Costa Rica. *Worldwide Hospital. Tour. Themes J.* 2014, 6(3), 244–260.

Sen, A. *Capability and well-being*. In *The Quality of Life. World Institute of Development Economics*; Nussbaum, M., Sen, A., Eds.; Clarendon Press: Oxford, 1993; pp 30–53.

Skerrit, D. and Huybers, T. The Effect of International Tourism on Economic Development: An Empirical Analysis. Asia Pacific Journal of Tourism Research. 2005. 10(1), 23-43.

Smeral, E. A structural view of tourism growth. *Tour. Econ.* 2003, 9(1), 77–94.

Spenceley, A.; Meyer, D. Tourism and poverty reduction: theory and practice in less economically developed countries. *J. Sustainable Tour.* 2012, 20(3), 297–317.

Steel, G.; Klaufus, C. Displacement by/for development in two Andean cities. Paper presented at the 2010 Congress of the Latin American Studies Association, Toronto, Canada, 2010.

Tang, C.; Jang, S. The tourism-economy causality in the United States: a sub-industry level examination. *Tour. Manage*. 2009, 30, 553–558.

Tasci, A.; Croes, R.; Bartels, J. Rise and fall of community-based tourism: facilitators, inhibitors and outcomes. *Worldwide Hospital. Tour. Theme J.* 2013, 6(3), 293–300.

Thirlwall, A. *Economic Growth in an Open Developing Economy. The Role of Structure and Demand*; Edward Elgar Publishing: Cheltenham, UK, 2013.

Underberg-Goode, N. Cultural heritage tourism on Peru's North Coast. *Worldwide Hospital. Tour. Theme J.* 2014, 6(3), 200–214.

Van der Duim, R.; Caalders, J. Tourism chains and pro-poor tourism development: an actor-network analysis of a pilot project in Costa Rica. *Curr. Iss. Tour*. 2008, 11(2), 109–125.

Vanegas, M. The triangle of poverty, economic growth, and inequality in Central America: does tourism matter? *Worldwide Hospital. Tour. Theme J.* 2014, 6(3), 277–292.

Vanhove, N. *The Economics of Tourism Destinations*; Butterworth-Heinemann: Oxford, UK, 2005.

Walker, J. Reflections on archeology, poverty and tourism in the Bolivian Amazon. *Worldwide Hospital. Tour. Theme J.* 2014, 6(3), 215–228.

Wattanakuljarus, A.; Coxhead, I. Is tourism-based development good for the poor? A general equilibrium analysis for Thailand. *J. Policy Model*. 2008, 30(6), 929–955.

Williams, A.; Shaw, G. *Tourism and Economic Development: European Experiences*, 3rd ed.; Wiley Publication: Chichester, NY, 1998.

Winters, P.; Corral, L.; Mora, A. Assessing the role of tourism in poverty alleviation: a research agenda. *Dev. Policy Rev*. 2013, 31(2), 177–202.

wiZhang, J.; Jensen, C. Comparative advantage: explaining tourism flows. *Ann. Tour. Res*. 2007, 34(1), 223–243.

Zhou, D.; Yanagida, J.; Chakravorty, U.; Leung, P. Estimating economic impacts from tourism. *Ann. Tour. Res*. 1997, 24(1), 76–89.

Zortuk, M. Economic Impact of Tourism on Turkey's Economy: Evidence from Cointegration Tests. International Research Journal of Finance and Economics 2009. 25, 231-239.

## ENDNOTES

[1]See, for example, Hawkins and Mann (2007).

[2]See, for example, Winters et al. (2013).

[3]For a discussion on the Bolivian Amazon tourism potential, see, for example, Walker (2014).

[4]For a discussion on the role of heritage sites in attracting international tourists, see, for example, Arezki et al. (2009).

[5]Spenceley and Meyer (2012, p. 299) remark "Rich cultural and natural assets exist in some of the poorest regions of the world, and they offer great potential for travel itineraries. Tourism can provide one possible mechanism to re-distribute from the rich to the poor. As tourists travel to impoverished regions in the world for a variety of reason, they spend money on travel, accommodation, excursions, food, drinks and shopping. In many tourism destinations,

the poor have the potential to capture some of this spending through employment, and, probably, most importantly through providing goods and/or services that the tourism sector and tourists need."

[6]See, for example, Hawkins and Mann (2007).

[7]See http://step.unwto.org/en/content/main-publications.

[8]For a discussion of the role of international organizations in advocating for a more prominent role for tourism in development programs, see, for example, Hawkins and Mann (2007). Winters et al. (2013) also discuss the role of the Inter-American Development Bank in promoting tourism development in Cancun, Mexico, and the lagging Northeastern region of Brazil through the PRODETUR program.

[9]See, for example, Vanegas (2014).

[10]See, for example, Mitchell and Ashley (2010).

[11]The delivery of the tourist experience depends on the nature of the interaction among multiple stakeholders at a destination. For a discussion about the collaborative challenges in the design, packaging, delivery, and sustainability of tourism products in Costa Rica, see, for example, Semrad and Bartels (2014) and Tasci et al. (2013).

[12]See, for example, Steel and Klaufus (2010) and Underberg-Goode (2014).

[13]See, for example, Ferroni et al. (2008), and Mak (2003).

[14]For a recount on the numerous victims of violence in Guatemala, see the Guatemalan Commission for Historical Clarification Report in 1999.

[15]See, for example, Van der Duim and Caalders (2008).

[16]See Dollar and Kraay (2000) and Easterly (2002).

[17]For further discussion see Pablo-Romero and Molina (2013).

[18]See Jin (2004) and Sachs (2005).

[19]See Gray (1982 and 1970).

[20]See Sahli and Nowak (2007).

[21]See Zhang and Jensen (2007).

[22]For further discussion, see Adamou and Clerides (2010) and Ridderstaat et al. (2012).

[23]See Archer (1973), Mathieson and Wall (1992), Zhou et al. (1997), Mihalic (2002), Mak (2004), and Vanhove (2005).

[24]See, for example, Croes (2006).

[25]Croes (2014) grounded his research in Central America on the Kaldor approach. For information on the Kaldor approach see Kaldor (1967, 1970).

[26]For further discussion, see Croes (2011).

[27]For further discussion, see Thirlwall (2013).

[28]Tourist behaviors and motivations seem to be in flux due to changing demand factors and market niches. For example, tourists that are more interested in the search for identity and authenticity may engage in forms of experimental tourism by interacting with the local's daily life more than mass tourists. Typical products and attractions of a destination may seem to be

in constant vogue, as evident by destinations' efforts to distinguish diverse market segments that could ultimately become a market segment advantage for the destination.

[29]See Benković and Mejia (2008).

[30]See Winters et al. (2013).

[31]See Mitchell and Ashley (2010).

[32]See Croes and Vanegas (2008).

[33]See Blake et al. (2008).

[34]See Wattanakuljarus and Coxhead (2008).

[35]See Vanegas (2014).

[36]For a critical analysis on the role of economic growth and poverty reduction, see, for example, Olavarria-Gambi (2003).

[37]See Copeland (1991).

[38]See Smeral (2003).

[39]See Oh (2005).

[40]See Tang and Jang (2009).

[41]See Dritsakis (2004) for Greece and Lee and Chang (2008) for Taiwan.

[42]See Hazari and Ng (1993) and Hazari and Sgro (1995).

[43]See, for example, Balakrishnan et al. (2013).

[44]See Williams and Shaw (1998) and Mazzanti (2002).

[45]See Sen (1993, p. 31).

## CHAPTER 4

# THE POWER OF TOURISM IN POVERTY ALLEVIATION: THE EMPIRICAL NEXUS TOURISM, GROWTH, INEQUALITY, AND POVERTY

## CONTENTS

## INTRODUCTION

This chapter examines the empirical relationship between tourism growth and poverty reduction. In the previous chapter, we laid down the theoretical foundations of the connection through the poverty obliteration paradigm. We hypothesize that tourism growth has a double barrel effect on poverty: directly and indirectly through economic growth. We also investigate the conditions that may attenuate the power of tourism in poverty alleviation. We illustrate this hypothesis through six cases. Five of the eight countries are from Central America. They are Costa Rica, El Salvador, Guatemala, Honduras, and Nicaragua. The other case is from Ecuador, located in South America.[1]

All these cases are related to developing countries that practice different stages of tourism development and reveal discrete incidence of poverty. They all have in common the fact that they are realigning their economy with tourism as a centerpiece. We find that direct effects of tourism are evident, though stalled by inequality and weak institutions. Also, we find that tourism matters for the poor in all countries, but in varying measures, contingent upon the area. Finally, tourism development seems an effective strategy in addressing poverty issues in developing countries. Apart from agriculture, tourism development has outperformed all other economic sectors in poverty alleviation.

## TOURISM DEVELOPMENT IN CENTRAL AMERICA

The region of Central America comprises seven countries: Belize, Costa Rica, El Salvador, Guatemala, Honduras, Nicaragua, and Panama. The countries vary in terms of land area and population. Belize is the smallest country both in land size and population: 22,810 $km^2$, with a population of 356,600. On the other hand, Nicaragua is the country with the largest land area (120,340 $km^2$), while Guatemala has the largest population with 14.8 million. Figure 4.1 reveals the map from Central America, which includes some socioeconomic general information.

One of the hallmarks of the region is its disturbing trend of violence throughout time. The region is rife with civil wars, social and ideological conflicts, dictatorship, underdevelopment, economic exploitation, and undue foreign influence in shaping political and economic decisions. Drug cartels are creating havoc, instilling terror and inciting crime to unprecedented levels. Central America is the region with the highest homicide numbers in the world, according to a 2010 report from the United Nations. Honduras, El Salvador, and Guatemala (called the Northern TrianSgle of Central America) are in the top 10 in the list of the most dangerous countries in the world.[2]

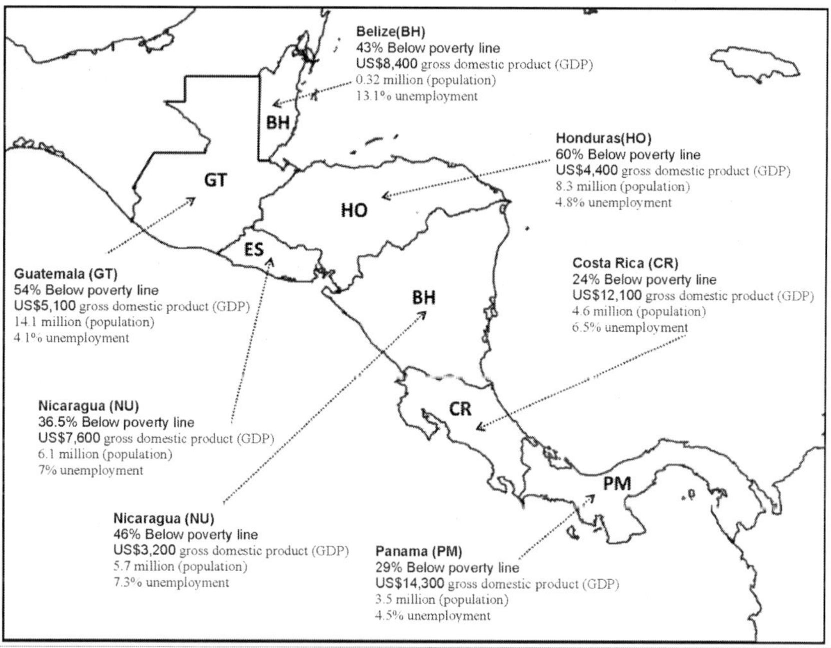


**FIGURE 4.1** Map of Central America with Selected Indicators.
(Prepared by authors [data source CIA World Factbook (2010): https://www.cia.gov/library/publications/the-world-factbook/].)

The region has received feeble interventions from the United States, mainly to safeguard the interests of the United Fruit Company. For example, in 1954, the United Fruit Company, supported by the American government, was instrumental in toppling a democratically elected president in Guatemala to secure its economic interest. Schlesinger and Kinzer tell this sad story of the American involvement deposing the Guatemalan president Jacobo Arbenz, reversing the implementation of the land reform program aimed at reducing inequality.[3]

The regions are very diverse in economic output, with Guatemala being the largest economy, with a total economic output of US$47.6 billion in 2011, while Belize is the smallest economy, with a total economic output of US$1.5 billion. Costa Rica leads the region in terms of quality of life measured by the income per capita and human development index (HDI). Costa Rica's income per capita is US$8,647 (2011) with an HDI of 0.771, which positions Costa Rica in the high human development group by United Nations' standards. Costa Rica ranks 62 out of 187 countries and territories. At the bottom is Nicaragua, with an income per capita of US$1,587 (2011) and an HDI of 0.599 trailed only by Guatemala with an HDI of 0.581. Nicaragua ranks number 129 on the global HDI list and is positioned in the bottom half of "medium development countries". Table 4.1 reveals some selected descriptive statistics from the region.

**TABLE 4.1** Central America: Country Description

| **Country** | **Area (km$^2$)** | **Population** | Gross Domestic Product **(GDP) Per Capita in US$** | **GDP Growth (%)** | **Poverty Headcount Ratio[a] (%)** |
|---|---|---|---|---|---|
| Belize[2] | 22,966 | 324,060 | 4,721 | 5.3 | NA |
| Costa Rica[1] | 51,100 | 4,805,295 | 9,386 | 5.1 | 20.3 |
| El Salvador[1] | 21,040 | 6,297,394 | 3,790 | 1.9 | 34.5 |
| Guatemala[2] | 108,889 | 15,082,831 | 3,331 | 3.0 | 53.7 |
| Honduras[3] | 112,492 | 7,935,846 | 2,323 | 3.9 | 60.0 |
| Nicaragua[4] | 130,375 | 5,991,733 | 1,754 | 5.2 | 42.5 |
| Panama[2] | 75,517 | 3,802,281 | 9,534 | 10.7 | 27.6 |

**Source:** [1]World Bank (2014), [2]World Bank (2011), [3]World Bank (2010), and [4]World Bank (2009)

[a]Based on national poverty line (% of population).

Central America is one of the poorest regions in the world. Almost half of its population lives in poverty. The region is the poorest after Haiti. Seven people out of every ten people in Honduras live in poverty. In Nicaragua, poverty is revealed in six of every ten people living in the country.[4] When the meaning of poverty moves beyond the unidimensionality of income and includes water, sanitation, energy, dwelling, and education, the poverty situation in Central American countries become more pronounced.[5] The multidimensional meaning of poverty reveals that 71% of the population in Nicaragua, 69% in Guatemala, and 63% in Honduras live in deprivation. A 2014 Economic Commission for Latin America and the Caribbean (ECLAC) report attributes the high incidence of poverty in Central American countries to housing (overcrowding and makeshift materials), energy (lack of electricity and cooking fuel), and lack of social protection (enrollment in social protection programs).

The region was able to reduce its indigence poverty from 23.9% in the decade of the eighties to 17.6% in the first decade of the twenty-first century, which is equivalent to a 36% reduction. El Salvador reduced its indigence poverty by 30.1% during that time span, followed by Nicaragua. While these accomplishments in poverty reduction are commendable, only Costa Rica among the other Central American countries has achieved its poverty reduction target according to the Millennium Development Goals. Table 4.2 reveals the achievements in reducing poverty by the countries in Central America from 1980 to 2012.[6]

## UNEVEN RESULTS OF POVERTY REDUCTION

Although poverty has decreased over the last 30 years, results of reducing poverty have been uneven in the region, and still too many remain poor and vulnerable, and slide back into poverty. Hunger, undernutrition, and lack of jobs are among the region's most pressing problems.[7] The region shows a remarkable divergence in terms of poverty. Costa Rica has the lowest indigence poverty level in 2011, with 6.3% of the population living under the national indigence poverty line. El Salvador has the largest portion of its population (18.21%) in 2011 living under the national indigence poverty line, followed by Guatemala (17.27%) and Nicaragua (14.86%). The unfolding of the global recession intertwined with food/fuel crisis spawned cumulative effects exacerbating food insecurity, malnutrition, unemployment, and underemployment, intensifying the vulnerability of the poor.[8]

**TABLE 4.2** Central America Evolution of Population Living Below the National Indigence Poverty Line 1: Average Head Count Ratio, % (1980–2012)

| Country | 1980–1990 | 1990–2000 | 2000–2010 | 2011 | 2012 |
|---|---|---|---|---|---|
| Costa Rica | 10.06 | 7.27 | 4.92 | 6.31 | 6.19 |
| El Salvador | 27.19 | 21.78 | 18.81 | 18.21 | – |
| Guatemala | 23.48 | 20.86 | 17.72 | 17.27 | – |
| Honduras | 49.31 | 48.19 | 44.00 | – | – |
| Nicaragua | 24.14 | 23.40 | 17.10 | 14.86 | 14.34 |
| Central America[a] | 26.84 | 24.30 | 20.35 | – | – |
| Central America[a] | 23.92 | 21.54 | 17.59 | – | – |

Source: Adopted from Vanegas (2014)
[a]As defined by the country's specific national indigence (or extreme) poverty line. It is defined as the share of the country's population whose income or consumption is below the poverty line, that is, the percentage of population that cannot afford to buy a defined basic basket of goods.

Among the Latin American region, the countries in Central America are the most unequal in terms of income distribution in the Americas, and perhaps the world, with the exception of Sub-Saharan Africa. According to Vanegas, the inequality in income distribution during the past 20 years remained almost unchanged in Central America[9]. From 1990 to 2000, the Gini coefficient was 49.75, while from 2000 to 2010, the coefficient was 49.30.[10] Table 4.3 reveals how income distribution has evolved in Central America. It reveals how persistent inequality is among the Central American countries, indicating slow movement in reducing inequality with the exception of Nicaragua and Guatemala. Costa Rica is the country with the most dramatic reversal of inequality reduction, indicating a substantial increase in 2011.

**TABLE 4.3** Evolution of Income Distribution in Central America: Gini Coefficient (1980–2012)

| Country | 1980–1990 | 1990–2000 | 2000–2010 | 2011 |
|---|---|---|---|---|
| Costa Rica | 41.60 | 35.46 | 36.11 | 51.47 |
| El Salvador | 53.97 | 50.42 | 51.23 | 47.88 |
| Guatemala | 55.21 | 54.57 | 51.39 | 48.79 |
| Honduras | 53.68 | 51.78 | 51.74 | NA |

**TABLE 4.3** *(Continued)*

| Country | 1980–1990 | 1990–2000 | 2000–2010 | 2011 |
|---|---|---|---|---|
| Nicaragua | 56.19 | 56.54 | 51.05 | 48.24 |
| Central America[a] | 52.13 | 49.75 | 49.30 | 47.84 |
| Central America[b] | 50.99 | 48.62 | 47.56 | 49.10 |

Source: Adopted from Vanegas (2014)
[a]Unweighted average.
[b]Weighted average.

The region has embraced tourism as a development strategy to reduce poverty and enhance development.[11] Except Costa Rica and Belize, tourism is relatively new to the Central American region, which suffered from political turmoil and violence during the eighties. The 1996 Declaration of Montelimar, Nicaragua, signed by the seven Central American countries recognized tourism as a driving force for economic development and diversification.[12] Tourism trumped as a feasible and effective development strategy by international organizations, and policy makers in Central America slowly began to use tourism in their efforts to alleviate their huge socioeconomic challenges. The 1996 Declaration of Montelimar, signed by the seven Central American countries, recognized tourism as a driving force for economic development and diversification.

From its inception, the Declaration sought for the tourism development project in Central America to promote private sector (usually foreign) investment and to achieve "poverty reduction" goals. One of the main reasons for the growing prominence of tourism as a development strategy is the restructuring of economies away from traditional agriculture and toward services and manufacturing.[13] This restructuring was necessary in view of the declining competitiveness of the agricultural sector and the need to improve competitiveness in nontraditional sectors. The traditional economic sectors were devastated by violence in the region. Consequently, the region has recently become an active participant in attracting tourism. Between 2000 and 2008, Central America experienced 8.4% growth in the arrival of international tourists, the highest rate among the world.[14] The Central American countries are allocating an important amount of scarce resources to tourism development.

Tourism development has been uneven in the region, with some countries having a longer history of tourism development than others. Similarly, some countries have been more successful in attracting tourists than others. Table 4.4 reveals tourism performance in the region. Panama has become the largest recipient of tourism receipts, overtaking Costa Rica, which has been the regional leader up until recently. However, Costa Rica remains a strong destination in the region, experiencing the largest market share in 2011 in terms of international arrivals. Tourism is showing strong performance in Nicaragua as the upcoming destination in the region. Tourism's contribution to Nicaragua's gross domestic product (GDP) was 6.4% on average between 2003 and 2008, while its contribution to employment was 5.2%.[15]

**TABLE 4.4** Central America: Tourism Overview (2012)

| Country | Arrivals | Arrivals% Change from 2011 | Market Share (%) | Tourism, Receipts in (Current US$) (M) | Tourism Receipts Per Arrival (US$) |
|---|---|---|---|---|---|
| Belize | 277,000 | 10.8 | 2.9 | 299 | 1,079 |
| Costa Rica | 2,343,000 | 6.9 | 24.6 | 2,544 | 1,086 |
| El Salvador | 1,255,000 | 6.0 | 13.2 | 894 | 712 |
| Guatemala | 1,951,000 | 7.0 | 20.5 | 1,419 | 727 |
| Honduras | 895,000 | 2.8 | 9.4 | 666 | 744 |
| Nicaragua | 1,180,000 | 11.3 | 12.4 | 422 | 358 |
| Panama | 1,606,000 | 9.0 | 16.9 | 3,784 | 2,356 |
| Total | 9,507,000 | 7.7[a] | 100 | 10,028 | 7,062 |

Source: UNWTO (2014)
[a]Average of arrivals% change from 2011.

The heterogeneity of the region is also manifested in the tourism structure of each country. For example, tourism specialization has the largest incidence in Belize (17.2%), followed by Panama with 9.3% and Costa Rica with 4.9%. Tourism specialization in the other countries in Central America oscillates between 2.7% and 4%. Incidentally, the countries with lowest incidence of tourism specialization are also the poorest countries in the region.

## ECUADOR: LOOKING SOUTH TO TOURISM DEVELOPMENT

Ecuador is one of the smallest countries in South America. In terms of total land area, the country ranks ninth in South America, with 283,560 km$^2$. As a central Andean country, Ecuador consists of three distinct areas: the lowlands in the west (*la costa*), the Andean highlands (*la Sierra*), and the Amazon. The country had a population of 15.8 million people in 2013 and is overwhelmingly *mestizo*.[16] Over 70% of its population lives in urban areas, in particular, Quito and Guayaquil, while 32% lived in rural areas in 2012, according to the World Bank. The urban–rural divide is pronounced, with rural areas experiencing major challenges with regard to accessibility to services such as water supply and sanitation.

The GDP at purchasing power parity (PPP) in 2012 was US$134,805 million, ranking it seventh in South America. The economic activities in Ecuador are characterized by a high primary commodity export concentration ratio for the leading primary products (the exports are crude petroleum, bananas, and shellfish). Its GDP at PPP per capita was US$8,510, which is equivalent to 71.2% of the Latin American and the Caribbean average. Overall, Ecuador ranks ninth in terms of GDP adjusted PPP per capita in South America. The United Nations' Development Program considers Ecuador a country with high human development with an HDI of 0.724, which ranks it eighth and 89 in South America and the world, respectively. Table 4.5 reveals selected socioeconomic characteristics for Ecuador.

**TABLE 4.5** Selected Socioeconomic Characteristics for Ecuador (2009–2012)

| Socioeconomic Indicator | 2009 | 2010 | 2011 | 2012 |
|---|---|---|---|---|
| Gross domestic product per capita (constant 2005 US$) | 3,210 | 3,251 | 3,449 | 3,568 |
| Gini index (%) | 49.43 | 49.26 | NA | NA |
| Human development index | 0.716 | 0.719 | 0.722 | 0.724 |
| International tourism, number of arrivals ('000) | 968 | 1,047 | 1,141 | 1,272 |
| International tourism, receipts (% exports in M) | 4.28 | 4.01 | 3.44 | 3.93 |
| International tourism receipts (current US$ in M) | 674 | 786 | 849 | 1,039 |
| Internet users (per 100 people) | 24.60 | 29.03 | 31.40 | 35.13 |
| Poverty head count ratio at national poverty line | 36.0 | 32.8 | 28.6 | 27.3 |
| Poverty head count ratio at rural poverty line | 57.5 | 53.0 | 50.9 | 49.1 |
| Poverty head count ratio at urban poverty line | 25.0 | 22.5 | 17.4 | 16.1 |

Source: World Bank and United Nations' Development Program

Like so many developing countries, Ecuador also experienced political upheaval, particularly in the last decade of the twentieth century. Political instability, weak institutions, lack in transparency, nepotism, and weak economic performance are present in Ecuador and it counteracts the national economic growth and development.[17] Ecuador experienced chronic political instability, changing presidents eight times in a span of 13 years. Sociologist Leon Zamosc called Ecuador "one of the most, if not the most, unstable country in Latin America."[18] The political turmoil was aggravated by the uprising of the indigenous people in 1990, which paralyzed the country for months. There is a strong presence of indigenous people (Ecuadorean Amerindians) in the country comprising nearly 25% of the total population. Unlike Peru and Bolivia, the indigenous population has a strong political presence through the national political organization of Pachakutik.

Ecuador provides a good case study, as nearly half of the population lives in poverty despite unprecedented growth due to the oil boom in the seventies. The country suffers from a chronic malnutrition rate with reported stunting outcomes among children under 5 years of age, similar to the Sub-Saharan countries.[19] In recent years, the amount of people considered as poor by international standards has declined, however, from 35.3% to 32.2%, and indigence poverty from 13.8% to 12.9%, between 2011 and 2012. In 2005, 48.3% of the population was poor and 21.2% was considered as living in indigence poverty; by 2011, 35.3% were poor, while 13.8% were indigence poor. By 2012, the numbers were 32.2% and 12.9%, respectively.[20]

While these achievements are commendable, there are still too many people in Ecuador that remain poor and suffering and are deprived from engaging in economic and social opportunities. Too many people cannot meet their basic nutritional requirements even if their entire incomes were spent on food. In addition, massive income disparities are noticeable. The poorest quintile receives only 5.1% of total income, while the richest quintile received 48.8% in 2002; in 2012, it was 6.4% and 43%, respectively.[21] Ecuador remains one of the most unequal countries in South America with a Gini coefficient of nearly 50%. Figure 4.2 reveals the income distribution by quintile in Ecuador (2005–2010).

A flourishing sector that has evolved as a new alternative for promoting development and economic growth in Ecuador is tourism. Romano et al. (2005) unveiled the results of the Tourism Satellite Accounts' program for

Ecuador. Their findings indicate that tourism (domestic and international) constitutes 4.5% of the gross domestic product. In addition, an increase of 13% in international arrivals in 2008 demonstrates that tourism expansion does not coincide with the economic contractions and recession in Ecuador (World Travel and Tourism Council [WTTC], 2009). International arrivals have steadily increased in the first decade of the twenty-first century, reaching almost 1.4 million, which is less than 1% of the South American market. International tourism receipts have also grown significantly. For example, these receipts increased by 21% from 2011 to 2012, reaching US$1.25 billion, equivalent to only 0.5% of the South American market. Tourism has become the third largest foreign exchange source after agriculture and fisheries, comprising 4.3% of total export in 2013. Table 4.6 showcases selected tourism indicators in Ecuador. The tourism sector supports 337,500 direct and indirect jobs, representing 4.8% of the total employment in the country in 2013.[22]

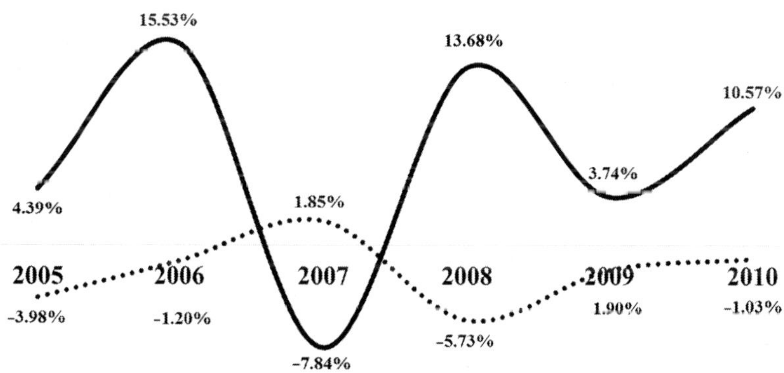


**FIGURE 4.2** Percentage Change of Incomes by Quintile from 2005 to 2010 in Ecuador.

**TABLE 4.6** International Tourism in Ecuador (2000–2012)

| Year | International Arrivals | International Receipts (Current US$) | Tourism Receipts Per Arrival (US$) |
|---|---|---|---|
| 2000 | 627,000 | 451,000,000 | 719 |
| 2001 | 641,000 | 438,000,000 | 683 |
| 2002 | 683,000 | 449,000,000 | 657 |
| 2003 | 761,000 | 408,000,000 | 536 |

TABLE 4.6 *(Continued)*

| Year | International Arrivals | International Receipts (Current US$) | Tourism Receipts Per Arrival (US$) |
|---|---|---|---|
| 2004 | 819,000 | 464,000,000 | 567 |
| 2005 | 860,000 | 488,000,000 | 567 |
| 2006 | 841,000 | 492,000,000 | 585 |
| 2007 | 937,000 | 626,000,000 | 668 |
| 2008 | 1,005,000 | 745,000,000 | 741 |
| 2009 | 968,000 | 674,000,000 | 696 |
| 2010 | 1,047,000 | 786,000,000 | 751 |
| 2011 | 1,141,000 | 849,000,000 | 744 |
| 2012 | 1,272,000 | 1,039,000,000 | 817 |

## ECONOMIES CAN LEVERAGE TOURISM TO ALLEVIATE POVERTY

Empirical studies examining the relationship of tourism growth and economic growth are very recent and still in their infancy. Most of the tourism literature investigating this issue has reached the conclusion that tourism is growth enhancing. In other words, tourism propels economic growth. The debate on whether or not countries should promote their tourism sector to achieve long-run economic growth is a recent issue. International tourism might be considered as an export in a nontraditional way since it implies a source of receipts and consumption at the destination.

However, allocating resources to tourism development, particularly in a resource-poor environment such as those in Central America and Ecuador without attempting to discern whether tourism is the most effective way of propelling economic growth is not a smart way to invest scarce resources. This policy question has not been asked enough in the tourism literature. Mainstream tourism literature assumed that tourism development is a smart investment, and therefore has examined the relationship between tourism and economic growth. Next, studies must examine if tourism development is more efficient than export of agricultural or manufacturing goods.

In evaluating these strategies, one must disaggregate the growth model into its economic sector components as the source of the differential growth impacts. Thus far, studies investigating the relationship between tourism growth and economic growth have not looked at the export composition and the role of tourism within that composition. Durbarry was the first study to consider tourism in an innovative way as a type of export. Using a production function, compatible with the new growth theory, Durbarry explained economic growth by physical capital, human capital, and exports, and applied his model to the island of Mauritius. His study includes disaggregated exports in the model, with international tourism as one form of export. While testing for Granger causality between total exports and economic growth, he disaggregated the export sector of Mauritius into its main components – sugar, manufactured goods, and tourism – and assessed the potential of tourism on growth from 1970 to 1999. The study used an econometric model and found that tourism had the most significant impact on the economy of Mauritius during the three decades under review, although sugar and manufacturing also had positive impacts on the economic growth of the island.[23]

The only other study to address the issue of the role of tourism as an export type was that done by Vanegas and Croes.[24] Their study applied a standard growth accounting function framework in order to assess the impact of tourism on growth in the case of Nicaragua. Export activities were divided into agriculture, manufacture, and tourism. The agricultural component was proxied by coffee export, which is the most important agricultural export of the country. Data covered the period 1980–2005. The results of the study indicate that tourism again had the most significant impact on economic growth, although coffee and manufacture also had positive impact on growth. It indicates that if tourism expansion increases by 5%, economic growth increases by 3.1%, while economic growth would increase by 2.52% if there were a similar increase in coffee exports, *ceteris paribus*. On the other hand, a 5% increase in manufacture would increase growth by 1.61%, *ceteris paribus*. The results of the study of Vanegas and Croes are consistent with Durbarry, providing empirical evidence that investing in tourism development to promote economic growth seems a sensible option for developing countries.

There is evidence to support the proposition that tourism is a powerful export activity compared to other export activities in supporting economic growth. However, the question remains whether tourism can directly reduce poverty. Vanegas and Croes examined this question in their study. Their study is one of the first studies to empirically assess the direct link between tourism and poverty reduction. Vanegas and Croes compared the impact of tourism, coffee, and manufacture on poverty and found again that tourism had the largest impact on poverty reduction. All three activities had a significant negative impact on poverty at the 5% level. The tourism coefficient was –0.617, while manufacturing was –0.441 and coffee was –0.333. One plausible reason that the gross domestic measure was unable to account for the full impact on poverty reduction may have been the large presence of an underground economy.[25] The International Labor Organization estimated informal employment at 47.7% in 2012 from a sample of thirteen Latin American countries.[26]

The study of Vanegas and Croes suggests that tourism has a significant direct effect on poverty reduction. Subsequently, Vanegas completed a separate study in 2014, confirming these results by examining five countries in Central America (excluding Belize and Panama).

Croes and Vanegas later examined the nexus tourism–growth–poverty more in depth in a study that considers the case of Nicaragua and applies a bivariate co-integration analysis. The study found that tourism has a positive long-run impact on economic growth (coefficient 0.7573 with a $t$-statistic =5.557). Unlike the previous study, this new study compared the strength of the impact of economic growth as well as tourism on poverty. The study found that both activities had a negative impact on poverty; economic growth reduced poverty by a coefficient of –0.2141 ($t = -2.703$), while the coefficient of tourism growth reducing poverty was –0.5076 ($t = -4.628$). This study suggests that tourism has a direct as well as an indirect effect on poverty through economic growth. Interestingly, the direct effects of tourism are stronger than the indirect effect through economic growth, suggesting conditions that may impair the indirect effects of tourism, such as inequality and weak institutions.

## TOURISM AND THE GROWTH POVERTY ELASTICITY

To test the direct and indirect negative impact of tourism on poverty, Croes expanded the econometric model from a bivariate framework to a multivariate one, and included Costa Rica together with Nicaragua in the same comparative study. The reason for applying a case study approach, according to the study, was to strengthen the proposition of the nexus tourism–economic growth–poverty reduction. Comparing Costa Rica and Nicaragua adds rigor to the analysis because both countries are enforcing tourism as a development strategy, while entertaining a dissimilar stage in their tourism life cycle. Costa Rica has a longer history with tourism development than Nicaragua. The study examined the growth elasticity of poverty, which means it examined the reduction in head count poverty as a result of tourism growth. The data covered the time period from 1980 to 2010.

The Nicaragua study found a long-run relation between tourism and economic growth; economic growth and poverty reduction; and tourism and poverty reduction. The study also estimated the growth elasticity of poverty induced by tourism as the coefficient of the long-run regression times the tourism share of GDP. The growth elasticity of poverty was equal to 1.23. This means that a 1% increase in tourism receipt would reduce the poverty rate by 1.23%. In the case of Costa Rica, the study found a different trajectory. While the study shows that tourism has a long-run positive relationship with economic growth, the study surprisingly found a long-run positive relationship with poverty as well. The long-term coefficient was 0.24 ($t = 1.78$). This means that tourism in Costa Rica does not seem to benefit the poor in the long run.

Costa Rica's stage in its life cycle seems to require quality offerings and services that are excluding the poor from the benefits from tourism. The unintended consequences of tourism in Costa Rica are excluding the poor from job opportunities and displacing them from the job market in the hospitality industry. For example, in the thriving tourism region of Guanacaste, most jobs went to higher educated *Ticos* from other regions within the country or foreigners.[27] People with higher education are more likely to have higher market contact, and they are more likely to respond quicker to emerging market opportunities because of specific skills and assets that they possess, perhaps more entrepreneurial spirit or simply luck.

It is clear from this study that tourism in Nicaragua and Costa Rica have different impacts on the poor. For Nicaragua, tourism matters, whereas for Costa Rica tourism benefits do not seem to reach the poor. The study came up with three main propositions: (1) tourism does not have systematic effects on the poor; (2) tourism matters most at lower levels of economic development; and (3) at higher levels of development, tourism matters less, hinting at attenuating conditions at play. One of these attenuating conditions may be inequality. The latter condition was factored by a study published by Vanegas in 2014 entitled "The Triangle of Poverty, Economic Growth, and Inequality in Central America: Does Tourism Matter?" Vanegas does a more in-depth investigation of the nexus between tourism, economic growth, and poverty.

By investigating the elasticity of income, the Vanegas study is different in two important ways: the study controlled for changes in inequality and expanded the sample of countries from two to six, comprising the whole Central American area. Controlling for inequality makes sense in the Central American context because this region is considered one of the most unequal regions in the world. Even Costa Rica, which has been considered the country with one of the least unequal income distributions in the region, has experienced a dramatic increase in inequality in the past 10 years. While Costa Rica's average Gini coefficient in the decade of 2000–2010 was 36.11, it jumped to 51.47 and 51.78 in 2011 and 2012, respectively.

The study of Vanegas builds on the poverty-distribution of income relationships approach. This approach basically says that income inequalities may affect the growth poverty elasticity. Similar to Croes, the study is also premised on the Kaldor approach, relating poverty reduction to the size of exports development structure, and not to income growth. Export is viewed as a channel to increase the domestic market. The data are from 1980 to 2012. The study found that poverty is negatively related to income changes and positively related to changes in income inequality. A 1% increase in income would reduce poverty by 0.79, while the same 1% increase in income inequality will increase poverty by nearly 1.4. The study also found substantial differences among the Central American countries in terms of the impact of income and inequality on poverty. The substantial variance in elasticities may be related to the initial poverty level, the initial level of income distribution, and the depth of poverty.

These same issues are examined considering the effects of tourism on poverty while controlling for income and inequality. The results are remarkable. Tourism matters for the poor in all countries, but tourism matters in some countries more than others in poverty reduction. For example, the tourism power in reducing poverty is stronger in Costa Rica (–0.62), Nicaragua (–0.63), and Guatemala (–0.56) compared to El Salvador (–0.29) and Honduras (–0.29). However, inequality has a substantial impact on poverty reduction. In all the countries that Vanegas examined, tourism has increased inequality, ranging from 0.86 in Costa Rica followed by Honduras (1.19), Guatemala (1.22), and Nicaragua (1.27) to El Salvador (1.31).

The implication is that inequality may be a powerful moderator in connecting tourism with the poor. While tourism directly reduces the poverty level, tourism also increases the level of inequality, and hence, the level of poverty. Tourism effects on the poor may cancel each other out, thereby increasing the army of poor. Thus, while initially the direct effects of tourism on poverty reduction seem substantial, when combined with the initial conditions of a country, such as the depth of poverty, the direct effects of tourism on poverty reduction may be limited. The power of tourism seems to reveal itself more clearly through economic growth. However, before we reach any definitive conclusion with regard to the quality of tourism growth, we need to move away from aggregate national data, because this type of data may conceal micro processes that hamper the understanding of the direct effects of tourism on poverty.

## THE QUALITY OF TOURISM GROWTH

We looked at the quality of tourism growth by applying a closed input–output (CIO) method to Ecuador and Nicaragua. Specifically, we explored the distributional effects of tourism development in these two developing countries. The CIO method includes businesses, different types of labor, and household incomes. This method is more appropriate for developing countries because it assesses more effectively the impact of any economic sector on the factors of production, including those of poor households.[28] In other words, the method further allows unveiling different income dimensions of poverty, which facilitates the direct assessment of poverty.

Applying this technique reveals three specific benefits. First, households are regarded as an industry, considering labor as their output. Second, the focus of the study is to determine whether poor households receive income directly from tourism-related activities and enables the comparison between households based on their incomes. Third, the study assumes that the poor are the best agents to freely decide how to consume any additional income. The focus on other mechanisms such as price and government transfers make choices for the poor and assume that the poor have the ability to influence government transfers: common assumptions embedded in computable general equilibrium studies.

The income categories follow those set by the United Nations. The US$1 threshold refers to the extreme poor; the US$2 threshold relates to poor; and the US$3 threshold refers to the vulnerability threshold. Vulnerability is a multidimensional situation that represents a stochastic hazard and is interconnected to the concept of poverty.[29] Household incomes were disaggregated in four groups: less than US$1/d; US$1.01/d and US$2.00/d; US$2.01/d and US$3.00/d; and US$3.01/d or more per day. The less than US$1/d threshold refers to extreme poor; US$2 relates to poor; and US$3 refers to the vulnerability threshold.

In the case of Nicaragua, the distribution for the change in demand for tourism was estimated based on the visitor's spending profile provided by the Cámara de Turismo de Nicaragua during a site visit by the researchers. As for Ecuador, the visitor's spending profile was adopted from the Plan Maestro De Desarrollo Turistico De la Provincia del Guayas. In both instances, the tourism dollars are assigned to two specific economic sectors (sector 6 [commerce/hotels/restaurants] and sector 7 [transportation] according to the distribution of the average total expenditures made by tourists in each country.

**TABLE 4.7** Direct Impact of Tourism in Nicaragua and Ecuador

| Economic Sector | Direct and Indirect (Ecuador) | | Direct, Indirect, and Induced (Ecuador) | |
|---|---|---|---|---|
| 6 | US$14,414,400 | 77% | US$7,890,799 | 75% |
| 7 | US$4,305,600 | 23% | US$2,675,649 | 25% |
| Total | US$18,720,000 | | US$10,566,448 | |

**Notes:** 6=, commerce/hotel/restaurants (International Standard Industrial Classification [ISIC]: 45–47; 55–56); 7=, transportation (ISIC: 49–53; l 58–63).

The study applied an experiment based on an estimation of a change in demand for tourism considering the real growth in international tourism receipts from 2000 to 2013 for each country. These estimates stem from the forecast conducted for each country by the WTTC (2013). The total change in demand for tourism in Nicaragua was estimated at US$18,720,000 (a 4.5% increase from 2012) and US$10,566,448 (a 1.1% increase from 2012) for Ecuador. The indirect impact refers to intersectoral linkages with nontourist sectors and Tables 4.7 and 4.8 reveal that tourism's direct and indirect contribution exceeds US$29.7 million and US$17.1 million in Nicaragua and Ecuador, respectively (see Table 4.8).

The indirect impact in Nicaragua is about 58.7% of the direct effects, while in the case of Ecuador, the proportion is 61.9%.

The Type I multipliers for tourism are 1.59 and 1.62 in Nicaragua and Ecuador, respectively. The total direct, indirect, and induced effects are presented in Tables 4.8 and 4.9. In the case of Nicaragua, the total induced effect from a change in demand from tourism is US$36.1 million and US$19.2 million for Ecuador.

**TABLE 4.8** Tourism Direct Economic Impact (Nicaragua and Ecuador)

| Economic Sector | Direct and Indirect (Nicaragua) (US$) | Direct and Indirect (Ecuador) (US$) |
|---|---|---|
| 1 | 1,676,080 | 346,475 |
| 2 | 351,358 | 241,451 |
| 3 | 567,897 | 2,548,646 |
| 4 | 5,819,487 | 332,885 |
| 5 | 136,300 | 63,493 |
| 6 | 15,012,705 | 8,462,975 |
| 7 | 4,721,987 | 4,340,702 |
| 8 | 738,078 | 714,974 |
| 9 | 692,405 | 64,170 |
| Total | 29,716,297 | 17,115,771 |

**Notes:** 1=, agriculture (International Standard Industrial Classification [ISIC]: 01–03); 2=, mining (ISIC: 05–09); 3=, manufacturing (ISIC: 10–33); 4=, utilities (ISIC: 35–39); 5=, construction (ISIC: 41–43); 6=, commerce/hotel/restaurants (ISIC: 45–47; 55–56)); 7=, transportation (ISIC: 49–53; 1 58–63); 8=, financial intermediaries (ISIC: 64–68); 9=, other services (ISIC: 69–98).

**TABLE 4.9** Total Tourism Economic Impact (Nicaragua and Ecuador)

| Economic Sector | Direct, Indirect, and Induced (Nicaragua) (US$) | Direct, Indirect, and Induced (Ecuador) (US$) |
|---|---|---|
| 1 | 2,759,589 | 509,319 |
| 2 | 535,112 | 319,287 |
| 3 | 750,009 | 3,377,309 |
| 4 | 8,884,444 | 402,783 |
| 5 | 176,440 | 79,279 |

**TABLE 4.9** *(Continued)*

| Economic Sector | Direct, Indirect, and Induced (Nicaragua) (US$) | Direct, Indirect, and Induced (Ecuador) (US$) |
|---|---|---|
| 6 | 15,381,631 | 8,687,520 |
| 7 | 5,180,166 | 4,616,776 |
| 8 | 937,170 | 1,043,235 |
| 9 | 1,553,339 | 197,546 |
| Total | 36,157,900 | 19,233,054 |

**Notes:** 1, agriculture (International Standard Industrial Classification [ISIC]: 01–03); 2, mining (ISIC: 05–09); 3, manufacturing (ISIC: 10–33); 4, utilities (ISIC: 35–39); 5, construction (ISIC: 41–43); 6, commerce/hotel/restaurants (ISIC: 45–47; 55–56)); 7, transportation (ISIC: 49–53; 1 58–63); 8, financial intermediaries (ISIC: 64–68); 9, other services (ISIC: 69–98).

The Type II multipliers are 1.93 and 1.82 in Nicaragua and Ecuador, respectively.[30] The results are clear: tourism spawns substantial economic benefits to Nicaragua and Ecuador. Tourism generates economic activities in other economic sectors by increasing business transactions as well incomes in both countries.

**TABLE 4.10** Income Multipliers (Nicaragua and Ecuador)

| | 1 | 2 | 3 | 4 | 5 | 6 | 7 | 8 | 9 |
|---|---|---|---|---|---|---|---|---|---|
| Nicaragua | | | | | | | | | |
| Less than US$1 ($H_1$) | 0.007 | 0.002 | 0.0009 | 0.003 | 0.002 | 0.003 | 0.002 | 0.0006 | 0.0009 |
| US$1.01 and US$2.00 ($H_2$) | 0.032 | 0.006 | 0.0060 | 0.012 | 0.015 | 0.014 | 0.009 | 0.0040 | 0.0050 |
| US$2.01 and US$3.00 ($H_3$) | 0.042 | 0.027 | 0.0280 | 0.034 | 0.079 | 0.041 | 0.037 | 0.0260 | 0.0200 |
| US$3.01 or more ($H_4$) | 0.083 | 0.039 | 0.1790 | 0.087 | 0.197 | 0.165 | 0.176 | 0.2770 | 0.0950 |
| Total | 0.164 | 0.073 | 0.2140 | 0.136 | 0.293 | 0.223 | 0.225 | 0.3070 | 0.1210 |

**TABLE 4.10** *(Continued)*

| | 1 | 2 | 3 | 4 | 5 | 6 | 7 | 8 | 9 |
|---|---|---|---|---|---|---|---|---|---|
| Ecuador | | | | | | | | | |
| Less than US$1 ($H_1$) | 0.003 | 0.0005 | 0.002 | 0.0008 | 0.001 | 0.0036 | 0.0006 | 0.002 | 0.005 |
| US$1.01 and US$2.00 ($H_2$) | 0.008 | 0.0020 | 0.004 | 0.004 | 0.003 | 0.0060 | 0.0010 | 0.003 | 0.013 |
| US$2.01 and US$3.00 ($H_3$) | 0.018 | 0.0003 | 0.005 | 0.004 | 0.004 | 0.0050 | 0.0020 | 0.007 | 0.015 |
| US$3.01 or more ($H_4$) | 0.143 | 0.0500 | 0.077 | 0.151 | 0.120 | 0.0850 | 0.0860 | 0.184 | 0.488 |
| Total | 0.172 | 0.0530 | 0.088 | 0.160 | 0.128 | 0.1000 | 0.0890 | 0.196 | 0.522 |

**Notes:** 1, agriculture (International Standard Industrial Classification [ISIC]: 01–03); 2, mining (ISIC: 05–09); 3, manufacturing (ISIC: 10–33); 4, utilities (ISIC: 35–39); 5, construction (ISIC: 41–43); 6, commerce/hotel/restaurants (ISIC: 45–47; 55–56); 7, transportation (ISIC: 49–53; 1 58–63); 8, financial intermediaries (ISIC: 64–67); 9, other services (ISIC: 69–98).

The income effects or household income multipliers for Nicaragua and Ecuador are presented in Table 4.10. For example, in the case of Ecuador, the income multiplier for the households that earn less than US$1/d can be used with the proposed $\Delta X$ of US$10,566,448 for Ecuador in Table 4.7 by considering $\Delta X_6$ = US$7,890,799 (commerce/hotels/restaurants) and $\Delta X_7$ = US$2,675,649 (transportation). For those earning less than US$1/d ($H_1$) the study includes a series of income multipliers (*ln*) for each element of $\Delta X$. Thus, total incomes for those earning less than US$1/d as a result from a change in demand for tourism in Ecuador can be estimated with the following formula: $H_1 = [(\Delta X_6)(l6)] + [(\Delta X_7)(l7)]$. In particular, for this example, $H_1$ = [(US$7,890,799) (0.0036)] + [(US$2,675,649) (0.0006)] or $H_1$ = US$28,059 + US$1,588 = US$29,647 (see Table 4.10 to Table 4.11).

Table 4.11 further reveals that in the case of Nicaragua, the lowest income category experienced an increase in their incomes at a higher rate than the other groups except for those in the highest income category (earning more than US$3.00/d). In the case of Ecuador, on the other hand, the lowest income earners saw their aggregate salaries increase at a larger rate than the other three income segments. Nevertheless, in Nicaragua and Ecuador, those earning more than US$3/d received 75% and 88% of the total salaries, respectively. The latter results imply that the highest income categories have received more income in absolute terms compared to the other income categories.

**TABLE 4.11** Tourism and Income Distribution

| | Total Change in Incomes by Income Group (US$) | Absolute Distribution (%) | Δ in Total Income by Group (%) |
|---|---|---|---|
| Nicaragua | | | |
| Less than US$1/d | 54,788 | 1 | 0.03086 |
| US$1.01/d and US$2.00/d | 246,005 | 6 | 0.02816 |
| US$2.01/d and US$3.00/d | 750,090 | 18 | 0.02923 |
| US$3.01/d or more per day | 3,129,954 | 75 | 0.03853 |
| Total | 4,180,837 | 100 | |
| Ecuador | | | |
| Less than US$1/d | 29,647 | 3 | 0.02870 |
| US$1.01/d and US$2.00/d | 50,542 | 5 | 0.02157 |
| US$2.01/d and US$3.00/d | 46,168 | 4 | 0.01406 |
| US$3.01/d or more per day | 900,556 | 88 | 0.01293 |
| Total | 1,026,913 | 100 | |

The study also compared the tourism income multipliers for each household category with other sectors of the economy in both countries. The tourism multiplier was considered the baseline for the analysis. The sign before the percentage reflects the distance (either positive or negative) of the assessed sector compared to tourism. Table 4.12 reveals the results of the comparison. When compared to the other economic sectors in both countries, tourism performed relatively well in favoring the poor. The agricultural sector did better than tourism for the poor in both cases. The construction sector in the case of Nicaragua seemed also to perform better for the income categories between US$1 and US$3, with the latter doing better than all the other categories. Only in the case of Ecuador, did other services outperform tourism.

**TABLE 4.12** Comparing Tourism Income Multipliers with Other Industry Sectors

| | Tour (%) | 1 (%) | 2 (%) | 3 (%) | 4 (%) | 5 (%) | 8 (%) | 9 (%) |
|---|---|---|---|---|---|---|---|---|
| Nicaragua | | | | | | | | |
| Less than US$1 ($H_1$) | 0.3 | 141.3 | -44.8 | -68.9 | -10.3 | -41.4 | -79.3 | -68.9 |
| US$1.01 and US$2.00 ($H_2$) | 1.3 | 141.8 | -57.4 | -52.8 | -5.7 | 12.5 | -73.3 | -65.7 |
| US$2.01 and US$3.00 ($H_3$) | 4.0 | 5.8 | -32.8 | -29.5 | -15.1 | 97.2 | -35.3 | -49.3 |
| US$3.01 or more ($H_4$) | 16.7 | -50.3 | -76.5 | 7.0 | -48.2 | 17.8 | 65.4 | -43.3 |
| Ecuador | | | | | | | | |
| Less than US$1 ($H_1$) | 0.3 | 9.1 | -82.4 | -26.0 | -71.8 | -61.2 | -47.2 | 79.5 |
| US$1.01 and US$2.00 ($H_2$) | 0.5 | 67.1 | -64.4 | -16.4 | -8.0 | -41.4 | -33.1 | 180.0 |
| US$2.01 and US$3.00 ($H_3$) | 0.4 | 307.8 | -93.1 | 20.7 | -15.7 | -13.4 | 68.6 | 250.8 |
| US$3.01 or more ($H_4$) | 8.5 | 67.2 | -40.8 | -10.1 | 77.3 | 41.0 | 115.9 | 472.5 |

**Notes:** 1, agriculture (International Standard Industrial Classification [ISIC]: 01–03); 2, mining (ISIC: 05–09); 3, manufacturing (ISIC: 10–33); 4, utilities (ISIC: 35–39); 5, construction (ISIC: 41–43); 6, commerce/hotel/restaurants (ISIC: 45–47; 55–56); 7, transportation (ISIC: 49 53; I 58–63), 8, financial intermediaries (ISIC: 64–68); 9, other services (ISIC: 69–98).

## *CASCADING EFFECTS OF TOURISM ON POVERTY*

What can we infer from the Ecuador and Nicaragua cases with regard to the quality of growth spawned by tourism? First, tourism development does help the poor increase their earnings, including those with the highest incidence of poverty, such as is the case for those earning less than US$1/d. Indigence conditions, then, may be alleviated in both countries through tourism development. This finding is consistent with the first definition of pro-poor growth being that growth increases income levels of the poor regardless of inequality (the absolute pro-poor definition). Tourism expansion has trickle-down effects from this perspective and market forces can assist poverty reduction if the poor have access to the market.

Second, the two cases also reveal inconsistent findings when comparing the distributional effects of tourism development. The poorest in Ecuador faired significantly better than all other income brackets, while the highest income bracket in Nicaragua reaped more benefits from tourism development than any of the lowest income groups. The relative increase in aggregate incomes of the lowest income group (less than US$1/d) was 54.9% higher than the highest income bracket (US$3 or more per day) in Ecuador. In Nicaragua, on the other hand, the relative increase in aggregate incomes of the lowest income bracket (less than US$1 a day) was 24.9% less than the highest income bracket (more than US$3 a day). Considering the second definition of pro-poor being growth benefiting the poor more than the nonpoor (the relative pro-poor definition), the findings reveal mixed results. Tourism development in Ecuador is pro-poor, while tourism development in Nicaragua cannot be considered pro-poor, according to the latter definition. Distribution seems purely incidental to tourism expansion.

Third, the actual differences in absolute income in both countries increased among the income groups due to tourism development. Thus, while the percentage growth rate could favor the poor more than the nonpoor income category, the nonpoor seem to receive substantially more income than the poor groups. In other words, the income increase will be higher for the highest income group; thus, the absolute differences will increase. The focus of the pro-poor growth should be relative to absolute inequality, because the latter touches the basic structure of equality in a developing country.

Lastly, tourism development seems an effective strategy in addressing poverty issues in developing countries. Apart from agriculture, tourism development has outperformed all other economic sectors in poverty alleviation. The distributional effects of tourism development are spread across all household incomes. Other sectors are much more intensive in their use of production factors, particularly those owned by the highest income groups, such as utilities and finance as illustrated in the case of Ecuador.

There are some theoretical and practical policy implications that warrant recognition from the previous findings. The inconsistency in results suggests that tourism development does not automatically alleviate the situation of a country's inequality. The impact of tourism development on the poor seems to be linked to the country's inequality level.[31] Ecuador is less unequal than Nicaragua based on the corresponding Gini coefficients and the former has less poor people than the latter. The inequality level in Ecuador was less severe than that of Nicaragua, possibly impacting the potential of tourism in alleviating indigence conditions in both countries. Furthermore, inequality seems persistent and is a barrier to poverty reduction. For example, Nicaragua witnessed a negative relationship between economic growth and poverty reduction. Inequality conditions in Nicaragua seem a potential barrier to reduce poverty levels as witnessed by the negative relationship between economic growth and poverty reduction. The country enjoyed a 7% increase of per capita income from 2001 to 2005; during the same time, poverty levels increased by 2.5%. Thus, the degree of inequality seems to matter in poverty alleviation.

Tourism connects directly to the poor, but in order to amplify its effects, policies integrating the poor into the market are required. Integrating the poor in the market is easier said than done. Weak institutions, corruption, crime, and a sizeable "underground economy" hamper the direct effects of tourism on poverty reduction efforts. Accelerating human development efforts that include the poor are intractable under these conditions. Thus far, we have only assessed the effects of tourism on average incomes and we provided an economic focus on poverty. In the next chapter, we will shift our focus on poverty by considering a human development perspective on poverty. We will assess the effects of tourism expansion on poverty by considering the Sen Poverty Index, which includes the head count ratio, the Gini coefficient, and the poverty gap.

## REFERENCES


Blake, A.; Arbache, J.; Sinclair, M.; Teles, V. Tourism and poverty relief. *Ann. Tour. Res.* 2008, 35(1), 106–127.

Budd, E. N. *Democratization, Development, and The Patrimonial State in the Age of Globalization*; Lexington Books: Maryland, 2003.

Cañada, E. *Turismo y Conflictos Socio-Ambientales en Centroamerica*; Editorial Enlace: Managua, Nicaragua, 2010.

Chaudhuri, S. Assessing Vulnerability to Poverty: Concepts, Empirical Methods and Illustrative Examples. 2003. http://info.worldbank.org/etools/docs/library/97185/Keny_0304/Ke_0304/vulnerability-assessment.pdf.

CIA, US. "The world factbook." *Retrieved August* 20 (2014): 2010.

Clark, A.; Becker, M.; Eds. *Highland Indians and the State in Modern Ecuador*; University of Pittsburg Press: Pittsburg, PA, 2007.

Croes, R. Tourism and poverty reduction in Latin America: where does the region stand? *Worldwide Hospital. Tour. Theme J.* 2014, 6(3), 261–276.

Croes, R.; Vanegas, M. Tourism and poverty alleviation: a co-integration analysis. *J. Travel Res.* 2008, 47(1), 94–103.

Croes, R.; Rivera, M.; Ramirez, X.; Pizam, A. *Plan Maestro de Desarrollo Turistico: Guayas*; Gobierno Provincial del Guayas y Camara de Turismo: Guayaquil, Ecuador, 2009.

Durbarry, R. Tourism and economic growth: the case of Mauritius. *Tour. Econ.* 2004, 10(4), 389–401.

ECLAC. *Social Panorama of Latin America 2013*; Santiago de Chile: ECLAC, 2014.

Honey, M.; Vargas, E.; Durham, W. Impact of tourism related development on the Pacific coast of Costa Rica, Center for Responsible Travel, Stanford University. 2010. http://www.responsibletravel.org/resources/documents/Coastal-tourism-documents/Summary%20Report/Summary_Report__Impact_Tourism_Related_Development_Pacific_Coast_Costa_Rica.pdf (accessed Jul 4, 2012).

FORLAC. Recent Experiences of Formalization in Latin America and the Caribbean. Program for the Promotion of Formalization in Latin America and the Caribbean. International Labor Organization. 2014. http://www.ilo.org/wcmsp5/groups/public/---americas/---ro-lima/documents/publication/wcms_245882.pdf. Retrieved July 22, 2015.

Isard, W.; Azis, I. J.; Drennan, M. P.; Miller, R. E.; Saltzman, S.; Thorbecke, E. *Methods of Interregional and Regional Analysis*; Ashgate Publishing Company: Aldershot, UK, 1998; Vol. 490.

Joseph, R. A. *Democracy and Prebendal Politics in Nigeria: The Rise and Fall of the Second Republic*; Cambridge University Press: Cambridge, MA, 1987.

Lejarraja, I.; Walkenhorst, P. *Diversification by Deepening Linkages with Tourism*; World Bank: Washington, DC, 2007.

Malik, K. "Human development report 2013." *United Nations Development Programme, New York* , 2013.

Miller, R. E.; Blair, P. D. *Input-Output Analysis*; University Press: Cambridge, MA, 1985.

Ravallion, M. *Pro-Poor Growth: A Primer. World Bank Policy Research*; World Bank: Washington, DC, 2004. [Working Paper].

Romano, S. M.; Falconí, J.; Aguinaga, C. *Una interpretación mesoeconómica del turismo en Ecuador*; Publicaciones Económicas, Banco Central del Ecuador: Ecuador, 2005.

Ruel, M.; Garrett, J.; Hawkes, C.; Cohen, M. The food, fuel and financial crises affect the urban and rural poor disproportionally: a review of the evidence. *J Food Nutr.* 2009, 140(1), 1705–1765.

Schlesinger, S.; Kinzer, S. *Bitter Fruit: The Untold Story of an American Coup in Guatemala*; Harvard University Press: Cambridge, MA, 1999.

Transparency International. TI Corruption Perceptions Index. 2008. http://www.transparency.org/policy_research/surveys_indices/americas (accessed Mar 31, 2009).

Ulate, G. La actividad turística en América Central: desarrollo y características. *Anuario de Estudios Centroamericanos*. 2006, 39(1), 9–35.

UNODC. *Transnational Organized Crime in Central America and the Caribbean: a Threat Assessment*; United Nations: Vienna, 2013.

United Nations World Tourism Organization. "UNWTO tourism highlights." (2014).

Vanegas, M. The Triangle of poverty, economic growth, and inequality in Central America: does tourism matter? *Worldwide Hospital. Tour. Theme J.* 2014, 6(3), 277–292.

Vanegas, M.; Croes, R. *Tourism, Economic Expansion and Poverty in Nicaragua: Investigating Cointegration and Causal Relations*; Staff Paper Series Department of Applied Economics, University of Minnesota: Minnesota, 2007. [Staff paper P 07-10].

Vos, R.; De Jong, N. *Rising Inequality During Economic Liberalisation and Crisis: Macro or Micro Causes in Ecuador's Case?*; International Institute of Social Studies of Erasmus University Rotterdam: Rotterdam, 2000. [ISS Working Paper].

World Bank. *Nutritional Failure in Ecuador. Causes, Consequences and Solutions*; World Bank: Washington, DC, 2007.

WTTC. Tourism Impact Data and Forecasts. 2009. http://www.wttc.org/eng/Tourism_Research/Tourism_Economic_Research/ (accessed Mar 24, 2009)

World Bank Group, ed. *World development indicators 2009*. World Bank Publications, 2009.

World Bank Group, ed. *World development indicators 2010*. World Bank Publications, 2010.

World Bank Group, ed. *World development indicators 2011*. World Bank Publications, 2011.

World Bank Group, ed. *World development indicators 2014*. World Bank Publications, 2014.

WTTC. Tourism Impact Data and Forecasts. 2013. http://www.wttc.org/eng/Tourism_Research/Tourism_Economic_Research/ (accessed Mar 24, 2009).

## ENDNOTES

[1]We illustrate these cases through studies from Croes (2014), Vanegas (2014), Croes and Vanegas (2008), and Vanegas and Croes (2007).

[2]See the UNODC (2013) report.

[3]See Schlesinger and Kinzer (1999).

[4]See, for example, ECLAC (2014).

[5]See ECLAC (2014, p. 17) report for the empirical analysis.

[6]For further discussion, see Vanegas (2014).

[7]For a discussion on the regions socioeconomic problems, see Malik (2013)

[8]See, for example, Ruel et al. (2009).

[9]See Vanegas (2014).

[10]Ibid iv. The Gini coefficient measures by how much there is a deviation from perfect equality in income distribution, when everybody has the same income. Zero means everybody has the same income (perfect equality) and one means that one person enjoys all the income indicating extreme inequality.

[11]See, for example, Croes (2014) and Vanegas (2014).

[12]Declaración de Montelimar. VII Cumbre de Presidentes Centroamericanos, Montelimar, República de Nicaragua, 3 April 1990. Montelimar, Nicaragua: Secretariat for Central American Economic Integration; 1990. Retrieved July 5, 2014, from http://www.sieca.int/site/Cache/17990000001145/17990000001145.pdf.

[13]For further discussion, see, for example,e Ulate (2006) and Cañada (2010).

[14]See the UNWTO World Tourism Barometer at http://mkt.unwto.org/barometer.

[15]See, for example, Cañada (2010).

[16]A mestizo is a term used in Spanish speaking countries and refers to mixed population from European and Native American descent.

[17]For examples about Ecuador see Budd (2003), Croes et al. (2009), Joseph (1987), Vos and De Jong (2000), and Transparency International (2008).

[18]See Clark and Becker (2007).

[19]See, for example, World Bank (2007).

[20]See, for example, ECLAC (2014).

[21]See ECLAC (2014).

[22]See the country report from WTTC (2014) about Ecuador. Retrieved June 19, 2014, from http://www.wttc.org/site_media/uploads/downloads/ecuador2014.pdf.

[23]See Durbarry (2004).

[24]See Vanegas and Croes (2007).

[25]The informal economy in Nicaragua represents 65% of the total economy.

[26]See FORLAC (2014).

[27]See, for example, Honey et al. (2010).

[28]For a discussion on the CIO method, see, for example, Isard et al. (1998) and Miller and Blair (1985).

[29]See, for example, Chaudhuri (2003).

[30]These figures are consistent with the findings of Lejarraja and Walkenhorst (2007) and Blake et al. (2008).

[31]We apply the Ravallion (2004) model to examine the poverty reducing effects of growth impacted by the income distribution on the two countries. The Ravallion model suggests that reduction in poverty is determined by economic growth and the Gini index and puts significantly more weight on the impact of inequality of growth on poverty reduction. We determine the average economic growth rate for Ecuador and Nicaragua at 3.6% and 3.7%, respectively, over 2000 and 2012, and a Gini index of 0.493 and 0.5657 for Ecuador and Nicaragua, respectively. We estimate the poverty reduction rate for Ecuador at 4.3% and for Nicaragua at 2.8%.

## CHAPTER 5

# TOURISM AND POVERTY INTENSITY

## CONTENTS

## INTRODUCTION

In the previous chapter, we assessed the relationship between tourism, growth, and poverty. We found that tourism reduces poverty, and now we must narrow the information space to fully grasp tourism's potential to help the poor. Positing that tourism, as a development tool, helps the poor implies that tourism decreases the number of people below the poverty line. But is this finding specific enough to direct programs to help the poor? In other words, does it tell us how much poverty is really out there? While we now know that tourism increases the income of everybody, our findings also hinted that incomes spawned by tourism may be unevenly distributed and insensitive to the distribution of incomes among the poor. Therefore, poverty measures by the head count rate ($H = q/r$) may not tell us much in terms of social welfare evaluation. We need a richer space of information to provide greater insights into the universe of poverty.

We are therefore shifting our focus to investigate the relationship between tourism and poverty. The conventional perspective investigates this relationship through the lens of economic development. This lens tells about head counts, about how individuals fall below the poverty line and how many individuals tourism can lift from underneath the poverty line. The conventional lens tells us nothing about whether tourism benefits the richest of the poor. If tourism is providing just barely enough income to lift someone from below the poverty line, then tourism as a development tool could be a controversial development strategy.

This chapter will look deep into the effects of tourism on the poor. It will investigate if the dollar reaches the poor and whether it will make some poor worse off or not. The main premise of this chapter is that economic growth alone cannot eradicate poverty. In his book *Development as Freedom* (1999), Sen argues for a human development perspective on poverty. This chapter takes on Sen's broader focus on poverty and investigates this perspective in the context of tourism development. It applies the Sen's poverty index (S index) to capture the broader meaning of poverty. The impacts of tourism on poverty are conceptualized by considering the poverty head count, the income shortfall of the poor, and Gini among the poor and will explore the application of the S index in the context of Ecuador.

## THE SEN POVERTY INDEX AND THE POVERTY OBLITERATION PARADIGM

The literature on classic theories of economic development, seen in the work of Rostow, Lewis, and Dos Santos, neither takes notice of the links between tourism and development nor mentions it as a contributor to the process.[1] However, this has not stopped tourism researchers from drawing extensively from such theories to evaluate tourism's contributions as they relate to development theory, dependency theory, tourism and economic development, community development and welfare, and socio-cultural development and well-being.[2] Although these studies cover important issues about the connections between tourism and development, they are all normative in nature and only give directive value judgments about what the potential impacts of tourism on development ought to be. Additionally, their information space to evaluate social welfare is narrow, focusing only on income as the yardstick for identifying poverty, and failing to integrate a broader perspective of the meaning of poverty that would include constraints that curb choices that people make.

We already saw in the previous chapters that the literature linking tourism expansion, development, and poverty shows an array of paradoxes. For every claimed relationship, for example, tourism and poverty reduction, there is a claim that either contradicts the magnitude of the effect or the causal connection. Therefore, the consideration for the phenomena under investigation necessitated a review of a body of knowledge well-grounded in theory. The first step for conceptualizing the proposed analytical framework is to converge on a set of two specific objectives for assessing the effects of tourism expansion on development (Figure 5.1).

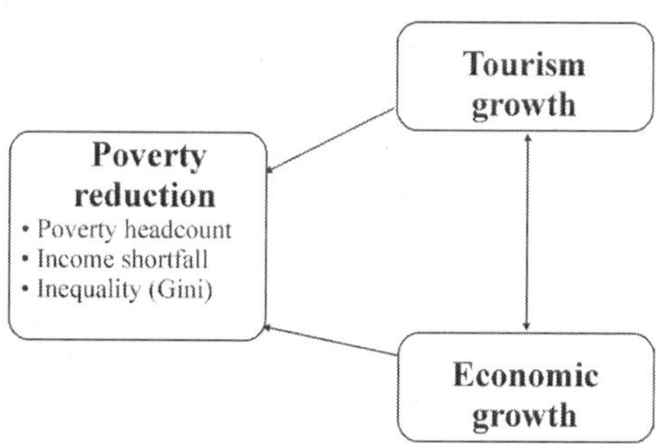


**FIGURE 5.1** Relationship Between Development and Poverty Obliteration Paradigm (Poverty).

The first objective, economic growth, has a strong foundation with two interrelated theories: neoclassical growth theory and endogenous growth theory. The former adheres to promoting free markets, exports, trade liberalization, and foreign investment in an attempt to spur efficiency and development.[3] The latter supports an active role of the state for promoting economic development through direct and indirect investment in human capital. A common feature is the focus on individual achievements through income and consumption, which are considered as the proper "space" for distributional assessments. Within the context of growth, tourism is viewed as a valuable export, and its effects on development, as supported by the tourism-led growth (TLG) hypothesis, occur when tourism stimulates the economy in the form of spillovers and externalities.[4]

As for the second objective, that of reducing poverty, this study embraces Sen's holistic approach, which is cemented in collective choice theory and considers the various predicaments and miseries that make up a society.[5] Under this framework, poverty is no longer defined as income deprivation or lack of command over commodities; poverty is now measured by the individual's income or consumption capabilities. Sen considers that the income paradigm revealed in poverty as a head count measure neglects the intensity of poverty and does not indicate how poor the poor really are. Instead, Sen claims that judgments about how well a society is doing should be based on cogent aggregative judgments about social welfare.

The ability of a person to freely choose the life valued depends, therefore, on many factors (some beyond the control of the individual), such as age (the needs of the young versus old person), by gender and social roles (women and family), and by location (drought and crime). Sen, as alluded to in Chapter 2, broadened the informational "space" of poverty and integrated the income distribution among the poor and the concept of inequality as important criteria to assess development. Sen was not only interested in capturing the incidence of poverty but also its depth and distribution. In this respect, the additional information resulting from this perspective facilitates a more comprehensive social welfare evaluation than just the focus on the incidence of poverty.

## USING THE SEN INDEX TO MEASURE POVERTY

The efforts to broaden the measure of poverty spawned specific indices that are closely related to Sen's notion of development, i.e., the S index.

Sen launched the S index in 1976 in his now famous article *Poverty: An Ordinal Approach to Measurement*. The S index measures poverty based on three axioms: the focus axiom, the monotonicity axiom, and the transfer axiom. The first axiom asserts that attention should be paid only to the poor; thus, any index is independent from the non-poor population. The second axiom includes an increase in overall poverty if the income of one person declines; and the third axiom states that poverty increases when the income of a poor person is transferred to someone with more income. His axioms yield the following index:

$$\text{Sen index} = H \times \left[ I + (1 - I) \times G \right]$$

- $H$ is the poverty head count and includes that segment of the population that has incomes lower than the poverty line. This is in conformity with the focus axiom held by Sen.
- I represents the income shortfall of the poor with regard to the poverty line.
- G, the last component of the index, represents the Gini coefficient and is a measure of the inequality of income among the poor. A higher value of each component means a lower level of social welfare due to poverty. Conversely, a lower value of each component means a higher level of social welfare due to lower poverty intensity.

The S index is applied from the perspective of the broader meaning of poverty. The impacts of tourism on poverty are conceptualized by considering the poverty head count, the income shortfall of the poor, and Gini. The index thus integrates three relevant and commonly used measures of poverty and inequality: the poverty rate (head counts), the poverty gap ratio, and a Gini index of the poor. The poverty rate refers to the number of people below the poverty line (head count); the poverty gap ratio is the number of people who on average fall below the poverty line; and the Gini index of the poor is a truncated income distribution including only the poor population. These three components measure the incidence, depth, and distribution of poverty, respectively.

## AN EMPIRICAL APPROACH FOR UNDERSTANDING THE DEVELOPMENT EXPERIENCE

The central focus of this chapter is the empirical model used to test the relationship between economic development and poverty obliteration paradigm (POP) presented in Chapter 4. We applied a co-integration technique based on the Granger representation theorem and tested the development propositions from the POP presented in Figure 5.1 (Mukherjee et al. 1998). For this purpose, we used annual time series data. A co-integration analysis requires that the properties of the time series under review are carefully and properly examined. For this purpose, several steps were undertaken in order to determine the form and pattern in which the data will be used for any estimation procedure. Whenever time series data are used in econometric models, any trend or seasonal component or any "memory" must be removed in order to avoid spurious results.

Most variables considered in tourism analysis seem nonstationary in the technical sense, i.e., their mean and variances alter over time. On the other hand, if the variables are stationary, then any arbitrary combination among them will also be stationary (Granger representation theorem).[6] This means that they move closely together over time and do not drift apart. In other words, there is some mechanism that pulls these variables back together. If this is the case, then the variables are said to be co-integrated. Engle and Granger posited that there is always an error correction representation that can depict the process of this relationship linking the variables. The co-integration procedure implemented in this study will determine if any pair of variables forms a long-term equilibrium combination. The Engle and Granger two-stage approach is used to test for co-integration.[7] If the results from the co-integration test indicate the existence of at least one co-integrating relationship, then long-term equilibrium exists among variables and the effects of hypothesized relationships can be tested.

This approach reveals a dynamic methodology that captures short term as well as long-term effects of variables interacting with each other. The dynamic methodology consists of four steps: (1) unit root testing, (2) co-integration, (3) error correction, and (4) Granger causality. These four methods answer four specific questions. The first question relates to the nature of the time series to discern patterns. The importance of the unit root testing is to determine the growth characteristics of aggregate economic behaviors (i.e., tourism arrivals, gross domestic product, and poverty) to identify if they grow in a secular way over long periods or if they just wander around without a fixed mean.

The second question pertains to the time variant component when variables interact and establish long-run relationships. Only if we can determine that at some point in time, tourism, economic growth, and poverty are pulled together by way of reaching a point of being stationary, will we know that they impact each other. The co-integration method will determine the time path of the impact of the variables among each other. Once a co-integration relationship has been established, the third step, the error correction model, answers our third question, which is related to how quick the variables move together. For example, how much time does it take for economic growth and tourism to impact poverty in the long run while simultaneously capturing the short-run effects. The last question we will address is the causality of the relationship. For example, are tourism and economic growth causing a reduction in poverty or is it the other way around?

The Granger test is applied only if co-integration between any set of two variables exists, which indicates that causality must then run in at least one direction.[8] According to the Granger representation theorem, in a bivariate context, causality boils down to the significance of the lagged residuals in the regression model. We make an a priori assumption that tourism expansion has an effect on economic growth, human development, and poverty. Therefore, the importance for establishing the causal relationship in a Granger sense is to validate such claims.

## DEVELOPMENT REALITY IN ECUADOR: CAPABILITIES, POVERTY, TOURISM, AND ECONOMIC GROWTH

We can test the relationships mentioned at the beginning of this chapter by understanding the measurement units and properties of the data employed for the analysis. In this section, we describe the data for poverty, tourism, and economic growth, and we use time series data from Ecuador.

While the incidence of poverty fluctuates around the world, the South American region draws attention because of the incessant political milieus and enduring poverty. Among the South American nations, Ecuador provides a good case study. From 2009 to 2013, during President Correa's first term, the country experienced a couple years of strong economic growth. The adoption of populist economic policies that included significant public investment, including cash transfer programs to those living in poverty, meaning those who cannot meet their basic nutritional requirements even if their entire incomes were spent on food, has helped combat poverty. For example, the poverty rate in urban areas has declined from 49% in 2002 to roughly 32% in 2011.[9] However, massive income disparities are still noticeable.[10] With a population of 16 million people, Ecuador continues to face high inequality. In 2006, Ecuador's Gini coefficient reached 0.54 and since then has decreased to 0.48 by the end of 2012.[11]

We first applied the S index to measure poverty in Ecuador. This index incorporates the head count ratio, the income gap or depth of poverty, and the Gini coefficient among the poor. The head count ratio is the proportion of people in a society who are living in poverty. The income gap is usually estimated as the distance between the mean income of the poor and the poverty line. The Gini coefficient is one of the most commonly used measures of income inequality. The Gini index is based on the Lorenz curve, which plots cumulative percentages of the population against their cumulative aggregate incomes. For the purpose of calculating the S index, distribution is measured by considering only those incomes below the poverty line. The latter is basically the truncated income distribution excluding the nonpoor population. The three factors are calculated to form the S index, which measures the incomes of the poorest persons more heavily than the incomes of persons closer to the threshold. The poverty line in Ecuador is based on a minimum consumption capability for basic goods.

The S index of Ecuador used for the analysis is from 1998 to 2005.[12] Figure 5.2 depicts the difference between stationary and nonstationary series for the S index. When looking at the Sen index in level form, the data are not stationary and have a unit root. The pattern of poverty in Ecuador yields some interesting information. First, the index indicates that income shocks are persistent, suggesting that tourism development may have lasting effects on alleviating poverty. The S index is particularly sensitive to income. When all poor individuals have zero income, the index is equal to the head count. When all poor individuals have an income equal to the poverty line, then the value of the index is zero. Therefore, persistence of income shocks means that once the poor receive income and are lifted from below the poverty line, it is difficult to revert to a situation below the poverty line.

Second, the poverty intensity is a dynamic process moving through different cycles. Figure 5.2 showcases three visible cycles. The first cycle includes the time period from 1990 to 1997, the second one from 1997 to 2000, and the third cycle refers to the period from 2000 to 2005. The first and the third periods reveal negative cycles, while the second time period exposes a positive cycle. And third, the rise and fall of the poverty intensity in Ecuador suggests that there is a constant shift in intensity of incidence, depth, and distribution of poverty in the country. Uncovering the dynamics among the main contributing factors in the change of poverty intensity in Ecuador provides insightful information to understand the multidimensional impact of tourism development on poverty.

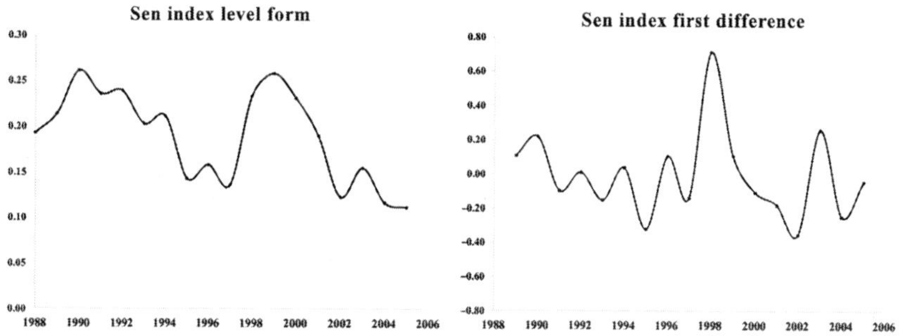


**FIGURE 5.2** Sen Poverty Index Ecuador.
Augmented Dickey–Fuller unit root test: with a drift and constant/levels = −1.406(1); with a trend and constant/levels = −2.238(1); with a drift and constant/first difference = −2.492(1)**; and with a trend and constant/1st difference = −2.331(1) (notes: ** denotes the rejection of the unit root hypothesis based on MacKinnon (1991) critical values at 5%. The optimal lag length is presented in brackets and is based on the SBIC and AIC criteria). Phillips–Perron unit root test: constant without trend/levels = −1.528(1); constant with trend/levels = −2.372(1); constant without trend/first difference = −4.170(1)*; and constant with trend/first difference = −4.111(1)* (notes: * denotes the rejection of the unit root hypothesis at 1% based on the Newey–West method. The optimal lag length is presented in brackets and is based on the SBIC and AIC criteria).

The latter pattern suggests that direct government grants to poor households through financial support may enable poor households to enjoy a virtuous cycle of increasing income. For example, the beginning of the second wave of negative trend in Ecuador, according to Figure 5.2, started about the year 2000. In 1999, the Ecuador government launched Bono Solidario, which became the Bono de Desarollo Humano (BDH) in 2003. The BDH is a cash transfer program for poor households. This program started with a US$15 monthly transfer to poor households in 2003 and grew to US$35 monthly transfer in 2009. The program is considered a positive influence on poor households.

Table 5.1 presents various poverty indicators in Ecuador. From 1987 to 2009, the average monthly per capita income/consumption expenditure in Ecuador has increased by 27% from US$190 to US$242.[13] During the same period, the number of people below the poverty line has also seen a dramatic decrease of 50% from 12.86% to 6.38%.[14] These figures can be seen as a sign or indicator of the possible obliteration of poverty. Individuals have not only seen an improvement in their overall incomes but have also migrated from below the poverty line. However, when looking at the POP, the issue of inequality is also a major concern when it comes to fighting poverty. The reduction of inequality in Ecuador has improved, however, at a lesser pace when compared to the other indicators. This could be attributed to the dollarization effect that took place in the year 2000. The figures in Table 5.1 indicate that the Gini coefficient for Ecuador increased to 60.13 during this time, and more recently, decreased to 49.43 in 2009.

**TABLE 5.1** Poverty Indicators in Ecuador

| Year | Average Per Capita Income (Month) (US$) | Poverty Head Count (%) | Gini Coefficient |
|---|---|---|---|
| 1987 | 190.30 | 12.86 | 50.49 |
| 1994 | 182.00 | 14.10 | 54.32 |
| 1999 | 151.20 | 23.92 | 60.13 |
| 2005 | 242.51 | 9.13 | 54.14 |
| 2006 | 266.45 | 6.14 | 53.2 |
| 2009 | 242.22 | 6.38 | 49.43 |

**Source:** http://iresearch.worldbank.org/PovcalNet/index.htm?2

To better assess the relationship between tourism development and poverty intensity, we need to look more closely at tourism patterns and their effects on poverty intensity. As we already discovered in the previous chapter, income through tourism has two channels through which it can reach the poor. The direct channel provides income right to the individual. For example, the individual can get a job in the hospitality industry. Income through tourism reaches the poor through the indirect channel when tourists spend their money in the economy and businesses pay taxes, and the government receives money that it can allocate to fund social programs. Therefore, in the next two sections, we will assess tourism and economic patterns in Ecuador.

A flourishing sector that has evolved as a new option for promoting development and economic growth in Ecuador is tourism. In 2005, the results of the Tourism Satellite Accounts program for Ecuador provided a welcome surprise for many. The report indicated that tourism (domestic and international) constitutes 4.5% of the gross domestic product.[15] In addition, an increase of 13% in international arrivals in 2008 demonstrates that tourism expansion does not coincide with the economic contractions and recession in Ecuador.[16] The World Travel and Tourism Council (WTTC) estimated that the contribution of travel and tourism to GDP in 2013 was US$1,657 million (1.9% of total GDP) in 2013 and is expected to rise by 3.4% in 2014. This represented 4.3% of total exports and 1.7% of total employment or 118,500 jobs.[17]

In the previous chapter, we described how important tourism has become in Ecuador in terms of its impact on economic growth and diversity, spillover potential to other sectors of the economy, and job creation and its impact on the poor. Tourism has become an important mainstay in the economy of Ecuador. International arrivals have steadily increased in the first decade of the twenty-first century, reaching almost 1.4 million, which is less than 1% of the South American market. International tourism receipts have also grown significantly. For example, these receipts increased by 21% from 2011 to 2012, reaching US$1.25 billion, equivalent to only 0.5% of the South American market. Tourism has become the third largest foreign exchange source after agriculture and fisheries, comprising 4.3% of total export in 2013.

Ecuador tourism expansion, based on international tourist arrivals figures from the WTTC, is not stationary in level form. Tourism arrivals in Ecuador are sensitive to external shocks, such as business cycles, 9/11 attacks, and the Great Recession. These shocks are persistent over time. The pattern of the data in Figure 5.3 shows a positive trend, indicating that visitor arrivals are continuously altered in a positive fashion. The data for tourism arrivals and the results for the unit root tests are presented in Figure 5.3.[18]

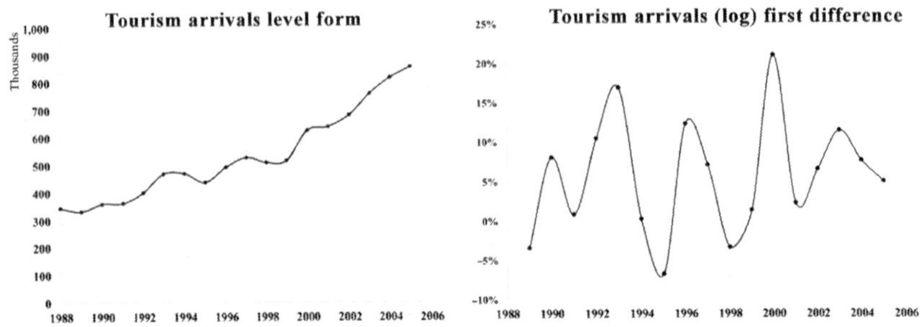


**FIGURE 5.3** Tourism Arrivals Ecuador.
Augmented Dickey–Fuller unit root test: with a drift and constant/levels = 0.318(3); with a trend and constant/levels = −1.034(3); with a drift and constant/first difference = −1.534(3)***; with a trend and constant/first difference = −1.663(3) (notes: *** denotes the rejection of the unit root hypothesis based on MacKinnon (1991) critical values at 10%. The optimal lag length is presented in brackets and is based on the SBIC and AIC criteria). Phillips–Perron unit root test: constant without trend/levels = 0.393(3); constant with trend/levels = 0.991(3); constant without trend/first difference = −5.554(3)*; and constant with trend/first difference = −5.402(3)* (notes: * denotes the rejection of the unit root hypothesis at 1% based on the Newey–West method. The optimal lag length is presented in brackets and is based on the SBIC and AIC criteria).

## ECONOMIC GROWTH

Despite Ecuador's efforts to reduce poverty and grow the tourism sector, a somewhat unstable political milieu seems to counteract against economic growth and development. Ecuador manifests most of the symptoms of developing countries, namely, political instability, weak institutions, lack in transparency, nepotism, and weak economic performance.[19] The economic activities in Ecuador are characterized by a high primary commodity export concentration ratio for the leading primary products (the exports are crude petroleum, bananas, and shellfish). In the past, the country's reliance on these exports has been devastating for the economy, demonstrated by the vulnerability to events such as the 1980 oil crises, and more recently, El Nino. Since then, the country has shifted from a state-oriented development model toward a neoliberal approach. President Correa's return to a state-oriented model spawned sizable contributions of welfare that is given to poor families, and the expansion of individual housing loans. In an attempt to drive the economy and promote businesses, his government has expanded the amount of credit available to small businesses, young people, and women. Many of these strategies are focused on social reforms as well as on boosting the country's economy.

Ecuador has shown strong economic performance in the first decade of the twenty-first century. Since 2000, its economic growth rate has been 5.5%, second to Peru with 7%. Ecuador has a low debt-to-GDP ratio, which is at 24% as compared to the United States, which has a ratio about 100%[20]; or Brazil, which has a ratio of 68.8.[21] A look at the Gross Domestic Product series in 2000 US$ indicates that the series are not stationary in the natural log level form. This means that the transition path to long-term growth is persistent in the case of Ecuador. The results presented in Figure 5.4 demonstrate that these series become stationary in first difference, thus integrated in the order of 1. The complete results from the unit root tests are provided in Figure 5.4.

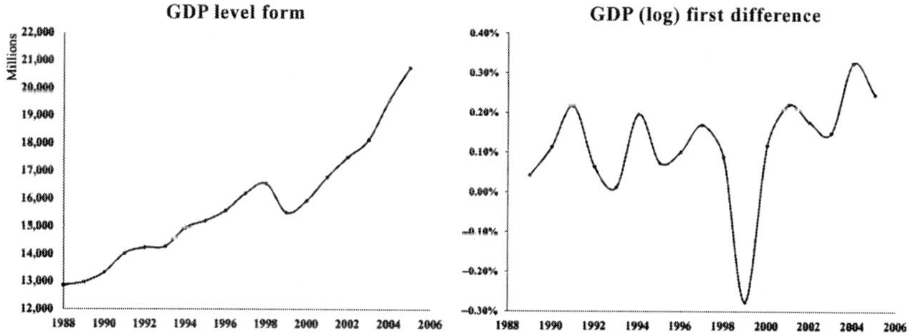


**FIGURE 5.4** Ecuador Gross Domestic Product (GDP).
Augmented Dickey–Fuller unit root test: with a drift and constant/levels = –1.406(1); with a trend and constant/levels = –2.238(1); with a drift and constant/first difference = –2.492(1)**; and with a trend and constant/first difference = –2.331(1) (notes: ** denotes the rejection of the unit root hypothesis based on MacKinnon (1991) critical values at 5%. The optimal lag length is presented in brackets and is based on the SBIC and AIC criteria). Phillips–Perron unit root test: constant without trend/levels = –1.528(1); constant with trend/levels = –2.372(1); constant without trend/first difference = –4.170(1)*; and constant with trend/first difference = –4.111(1)* (notes: * denotes the rejection of the unit root hypothesis at 1% based on the Newey–West method. The optimal lag length is presented in brackets and is based on the SBIC and AIC criteria).

Because all three time series, i.e., poverty, tourism, and growth are integrated in the first order (first difference stationary), it means that the possibility exists that their relationship will be linked or connected in the long run. What we learnt from Figures 5.1–5.4 is that while poverty is declining in the case of Ecuador, economic growth and tourism expansion have taken place simultaneously. The next section will formally test this relationship and determine the level to which the two are connected.

## CAN TOURISM DRIVE ECONOMIC GROWTH IN ECUADOR?

We applied a bivariate co-integration framework to investigate the potential connection between tourism expansion and economic growth. The variables for gauging tourism and economic growth are tourism arrivals and GDP. Since tourism arrivals and economic growth are integrated in the same order ($I(1)$), co-integration only exists if the residuals from the ordinary least square (OLS) regression between these two are $I(0)$, in other words, stationary. The unit root test for the residuals from regressing Tourism Arrivals on GDP are presented in Figure 5.5.

**FIGURE 5.5** Co-integration Between Tourism and Gross Domestic Product (GDP) in Ecuador.

Granger two-step co-integration test: $Y_{\text{growth GDP}_t} = 16.64 + 0.288X_{\text{tour}_t} + -0.588\Phi_{\text{dummy}+\epsilon_t}$ (notes: *t* value for $\alpha_t = 23.94$ ($P < 0.01$), *t* value for $8X_{\text{tour}_t} = 9.72 (P < 0.01)$, *t* value for $\Phi_{\text{dummy}}$ = ($p<.10$); $R^2$ = 0.94; $F(2,15) = 125.869$ (0.000); Durbin Watson = 1.66; $\Phi_{\text{dummy}}$ represents a dummy that captures the dollarization effects in Ecuador. The results from the augmented Dickey–Fuller test indicate that the residuals are stationary with and without a constant, with four lags at the 5% level ($t = -3.18$ and $t = -3.05$). As for the Phillips–Perron test, the results indicate that the residuals are also significant with and without a constant with four lags at the 5% level ($t = -3.05$ and $t = -2.99$)).

A cointegrating relationship thus exists between tourism arrivals and economic Growth. Arrivals are used because there is a strong correlation between international arrivals and jobs. Every 12 tourists visiting Ecuador create one job.[22] We examined if a long-term relationship exists by considering a single-equation error-correction model based on an Autoregressive Distributed Lag Model (ADL). The ADL equation to test the effects of tourism on economic growth is:

$$\Delta Y_{growth\ gdp_t} = \alpha_t + \beta_0 \Delta X_{tour_t} + \beta_1 X_{tour_{t-1}} + \gamma_{growth\ gdp_{t-1}} + \omega_t$$

To obtain the short term effects, long-term effects, and the adjustment speed coefficients, the error correction model can be simplified and written as:

$$\Delta Y_{growth\ gdpi_t} = \alpha_t + \beta_0 \Delta X_{tour_t} + \gamma [Y_{growth\ gdp_{t-1}} - \beta_3 X_{tour_{t-1}}] + \omega_t$$

where $\beta_0 \Delta X_{tour_{t-1}}$ is a first difference operator that represents the short term impact of tourism on economic growth, $\beta_3 X_{tour_{t-1}} = \frac{\beta_2 X_{tour_{t-1}}}{\gamma Y_{growth\ gdp_{t-1}}}$ and captures the long-term effect of tourism arrivals on economic growth, and $\gamma$ captures the rate at which the model moves toward equilibrium. This equation provides the long- and short-term elasticities for tourism on economic growth and the adjustment speed at which the system is restored to equilibrium. The results from the ADL single-equation error-correction model for tourism and economic growth are[23]:

$$\Delta Y_{growth\ gdp_t} = 8.9\alpha 1 + .069 \Delta X_{tour_t} - .523 Y_{growth\ gdp_{t-1}} + .25 X_{tour_{t-1}} + \omega_t$$

To obtain the long-term effects and adjustment coefficient, the error correction model can be simplified as:

$$\Delta Y_{growth\ gdp_t} = 8.9\alpha 1 + .069 \Delta X_{tour_t} - .523 \gamma [Y_{growth\ gdp_{t-1}} - .50 X_{tour_{t-1}}] + \omega_t$$

where the short-term effect is equal to 0.069 $\Delta X_{tour\ arrivals_{t-1}}$; the long-term effects is $\frac{.25 X_{tour_{t-1}}}{-.523 Y_{growth\ gdp_{t-1}}}$; and the rate of adjustment $\gamma$ is equal to -0.523. Therefore, the results signify there is a long-run relationship between tourism and poverty, and they have the correct sign.

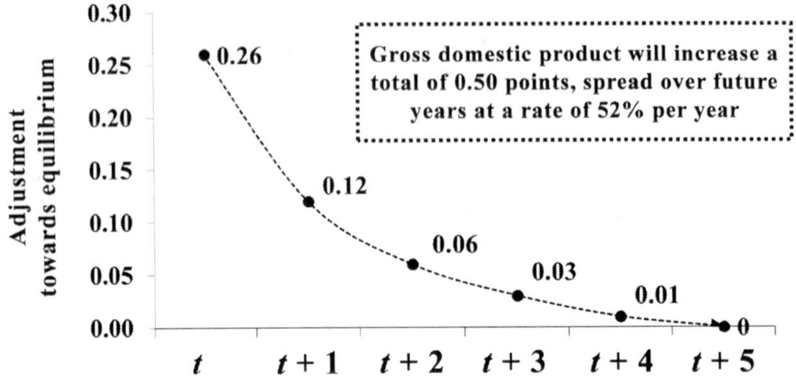


**FIGURE 5.6** Adjustment Toward Equilibrium: Tourism and Economic Growth.

This means that a 1% increase in tourism arrivals improves economic growth by 0.50% in the long term for the case of Ecuador. As for the short-term effects, the coefficient of 0.069 is not significant.[24] Moreover, the correction term is significant and equal to 0.523, thus implying that in the long run, economic growth increases at a rate of 52.3% per period. As presented in Figure 5.6, the total effects of tourism on economic growth in period t are complete by period t+5, meaning that it takes a total of five additional years to adjust toward equilibrium.

The last important issue to be addressed is how the long-run relationship between tourism arrivals and economic growth is causally related. The evidence of a co-integrating relationship indicates that tourism arrivals and economic growth move together over time; however, the questions of whether economic growth actually drives tourism or whether tourism drives economic growth are open. In other words, is the current level of economic growth better explained by using past values of tourism than by not doing so? Or, is the current level of tourism better explained by using past values of economic growth than by not doing so?

The results from the Granger test indicate that the null hypothesis "economic growth does not Granger cause poverty" can be rejected at the 1% level, evidencing that economic growth "Granger causes" tourism.[25] The results also indicate that the null hypothesis that tourism does not Granger cause economic growth can be rejected at the 5% level,[26] thus concluding that a two-way relationship exists running from economic growth to tourism and the other way around. The finding means that as the economy expands, there are more resources invested in the hospitality industry through the expansion of supply factors, such as accommodation, restaurants, and attractions, as well as infrastructural projects that support tourism.

In addition, resources are allocated to enhance the quality of human capital and to fund marketing and promotion in the international market. The government of Ecuador just recently announced an unprecedented budget of more than 600 million U.S. dollars investment to be used between 2014 and 2017 to support tourism in the country.[27] The improved economic situation in Ecuador combined with the potential of tourism as a powerful source of jobs triggered the decision of the government to commit this sizeable investment in tourism development.

Conversely, more arrivals means greater economic activity in the hospitality industry and other economic sectors. Tourism has a significant impact on the national economy. In the previous chapter, we already revealed the spillover effects of tourism to other economic sectors in Ecuador. These spillover effects are also revealed in the WTTC report in 2014. The report recounted that the total economic contribution of tourism was 5.3% of the GDP in 2013 and represented 4.3% of total investment in the economy. Tourism supported 337,500 jobs, equivalent to 4.8% of total employment in the country.[28] Tourism is a powerful job generator with significant potential for Ecuador. For each 12 arrivals a new job is created in Ecuador. Job creation is a powerful way to lift people out of poverty. These findings are consistent with the claim made by Mitchell and Ashley (2010) in their work *Tourism and poverty reduction: pathways to prosperity* that tourism entertains three main channels (i.e., direct, secondary and dynamic effects) through which it impacts the economy and poverty. They suggested pathways for making the nexus of tourism, economy and poverty stronger.

The findings reveal an interesting trend regarding the role of tourism as a strategy for growth. In the case of Ecuador, it was found that tourism arrivals and economic growth cause each other. These findings contradict our initial position, in which we argued that the expansion of tourism promoted economic growth. These results are in line with previous studies discussed in previous chapters.[29] The existence of a mutual influence in which higher levels of economic growth lead to higher levels of tourism development and vice versa deserves a different policy set and will result in more complex implications in terms of sustainability and long-run impacts for development in Ecuador. The results also reflect the tourism literature. The mutual reinforcing effects of tourism and growth reveal that tourism in the case of Ecuador has served as a significant input in expanding economic output, and the growth in output has been employed to further promote tourism.[30]

The tourism literature reveals that international tourism is a source of long-run growth through several channels, such as leveraging the increase in foreign exchange to increase imports of capital goods. Additionally, an increase in tourism has important spill-over effects in other sectors of the economy such as higher level of accumulation and efficiency of tourism resources as well as higher levels of investment and human capital accumulation in tourism activities. In Ecuador, we are seeing an increase in investment in infrastructure such as hotels, roads, transport, and airports. The growth of investments has facilitated the establishment of a tourism infrastructure supply that fosters the expansion of tourism demand. The Minister of Tourism of Ecuador recently announced that the Ecuador government will spend US$660 million over the next four years to boost tourism promotion and to expand and upgrade the tourism infrastructure.[31]

Tourism is the third most important economic sector in the country after the oil and agricultural industries. Tourism played a pivotal role in the economic recovery of the 1990s and in stimulating economic growth in the first decade of the twenty-first century. The increased prominence of the tourism sector in the growth and diversification strategy of the country was revealed in the recent announcement of the unprecedented budget to support tourism growth by the Ecuadorian Minister of Tourism. The aggressive tourism promotion and marketing is to boost demand, which is heavily linked to job creation. Every 12 new arrivals create one job, and jobs are crucial in the country's poverty reduction strategy.[32]

## CAN TOURISM REDUCE POVERTY IN ECUADOR?

We can proceed to test the impact of tourism on poverty via an error correction model. We will follow a similar procedure as the previous one to answer this question. The results from the unit root test presented in the previous section indicate that tourism arrivals and poverty are integrated in the same order (I(1)). We also determined that the series are co-integrated through the unit root test for the residuals from regressing Tourism Arrivals on Poverty. The results are presented in Figure 5.7.

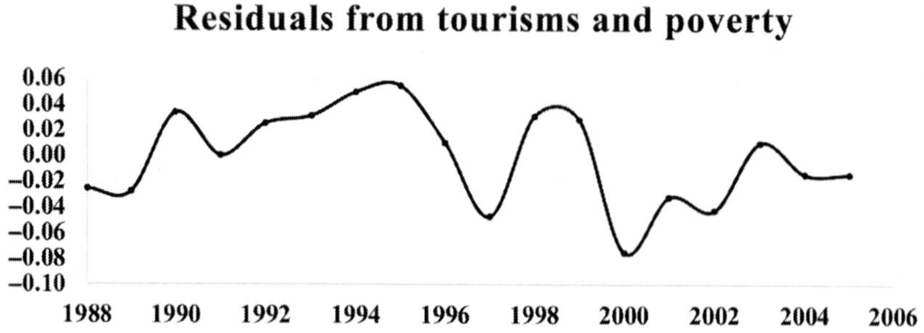


**FIGURE 5.7** Co-integration Between Tourism and Poverty in Ecuador.

Granger two-step co-integration test: $Y_{\text{Sen}_t} = 3.92 - 0.29X_{\text{tour}_t} + 0.07T_{\text{trend}} + \in_t$

(notes: $t$ value for $\alpha_t = 2.05$ ($P < 0.10$), $t$ value for $X_{\text{tour}_t} = -1.79(P<0.10)$, $t$ value for $T_{\text{trend}} = -1.16$ ($P > 0.10$); $R^2 = 0.45$; $F(2,15) = 6.14(0.01)$; Durbin Watson = 1.38; $T_{\text{trend}}$ a trend as suggested by the Phillips–Perron (PP) test. The results of the augmented Dickey–Fuller and PP tests without a constant and trend indicated that residuals were $I(0)$ and stationary at the 5% level ($t = -3.023$, $P < 0.05$ and $t = -3.034$, $P < 0.05$, respectively)).

We confirmed the long-term relationship between tourism and poverty by considering a single-equation error-correction model based on an Autoregressive Distributed Lag Model (ADL). The ADL error-correction equation tested the effects of tourism on poverty is:

$$\Delta Y_{sen_t} = \alpha_t + \Delta\beta_0 X_{tour_t} + \beta_2 X_{tour_{t-1}} + \gamma Y_{sen_{t-1}} + \omega_t$$

To obtain the short-term effects, long-term effects, and the adjustment coefficient, the error-correction model can be simplified and written as:

$$\Delta Y_{sen_t} = \alpha_t + \beta_0 \Delta X_{tour_t} + \gamma [Y_{sent-1} - \beta_3 X_{tour_{t-1}}] + T_{trend} + \omega_t$$

where $\beta_0 \Delta X_{tour\ arrivals_{t-1}}$ is a first difference operator that represents the short term impact of tourism on poverty, $\beta_3 X_{tour_{t-1}} = \dfrac{\beta_2 X_{tour_{t-1}}}{\gamma Y_{sen_{t-1}}}$ and captures the long-term effect, $\gamma$ captures the rate at which the model moves toward equilibrium, and $T_{\text{trend}}$ is a trend. This equation provides the long- and short-term elasticities for tourism arrivals and the adjustment speed

at which the system is restored to equilibrium. The results from the ADL error correction model for tourism and poverty are[33]:

$$\Delta Y_{sen_t} = 4.85\alpha_t - .159\Delta X_{tour_t} - .37X_{tour_{t-1}} - .684Y_{sen_{t-1}} + .015T_{trend} + \omega_t$$

To obtain the long-term effects and adjustment coefficient, the error-correction model can be simplified and written as:

$$\Delta Y_{sen_t} = 4.85\alpha_t - .159\Delta X_{tour_t} - .68\gamma[Y_{sen_{t-1}} - .54X_{tour_{t-1}}] + .015T_{trend} + \omega_t$$

where the short term effect is equal to -0.159 $\Delta X_{tour_{t-1}}$; the long term effects is $-.54X_{tour_{t-1}} = \frac{.37X_{tour_{t-1}}}{-.684Y_{sen_{t-1}}}$; and the rate of adjustment is equal to -0.68.

The results therefore posit that there is a long-run relationship between tourism and poverty and both have the correct sign. This means that a 1% increase in tourism arrivals reduces the S index by 0.54% in the long term for the case of Ecuador. Moreover, the correction term is significant and it implies that in the long run, poverty is reduced at a rate of 68% per period. The total effects of tourism on poverty in period *t* are complete by period *t+3*, meaning that it takes a total of three additional years to adjust towards equilibrium. It is important to note that the short-term coefficient of tourism is not significant[34] (Figure 5.8).

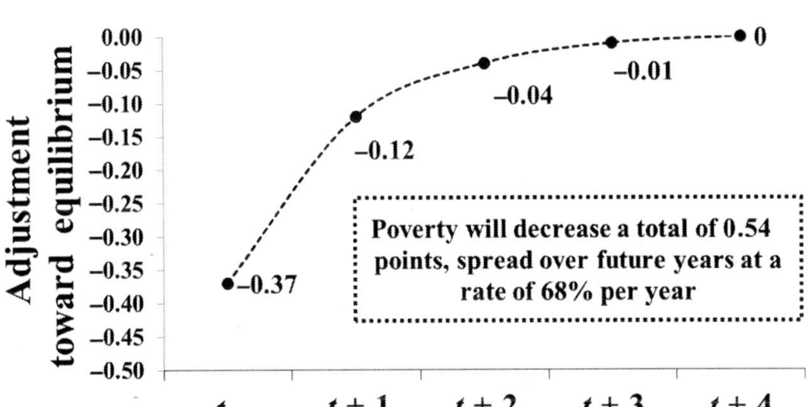


**FIGURE 5.8** Adjustment Toward Equilibrium: Tourism and Poverty.

The findings show tourism as a pro-poor long-term development strategy in Ecuador. However, such assertions cannot be made until the direction of causality is established. The evidence of a co-integrating relationship indicates that tourism and poverty reduction move together over time; however, the question of whether tourism actually drives poverty reduction or poverty reduction drives tourism arrivals remains open. The results from the Granger tests indicate that the null hypothesis "tourism does not Granger Cause poverty" can be rejected at the 1% level, evidencing that tourism Granger Cause poverty reduction.[35] The results also indicate that the null hypothesis "poverty does not Granger cause tourism" cannot be rejected at the 1% level, concluding that a one-way relationship exists running from tourism to poverty reduction.[36]

There are three possible explanations regarding the relationship between tourism and poverty. First, not finding an immediate or short-term impact of tourism arrivals on poverty can suggest that the effects of tourism might not rapidly reduce income inequalities. These findings are in line with the Kuznets hypothesis, in which rapid economic expansion triggers an increase in income inequality.[37] A cursory look at Figure 5.9 demonstrates that as tourism arrivals increase, the income of the top quintile (the rich) also increases over time. This is an indicator that the rich rapidly capture potential benefits from the expansion of the tourism sector. We saw in the previous chapter that higher income categories captured more benefits in absolute terms from tourism compared to the lowest income categories.

Nevertheless, the same is not sustained for the relationship between tourism arrivals and the income of the bottom quintile (the poor), as structural breaks seem to exist. A plausible explanation could be that the severity of income inequality for the bottom quintile places them at a disadvantage (see Figure 5.9). However, this imbalance repositions itself or moves back to equilibrium in the long term, as poverty is reduced in the long term. More specifically, this could be explained by the conditions of income inequality that were in existence prior to the year 2000.

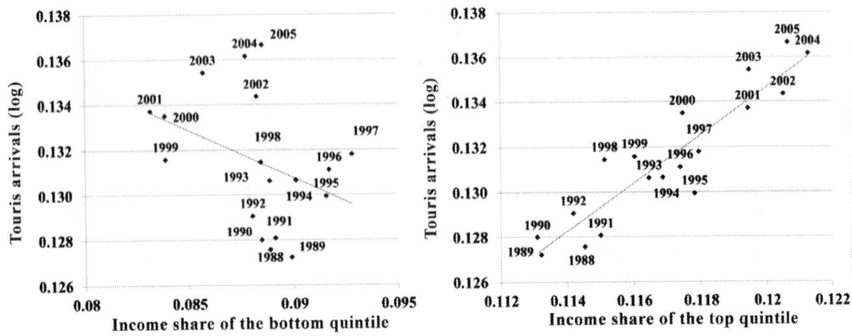


**FIGURE 5.9** Tourism Arrivals and Income Share (Top and Bottom Quintiles).

## CAN ECONOMIC GROWTH REDUCE POVERTY?

We will now turn our investigation toward the global question of whether economic growth and poverty are connected. We established that the residuals from the OLS regression between these two are I(0), in other words, stationary (Engle and Granger), thus demonstrating that a co-integrating relationship exists between economic growth and poverty. The unit root test for the residuals by regressing Economic Growth on Poverty is revealed in Figure 5.10.

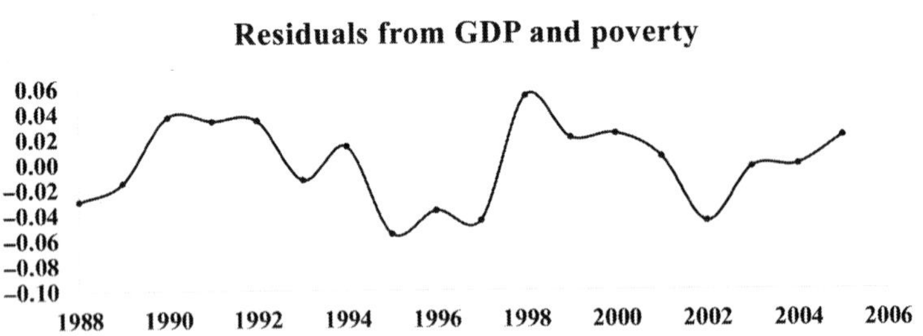


**FIGURE 5.10** Co-integration Between Gross Domestic Product (GDP) and Poverty in Ecuador.

Granger two-step co-integration test: $Y_{\text{Sen}_t} = \alpha_t + \beta_1 X_{\text{growth GDP}_t} + T_{\text{trend}} + \Phi_{\text{dummy}} + \epsilon_t$ (notes: $t$ value for $\alpha_t = 2.81$ ($P < 0.05$), $t$ value for $X_{\text{growth GDP}_t} = -2.77\,(P < 0.05)$, $t$ value for $T_{\text{trend}} = -1.89$ ($P > 0.10$); $t$ value for $\Phi_{\text{dummy}} = 0.77$ ($P > 0.10$); $R^2 = 0.57$; $F(3,14) = 6.23(0.006)$; Durbin Watson = 1.50; $T_{\text{trend}}$ represents a trend, and $\Phi_{\text{dummy}}$ represents a dummy to capture the effect of dollarization in Ecuador. The results of the augmented Dickey–Fuller and Phillips–Perron tests without a constant and trend indicated that residuals were $I(0)$ and stationary at the 5% level ($t = -3.137$, $P < 0.05$ and $t = -3.175$, $P < 0.05$, respectively)).

We confirmed a long-term relationship between growth and poverty through a single-equation error-correction model based on an Autoregressive Distributed Lag Model (ADL). The ADL error correction equation to test the effects of economic growth on poverty is:

$$\Delta Y_{sen_t} = \Delta_t + \Delta\beta_0 X_{growth\ gdp_t} + \beta_2 X_{growth\ gdp_{t-1}} + \gamma Y_{sen_{t-1}} + \omega_t$$

To obtain the short term effects, long term effects, and the adjustment coefficient, the error correction model can be simplified and written as:

$$\Delta Y_{sen_t} = \alpha_t + \beta_0 \Delta X_{growth\ gdp_t} + \gamma [Y_{sen_{t-1}} - \beta_3 X_{growth\ gdp_{t-1}}] + \omega_t$$

where $\beta_0 \Delta X_{growth\ gdp_t}$ is a first difference operator that represents the short-term impact of economic growth on poverty, $\beta_3 X_{growth\ gdp_{t-1}} = \frac{\beta_2 X_{growth\ gdp_{t-1}}}{\gamma Y_{sen_{t-1}}}$ and captures the long-term effect of tourism on poverty, and $\gamma$ captures the rate at which the model moves toward equilibrium. The results from the ADL error correction model for economic growth and poverty are[38]:

$$\Delta Y_{sen_t} = 2.66\alpha_t - .613\Delta X_{growth\ gdp_t} - .173 X_{growth\ gdp_{t-1}} - .7 Y_{sen_{t-1}} + \omega_t$$

To obtain the long-term effects and adjustment coefficient, the error correction model can be simplified and written as:

$$\Delta Y_{sen_t} = 2.66\alpha_t - .613\Delta X_{growth\ gdp_t} - .70\gamma [Y_{sen_{t-1}} \quad .24 X_{growth\ gdp_{t-1}}] + \omega_t$$

where the short-term effect is equal to -0.613 $\Delta X_{growth\ gdp_{t-1}}$; the long-term effects is $-.24 X_{growth\ gdp_{t-1}} = \frac{.173 X_{growth\ gdp}}{-.70 Y_{sen_{t-1}}}$; and the rate of adjustment is -0.70γ.

The results demonstrate the existence of a long-run relationship between economic growth and poverty and both have the correct sign. This means that a 1% increase in economic growth reduces poverty by 0.24% in the long term in the case of Ecuador and 0.61% in the short term. The correction term is also significant, thus implying that in the long run, poverty is reduced at a rate of 70% per period. As presented in Figure 5.11, the total effects of economic growth on poverty in period *t* are complete by period *t+2*, meaning that it only takes two additional years for the system to adjust toward equilibrium.[39]

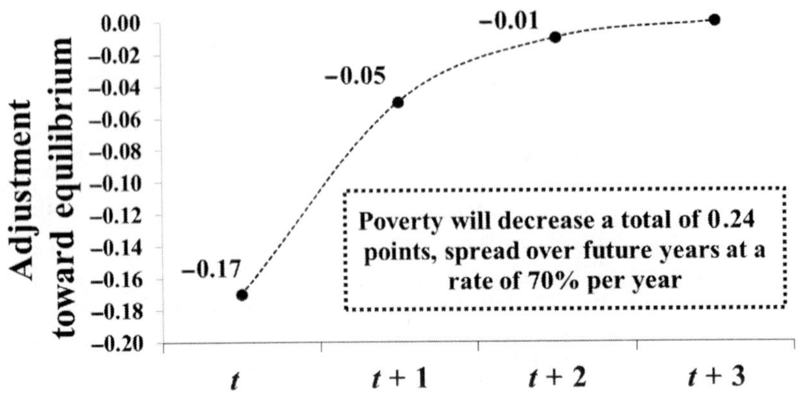


**FIGURE 5.11** Adjustment Toward Equilibrium: Economic Growth and Poverty.

The evidence of a co-integrating relationship indicates that economic growth and poverty move together over time. The results from the Granger tests indicate that the null hypothesis "economic growth does not Granger cause poverty" can be rejected at the 1% level, evidencing that economic growth "Granger causes" poverty.[40] The results also indicate that the null hypothesis that poverty does not "Granger cause" economic growth cannot be rejected at the 1% level, thus concluding that a one-way relationship exists running from economic growth to poverty reduction and not the other way around.[41]

In summary, we have found that a long-run causal relationship exists between economic growth and poverty. This relationship was not only significant, but the magnitude of 1% increase in economic growth results in 0.21% reduction of the S index in the long run. The error correction term was also significant and smaller than one, suggesting that the system is restored back to equilibrium at a rate of 70% per period and completely phased out by period t+3. Moreover, in the short term, economic growth reduces poverty. This suggests that an opportunity exists to develop pro-growth policies in order to combat poverty in Ecuador. It can be observed that immediate effects on reducing poverty are channeled directly through economic growth and not tourism, as the effects of tourism on poverty reduction are not direct, but instead are channeled through economic growth.

## THE DUAL CHANNELS OF TOURISM IN OBLITERATING

Lee, C. C.; Chien, M. S. Structural breaks, tourism development, and economic growth: evidence from Taiwan. *Math. Comp. Simul.* 2008, 77(4), 358–368.

MacKinnon, J.G. "Critical values for cointegration tests, Chapter 13 in Long-Run Economic Relationships: Readings in Cointegration, ed. RF Engle and CW J. Granger." (1991).

Mihalic, T. *Tourism and economic development issues*. In *Tourism and Development: Concepts and Issues*; Sharpley, R., Tefler, D. J., Eds.; Chanel View Publications: London, UK, 2002.

Mitchell, J.; Ashley, C. *Tourism and Poverty Reduction: Pathways to Prosperity*; The Cromwell Press Group: London, UK, 2010.

Mowforth, M.; Munt, I. *Tourism and Sustainability: New Tourism in the Third World*; Routledge: London, UK, 1998.

Mukherjee, C.; White, H.; Wuyts, M. *Econometrics and Data Analysis for Developing Countries*; Routledge: London, UK, 1998.

Nafziger, E. W. *The Economics of Developing Countries*; Prentice Hall: Upper Saddle River, N.J, 1997.

Romano, S. M.; Falconí, J.; Aguinaga, C. *Una interpretación mesoeconómica del turismo en Ecuador*; Publicaciones Económicas, Banco Central del Ecuador: Quito, Ecuador, 2005.

Sen, A. Poverty: an ordinal approach to measurement. *Econometrica*. 1976, 44(2), 219–231.

Tefler, D. *The evolution of tourism and development theory*. In *Tourism and Development: Concepts and Issues*; Sharpley, R., Telfer, D. J., Eds.; Chanel View Publications: London, UK, 2002.

Timothy, D. *Tourism and community development issues*. In *Tourism and Development: Concepts and Issues*; Sharpley, R., Telfer, D. J., Eds.; Chanel View Publications: London, 2002.

Todaro, M. P.; Smith, S. C. *Economic Development*; Pearson Addison Wesley: Ann Arbor, MI, 2009.

Transparency International. TI Corruption Perceptions Index. 2008. http://www.transparency.org/ (accessed Mar 31, 2014).

UNWTO. World Tourism Barometer [Electronic Version], 6. 2008. http://pub.unwto.org/epages/Store.sf/?ObjectPath=/Shops/Infoshop/Products/1324/SubProducts/1324-1 (accessed Jan 6, 2009).

USAID. Regional Overview: Ecuador. 2002. http://usaidlandtenure.net/sites/default/files/country-profiles/full-reports/USAID_Land_Tenure_Ecuador_Profile.pdf (accessed Mar 31, 2014).

Vos, R.; De Jong, N. *Rising Inequality During Economic Liberalisation and Crisis: Macro or Micro Causes in Ecuador's Case?*; Institute of Social Studies: The Hague, The Netherlands, 2000. [ISS Working Paper No. 326].

## ENDNOTES

[1]See Todaro and Smith (2009, p. 103).

[2]For tourism and economic development, see Mihalic (2002). For community development, see Hall and Brown (2006). For sociocultural development and well-being, see Hashimoto (2002), Mowforth and Munt (1998), Timothy (2002), and Tefler (2002).

[3]See Nafziger (1997).

[4]See, for example, Balaguer and Cantavella-Jorda (2002) and Gunduz and Hatemi-J (2005).

[5]See Sen (1976).

[6]For more details on unit root tests see Dickey and Fuller (1979, 1981).

[7]See Engle and Granger (1987).

[8]For details on causality tests, see Granger (1969).

[9]For full statistics, see the United Nations' Economic Commission for Latin America and the Caribbean's Social Panorama of Latin America 2012 Briefing Paper, November 2012 (http://fas.org/sgp/crs/row/R43135.pdf).

[10]In 2002, according to USAID, the highest 20% of the income earners receive 80% of the income share of gross domestic product.

[11]Poverty figures available from PovcalNet:

(http://iresearch.worldbank.org/PovcalNet/index.htm?2).

[12]Data for the Sen index was provided by the Oficina Sistema Integrado de Indicadores Sociales del Ecuador (http://www.siise.gob.ec/).

[13]The average monthly per capita income/consumption expenditure from the survey is in 2005 Purchasing Power Parity (PPP). The default option is the PPP rates for consumption in 2005 estimated by the World Bank's Development Data Group.

[14]Any variation in poverty headcount could be attributed to the poverty line value. The default poverty line is US$38.00/mo. This is the World Bank US$1.25/d poverty line (US$38 = US$1.25 × 365/12).

[15]See Romano et al. (2005).

[16]See United Nations' World Tourism Organization (2008).

[17]See the Travel and Tourism Impact 2014: Ecuador from the Word Travel and Tourism Council. Available at http://www.wttc.org/site_media/uploads/downloads/ecuador2014.pdf.

[18]Data for International Tourist Arrivals was obtained from http://www.wttc.org/.

[19]For details about Ecuador political instability, see Budd (2003), Joseph (1987), Vos and De Jong (2000), and Transparency International (2008).

[20]For a further discussion, see a study by the United Nations' Economic Commission for Latin America and the Caribbean. Retrieved July 23, 2014. from http://www.cepal.org/publicaciones/xml/3/48593/Ecuador_ing.pdf.

[21]See, for example, IMF World Economic Outlook Database, October 2010.

[22]See, for example, "Ecuador Government Earmarks $600 Million for Tourism Promotion" retrieved on July 24, 2014, from http://www.travelpulse.com/news/destinations/ecuador-government-earmarks-600-million-for-tourism-promotion.html.

[23]Note:

$\alpha(t = 2.49, P < 0.05)$; $\ddot{A}X_{tour_t}$ $(t = -0.76, P > 0.10)$; $X_{tour_{t-1}}$ $(t = 3.08, P < 0.01)$; $Y_{growth\ GDP_{t-1}}$ $(t = -2.60, P < 0.05)$; $F(4,11) = 3.64$; $P < 0.01$; DW $= 1.36$; $R^2 = 0.61$; adjusted $R^2 = 0.48$.

[24]The results of the Durbin Watson (DW) test (DW = 1.36) and the Breusch–Godfrey (BG) test (BG=2.55, $P > 0.01$) indicate that the null hypothesis of no serial correlation can be rejected. In addition, the results of the Breusch–Pagan (BP) test for heteroskedasticity indicate that the null hypothesis of no heteroskedasticity is accepted (BP = 4.24, $P < 0.001$).

[25]Null hypothesis: $Y_{growth\ GDP}$ does not Granger cause $X_{tour}$ ($F$-statistic = 10.53; $P < 0.001$).

[26]Null hypothesis: $X_{\text{tour}}$ does not Granger cause $Y_{\text{growth GDP}}$ ($F$-statistic = 2.25; $P < 0.05$).

[27]See, for example, "Ecuador Government Earmarks $600 Million for Tourism Promotion" retrieved on July 24, 2014, from http://www.travelpulse.com/news/destinations/ecuador-government-earmarks-600-million-for-tourism-promotion.html.

[28]See World Travel and Tourism Council, Economic Impact 2014 Ecuador, retrieved July 25, 2014, from http://www.wttc.org/site_media/uploads/downloads/ecuador2014.pdf.

[29]For example, see Chen and Chiou-Wei (2009), Cortés-Jiménez and Pulina (2006), Dritsakis (2004), Katircioglu (2009), Kim et al. (2006), and Lee and Chien (2008).

[30]The findings conform to the postulates of the Tourism Capital Imports to Growth and the TLG hypothesis. For further discussion, see Cortés-Jiménez and Pulina (2010).

[31]See "Ecuador Government Earmarks $600 Million for Tourism Promotion" retrieved July 24, 2014, from http://www.travelpulse.com/news/destinations/ecuador-government-earmarks-600-million-for-tourism-promotion.html.

[32]See footnote xviii. On the relevance of job creation for the poverty reduction strategy, see, for example, http://www.telesurtv.net/english/news/UN-Ecuador-Has-Reduced-Poverty-by-50-20140725-0052.html, retrieved July 29, 2014.

[33] $\alpha_1 (t = 1.88, P < 0.10), X_{tour\ arrivals_{t-1}} (t = -1.80, P < 0.10),$
$\gamma(t = -2.84, P < 0.05), \Delta X_{tour\ arrivals_t} (t = -0.96, P > 0.10),$
$T (t = -1.38, P > 0.10); F(3.13) = 2.49, P < 0.10; DW = 2.08;$
$R^2 = 0.48; adjusted\ R^2 = 0.27.$

[34]The results of the DW test (DW = 2.08) and the BG test (BG = 0.029, $P > 0.01$) indicate that the null hypothesis of no serial correlation can be rejected. In addition, the results of the BP test for heteroskedasticity indicate that the null hypothesis of no heteroskedasticity is accepted (BP = 0.92, $P < 0.001$).

[35]$X_{\text{tour}}$ does not Granger cause $Y_{\text{Sen}}$ ($F$-statistic = 19.273, $P < 0.0001$).

[36]$Y_{\text{Sen}}$ does not Granger cause $X_{\text{tour}}$ ($F$-statistic = 2.442, $P > 0.10$).

[37]See Kuznets (1963, p. 68).

[38]Note: $\alpha_1 (t = 2.25, P < 0.10), X_{\text{GDP growth}_{t-1}} (t = -1.87, P < 0.10), \gamma Y_{\text{Sen}_{t-1}} (t = -2.98, P < 0.05), X_{\text{growth GDP}_{t-1}} (t = -2.05, P < 0.10).$

[39]The results of the DW test (DW = 2.17) and the BG test (BG = 0.431, $P > 0.01$) indicate that the null hypothesis of no serial correlation can be rejected. In addition, the results of the BP test for heteroskedasticity indicate that the null hypothesis of no heteroskedasticity is accepted (BP = 0.306, $P < 0.001$).

[40]$X_{\text{growth GDP}}$ does not Granger cause $Y_{\text{Sen}}$ ($F$-statistic = 0 .264, $P = 0.67$).

[41]$Y_{\text{Sen}}$ does not Granger cause $X_{\text{growth GDP}}$ ($F$-statistic = 10.05, $P = 0.002$).

## CHAPTER 6

# TOURISM WITH A HUMAN FACE

## CONTENTS

## INTRODUCTION

We explore in this chapter the relationship between tourism development and human development from Sen's perspective revealed in his capability approach. More specifically, we will expand the information base of human development from Sen's poverty index (S index) to include the human development index (HDI). We noticed in the previous chapter that the S index reveals information regarding the incidence of poverty, how poor is the poor, and how income is distributed among the poor. Incidence, depth, and distribution of income among the poor recounts those among the poor who get more income. The S index provides valuable information with regard to the role of tourism in reaching out to the poor and lifting them out of poverty, as illustrated in the case of Ecuador[1].

The S index suggests that the most impactful effects from tourism are through economic growth, suggesting an important role of social programs. Additional income will provide individuals the opportunity to decide how discretionary funds will be spent. However, this choice may be motivated by conflicting life desires and necessities. Desires may absorb the opportunity to alleviate poverty. The S index does not tell us what the poor care about and how they allocate their resources. In this chapter, we will investigate the nexus between tourism development and human development.

## TOURISM AND HUMAN DEVELOPMENT

Human development is relevant for poverty reduction because the framework provides a richer information context to both theory and practice. According to the first human development report, "The basic objective of development is to create an enabling environment for people to enjoy long, healthy and creative lives" (United Nations' Development Program [UNDP], 1990, p. 9). The report defines human development as "a process of enlarging people's choices" (UNDP, 1990, p. 10). Surely, education and health are considered the twin pillars of this conceptualization of human development.[2] There is ample empirical evidence suggesting a clear connection between human development and economic growth. Economic growth provides the resources to improve human development, while human development improves the quality of labor, improving productivity, and hence, economic growth.

While the bidirectional connection between economic growth and human development is clear, the implications of this connection are clouded by the allocation of income growth to human development among the poor[3]. For example, the impact of an increase in household income on human development depends on how much more income is spent on food, education, and health, and who controls the spending behavior of the household. However, the empirical evidence indicates that when income rises, expenditures on human development items increase as well. Higher levels of human development in turn have an impact on growth through their enhanced capabilities and creativity. Evidence suggests that healthier, better nourished, and educated people contribute more to economic growth through higher labor productivity, improved technology, and higher exports. Similarly, the chapter applies the HDI to poverty.

Similar to the previous chapter, this chapter will explore the application of these indices in the context of Ecuador and Central America. This index combines the three main capabilities of health, education, and a decent standard of living. The question is whether there is a role for tourism development in enhancing this connection, and if there is, what exactly is the role of tourism development in connecting human development, economic expansion, and poverty reduction?

The main objective of this chapter is social welfare. Social welfare is supported by three pillars: opportunities (capabilities); achievements (functioning); and freedom to choose, take actions, and seize opportunities. Development from this perspective is the result of the ability of a person (not the potential) to leverage her/his own capabilities as a free human agent. Capabilities refer to the ability to convert commodities into achievements. Sen states that "the conversion of commodity-characteristics into personal achievements of functionings depends on a variety of factors—personal and social" (Sen 1985, p. 17). This conversion ability is at the heart of Sen's analysis of poverty. This ability is determined by communities, families, and individuals.

## HUMAN DEVELOPMENT: THE NEXUS WITH ECONOMIC GROWTH AND TOURISM

In his book *Development as Freedom* (1999), Sen argues for a human development perspective on poverty with the main premise that economic growth alone cannot eradicate poverty. Sen claims that more income will not necessarily result in a better quality of life. The automatic connection between economic development and human development according to the conventional perspective does not exist in Sen's view. The connection depends on the individual's ability to convert resources into capabilities. It is not about potential, but everything is about the ability of the individual.

What matters, according to Sen, is how people are able to function with the resources at their disposal. Investigating the effects of resources on the human being seemingly enabled Sen to unlock the mystery of how resources and achievements are related. He discovered the multidimensional nature of individuals, thereby positing that an income metric is inadequate in capturing the full array of the diversity of human beings. According to Sen, development and well-being should be more directly linked to their foundational roots and not to their instrumental antecedents.

The construct of capabilities is therefore the range of opportunities present for an individual to pursue the lifestyle that he/she values and determines the range of achievements (functionings) possible for the individual, such as a good job. Achievements, or what Sen terms "functionings", depend on an individual's ability or "capabilities" to choose among available options. Freedom to choose what one values in life is crucial in shaping well-being. Capabilities refer to the ability of an individual to function, seize opportunities, make choices, and take actions. This ability is contingent upon objective elements, such as quality of education, life expectancy, poverty, employment, discrimination, and subjective elements such as memory, ethics, common sense, and reason.

The ability of a person combined with the role of the social environment affect human choice and agency, and then determines the opportunities available for a person (Sen, 1999). The ability of a person to freely choose the life he or she valued depends, therefore, on many factors, some of which are beyond the control of the individual. These factors include age (the needs of the young versus old person), gender and social roles (women and family), and location (drought and crime). Human diversity therefore is affected by personal and existing social arrangements. Sen, as alluded to in Chapter 2, broadens the informational "space" in defining poverty as the lack of opportunities. Lack of opportunities can push a person to unemployment, and hence lack of income results in the inability to meet basic needs. Lack of opportunities in the economic and political domains is the root cause of poverty from Sen's perspective.

Development from this perspective means broadening opportunities and reducing the constraints that curb opportunities. Understanding the process of widening opportunities is relevant in our understanding why marginalized segments in developing countries are removed from the benefits of development[4]. For example, given two persons with similar income, one can walk freely in his neighborhood while the other's freedom to walk is constrained by a crime-infested area. This would be the case in Central America, where the crime rate is three times higher than the world average. It appears that women (gender), older people (age), and minorities (exclusion) are more often victims of crime than other groups.[5]

Clearly, these people have a different quality of life. The lack of opportunity, according to Sen, is the result of not only the command of resources but is also the consequence of how these resources are distributed among individuals, and the degree to which individuals, households, and governments prioritize human development (education, longevity, nutrition, leisure, etc.) in the expenditures. Lack of capacity to make choices or take actions is viewed as poverty rather than the lack of income or the possession of commodities per se.

## THE HUMAN DEVELOPMENT MODEL: THE LACK OF OPPORTUNITIES

We evaluated the link between tourism development and human development by using a production process model **(See Table 6.1 for a selected overview of the tourism literature pertaining to this subject).** The model is built on the supposition that a person's achievements (functionings) hinge upon available resources and the capacity to utilize those resources. To be successful, the model requires both aspects: achievement and resources. The resources serve as inputs, which will later result in increased economic growth. For many, the only input resource they possess is labor power. However, gaining employment and earning livable wages is still necessary to complete the model. Without opportunity, they may be limited in their ability to buy food, find shelter, and participate in their communities.

Expanding resources, like income, will depend on capabilities. The production process model describes achievements serving as outputs. The conversion of input to output is not, however, a direct and observable relationship. The capabilities are the mediating force to move toward achievements. Poverty thus viewed as the lack of opportunities is measured by the HDI. We gage well-being using standard economics and revealed achievements, such as literacy rate, income, and life expectancy. The achievements can be viewed as functionings and interpreted with the lens of Sen's frugal premise. The relationship between human development and the POP paradigm is revealed in Figure 6.1.

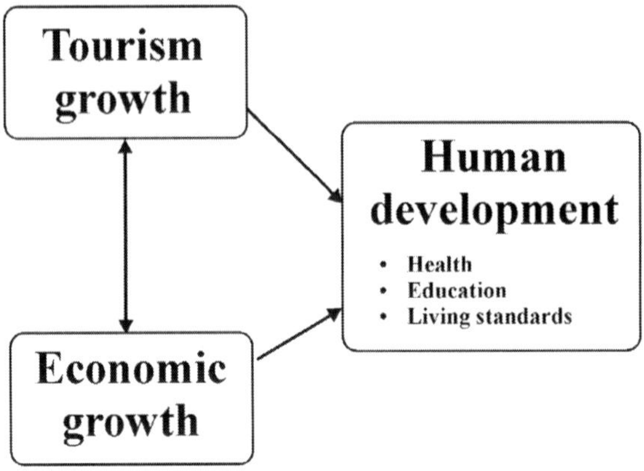


**FIGURE 6.1** Relationship Between Development and Poverty Obliteration Paradigm (Capabilities).

Enlargement of capabilities is an important contributor to the expansion of resources (e.g., incomes). However, this ability or capabilities (qualities of a person) to achieve functionings cannot be observed directly. It is assumed that capabilities are a mediating force in the conversion of resources into functionings.

**TABLE 6.1** Tourism and Human Development

| Authors | Country | Empirical Methods | Main Findings |
|---|---|---|---|
| Barros et al. (2012) | Mozambique | Logistic regression for randomized response data | The improvements of the destination associated with tourism had a positive effect on the subjective evaluation of tourism contribution to human development |
| Croes (2012) | Nicaragua and Costa Rica | Log-linear model, co-integration analysis and the error correction model | Tourism and human development were interconnected and mutually reinforcing in the case of Nicaragua<br>In the case of Costa Rica, however, this relationship was weak and did not hold in the long-term |
| Mehregan et al. (2012) | Iran | Autoregressive distributed lag model | The results supported positive and significant short- and long-term relationship between human development index and foreign tourist arrivals |
| Ridderstaat et al. (2013) | For example, Fiji, USA, Yemen, China, and Mexico | N/A | The research related to the impact of quality of life on tourism development was scarce<br>The effect of potential shocks on both quality of life and tourism development also remained largely unexplored |
| Ridderstaat et al. (2014) | Aruba | Multivariate co-integration analyses and Granger causality testing | The result supported the two-directional relationship between quality of life and tourism development |

The study employs revealed achievements (literacy rate, life expectancy, incomes), following standard economics, to gage a person's well-being. Revealed choices are measured through aggregate measures of benefits and are directly related to a person's behavior. Functionings are aspects of a person's life, of who he is or what he does, and can include "being happy", "being nourished", "being well educated", "being sheltered", "being able to move freely", and "avoiding premature mortality".

All these aspects of life are captured in this multi-dimensional construct of functionings. Resources impact these functionings and are observed through the concept of achievements. Achievements is conceived by Sen as outcome (achieved well-being) and as opportunity (conversion ability), and reveals a large information space to assess well-being.

**TABLE 6.2** Human Development Indicators in Ecuador

| Year | Life Expectancy at Birth | Expected Years of Schooling | Mean Years of Schooling | GNI Per Capita (2005 US$ Purchasing Power Parity) |
|---|---|---|---|---|
| 1980 | 62.9 | 11.8 | 5.4 | 5,487 |
| 1985 | 66.1 | 12.3 | 6 | 4,855 |
| 1990 | 68.9 | 11.5 | 6.6 | 4,777 |
| 1995 | 71.3 | 11.4 | 6.9 | 5,310 |
| 2000 | 73.4 | 11.4 | 7 | 4,903 |
| 2005 | 74.7 | 11.4 | 7.3 | 6,190 |
| 2010 | 75 | | | 7,880 |

Sen's capability approach is measured through the HDI, which combines three crucial human capabilities: health, education, and a decent standard of living. Health is captured through longevity and is measured by life expectancy. Education is captured through knowledge and is measured by a combination of adult literacy (two-third weight) and mean years of schooling (one-third weight). Finally, standard of living is measured by purchasing power parity (PPP) based on Real gross domestic product (GDP) per capita adjusted for the cost of living, thereby eliminating differences in national price levels (UNDP, 1990). The HDI computes an average value over different dimensions and then aggregates these values for the different dimensions in one overall index for each country, and ranks the countries according to a score of the overall index. The United Nations endorsed the HDI as the metric to measure the promotion of human development. The HDI metric is calculating as follows:

$$\text{HDI}_i = \left(H-\text{index}_i + E-\text{index}_i + Y-\text{index}_i\right)/3$$

The HDI series for Ecuador are from 1998 to 2005.[6] The data in Figure 6.2 depict the HDI in level form and in fist differences. In both instances, the data are stationary and free of unit root.[7] Overall, a review of Ecuador's progress in each of the HDI indicators since 1980 indicate life expectancy at birth increased by 12.9 years, mean years of schooling increased by 2.2 years, expected years of schooling increased by 1.9 years, and GNI per capita increase by almost 13% (see Table 6.2).[8]

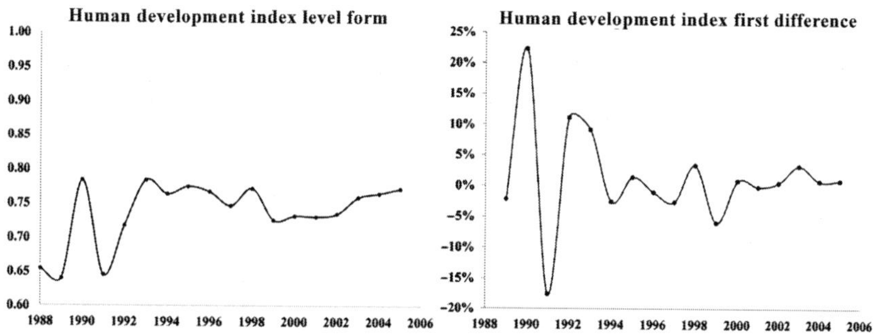


**FIGURE 6.2** Human Development Index (HDI) Ecuador.
Augmented Dickey–Fuller unit root test: with a drift and constant/levels = −3.300(4)*; with a trend and constant/levels = −3.074(4); with a drift and constant/first difference = −2.429(4)*; and with a trend and constant/first difference = −1.352(4) (notes: * and *** denotes the rejection of the unit root hypothesis based on MacKinnon (1991) critical values at 1% and 10%, respectively. The optimal lag length is presented in brackets and is based on the SBIC and AIC criteria. The critical values are obtained from STATA Version 9 and correspond to 18 observations). Phillips–Perron unit root test: constant without trend\levels = −3.676(4)*; constant with trend\levels = −3.936(4)**; constant without trend\first difference = −8.177(4)*; and constant with trend\first difference = −8.878(4)** (notes: * and ** denote the rejection of the unit root hypothesis critical values at 1% and 5% based on the Newey–West method. The optimal lag length is presented in brackets and is based on the SBIC and AIC criteria. The critical values are obtained from STATA Version 9 and correspond to 18 observations)[9].

## CAN ECONOMIC DEVELOPMENT IMPROVE HUMAN DEVELOPMENT IN ECUADOR?

We will now turn our investigation toward determining the existence of a link between tourism and economic growth with the HDI. While the S index looks at how income resonates in the poor households, the HDI is a lens to look how these incomes are used in health, education, and standard of living to enhance the quality of life of the poor. In Chapter 2, we notice that higher incomes to the poor do not necessarily result in enhanced human development. For example, Banerjee and Duflo found that in India a little more income does not correlate with the poor eating a little better. In other words, the premise that more income will lead to better nutrition among the poor is not necessarily true. This is a crucial issue because if individuals get more money and do not use that money for buying factors that improve nutrition (better food, care, and health), then malnutrition is unlikely to be reduced.

Throughout this book, we discuss the link between economic growth and tourism development with human development. In this section, we explore the relationship between these factors. In the case of tourism, economic growth, and the HDI, the results from the unit root test indicate that all series are integrated in the same order ($I(1)$), and therefore suitable for testing for co-integration. The results from the ordinary least square (OLS) regressions and the unit root test for the residuals are presented in Figures 6.3 and 6.4. The results confirm the residuals from OLS regressions between economic growth and human development and between tourism and human development are stationary, and both series are cointegrated.

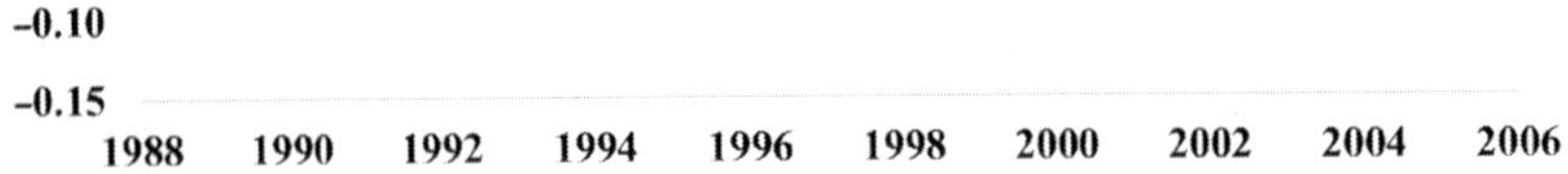


**FIGURE 6.3** Co-integration Between Tourism and Human Development.

Granger two-step co-integration test: $Y_{\mathrm{HDI}_t} = -0.290 - 0.078 X_{\mathrm{tour}_t} + \epsilon_t$ (notes: $t$ value for $\alpha_t$ = −0.650 ($P$ > 0.10), $t$ value for $X_{\mathrm{tour}_t} = -2.32(P < 0.01); R^2 = 0.2511; F(1,16) = 6.76(0.03)$; Durbin Watson = 1.85. The results of the augmented Dickey–Fuller and Phillips–Perron tests without a constant and trend indicated that residuals were stationary at the 1% level ($t = -4.000$ and $t = -4.002$, respectively)).[10]

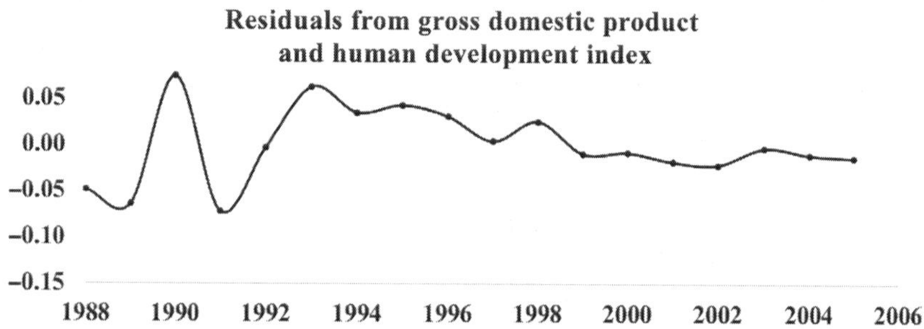


**FIGURE 6.4** Co-integration Between Economic Growth and Human Development.

Granger two-step co-integration test: $Y_{\text{HDI}_t} = 6.32 + 0.301X_{\text{growth GDP}_t} - 0.046\Phi_{\text{dummy}}$ (notes: $t$ value for $\alpha_t = -2.46$ ($P < 0.10$) $t$ value for $X_{\text{growth GDP}_t} = -1.51$ ($P > 0.01$); $R^2 = 0.35$; $F(2,15) = 5.36(0.03)$; Durbin Watson = 2.43; $\Phi_{\text{dummy}}$ represents a dummy that captures the dollarization effects in Ecuador. The augmented Dickey–Fuller and Phillips–Perron tests without a constant and trend indicated that residuals were stationary at the 1% level ($t = -4.24$ and $t = -4.25$, respectively)).

## ECONOMIC GROWTH AND HUMAN DEVELOPMENT: A LOPSIDED HUMAN DEVELOPMENT IN ECUADOR

In the previous section, we established that all the regressors are $I(1)$ and cointegrated. In this section, we are testing the relationship between economic growth and human development. Similar to the method used in Chapter 5, we apply an autoregressive distributed lag (ADL) model to test the long- and short-term effects of economic growth on human development[11]. The ADL equation is:

$$\Delta Y_{HDI_t} = \alpha_t + \Delta\beta_0 X_{growth\,GDP_t} + \beta_2 X_{growth\,GDP_{t-1}} + \gamma Y_{HDI_{t-1}} + \omega_t$$

To obtain the short-term effects, long-term effects, and the adjustment coefficient, the error-correction model can be simplified and written as

$$\Delta Y_{HDI_t} = \alpha_t + \beta_0 \Delta X_{growth\,GDP_t} + \gamma[Y_{HDI_{t-1}} - \beta_3 X_{growth\,GDP_{t-1}}] + \Phi_{dummy} + \omega_t$$

where $\beta_0 \Delta X_{growth\,GDP_{t-1}}$ is a first difference operator that represents the short-term impact of economic growth on human development,

$\beta_3 X_{\text{growth GDP}_{t-1}} = \beta_2 X_{\text{growht GDP}_{t-1}} / \gamma Y_{\text{HDI}_{t-1}}$ and captures the long-term effect of economic growth on human development, $\Phi_{\text{dummy}}$ captures the rate at which the model moves toward equilibrium, and $\Phi_{\text{dummy}}$ is a dummy used to capture the effects of dollarization. This equation provides the long- and short-term elasticities for economic growth and the adjustment speed in which the system is restored to equilibrium.

The results from the ADL error correction model for economic growth and human development is[12]

$$\Delta Y_{HDI_t} = -6.91\alpha - 0.314\Delta X_{growth\,GDP_t} - 1.22\gamma[Y_{HDI_{t-1}} - .27X_{growth\,GDP_{t-1}}] - 0.05\Phi_{dummy} + \omega_t$$

where the short term effect is equal to 0.314 $_{growth\,GDP_{-1}}$; the long term effects is $-0.27X_{\text{growth GDP}_{t-1}} = 0.33X_{\text{growth GDP}_{t-1}} / -1.22Y_{\text{HDI}_{t-1}}$; and the rate of adjustment $\gamma$ is equal to $-1.22$.

The results confirm the existence of a long-run relationship between economic growth and human development, and they have the correct sign. This means that a 1% increase in economic growth improves human development by 0.27% in the long term for the case of Ecuador.[13]

It is important to note that the short-term coefficient of economic growth is not significant. Interestingly, the error correction term is significant and >1, thus implying that in the long run the long-term effect of economic growth on human development increases over unity (overshooting). This means that progress in human development is outstripping the capacity of the economy to grow at a faster pace, implying an unsustainable situation over time. See Figure 6.5.

The imbalance between human capital progress and economic growth is the result of the still high inequality in Ecuador and controversial economic policies restricting high growth. We already saw in Chapter 5 how crucial the Bono de Desarrollo Humano was in alleviating poverty. Direct cash transfers to the poor enhanced human development. However, economic growth did not accelerate enough to absorb a more qualified human capital. Ecuador is plagued by high underemployment.[14] Clearly, the economic growth achieved in Ecuador is without enough jobs. Ranis et al. (2000) called this situation "lopsided human development", which is a situation in which there is progress in human capital combined with low economic growth.[15]

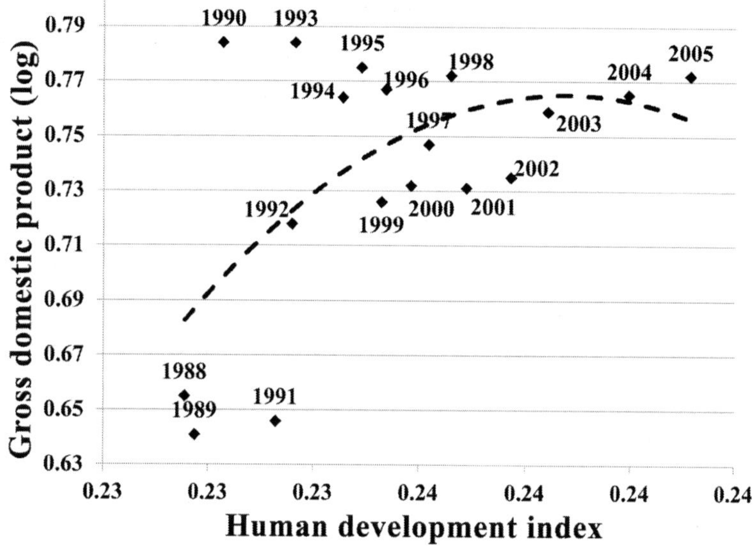


FIGURE 6.5 Overshooting: Economic Growth and Human Development.

However, the data regarding economic growth in the country may not reflect the economic reality in the country because the data do not include the informal economy. Developing countries and Latin American countries reveal a high incidence of informal economy.[16] For example, a recent report issued by the Latin American office of the International Labor Organization estimated that the informal economy includes nearly 48% of the employment affecting 130 million people in Latin America and the Caribbean. This high incidence of informality, according to the report is due to unfamiliarity with labor laws or simply it costs too much to be in the formal economy. The informal economy mainly affects the poor in Latin America.[17]

The economy of Ecuador is no exception. For example, more than half of the national economy consists of the informal sector –53.3% in 2012. Street vendors and improvised mom and pops stores decorate the streets of Quito and Guayaquil. When we visited Guayaquil for the first time in 2008, we were mesmerized by the number of small businesses on the street, some of them with tables, chairs, and scales as their only assets. They were selling sodas, *ceviche*, *patacones*, *bolon* (fried plantain with cheese), and *pan de yucca* on the street. In Cerro Santa Ana, the hallmark regeneration project in the city of Guayaquil, launched in 2000, each house on the hill had a business. We were surprised because these people were poor, and essentially lack income, access to credit sources, and finances, assuming high risks.

Banerjee and Duflo in their book *Poor Economics* also struggled with this observation. They documented that in Ecuador up to 44% of the rural poor operate a non-agricultural business with little assets of their own and with low productivity and profitability. Typically these businesses consist of family labor, but the profit generated by these businesses barely reached the US$2 PPP per day to pat one family member. When family labor is included in the production equation, most of these businesses have a negative profit. It is no wonder that this dismal situation of low productivity and low profitability spawn high informality. When combined with government red tape, there is little incentive left to incorporate a business.[18]

The Peruvian economist De Soto documented the enormous costs associated with the incorporation of a business in Lima, Peru. According to him it took 289 days at a cost of US$1,231, equal to 31 times the minimum wage to bring a business in the formal economy.[19] Torres found a similar situation in Yucatan, Mexico, where small farmers operated informally and were unwilling to provide a receipt to hotels.[20] A team of the University of Central Florida, realized an experiment in Guayaquil, Ecuador, in 2009 to incorporate a small hospitality business in Guayaquil. It took 92 working days at a cost of almost a year of a monthly minimum wage.[21] The World Bank ranks Ecuador as 176 among 189 countries in the ease of starting up in business.[22] Informality constrains economic growth because the state is prevented from raising enough taxes to enhance the quality of its services. The dismal government services in many of these countries may be another deterrent to join the formal economy.

The evidence of a cointegrating relationship indicates that economic growth and human development move together over time; however, whether economic growth actually drives human development or human development drives economic growth needs to be established. The results of the Granger tests indicate that the null hypothesis "economic growth does not Granger cause poverty" can be rejected at the 10% level, evidencing that economic growth "Granger causes" human development.[23] The results also indicate that the null hypothesis that human development does not Granger cause economic growth cannot be rejected at the 1% level, thus concluding that a one-way relationship exists running from economic growth to human development and not the other way around.[24] This result is consistent with the overshooting phenomenon where human development is not aligned with high economic growth, revealed in the words of Ranis et al. a "lopsided human development".

## TOURISM AND HUMAN DEVELOPMENT: THE POWER OF OVERSHOOTING EFFECTS

We now turn to investigate the relationship between tourism and human development. A co-integration relationship between tourism arrivals and human development is established, and consequently, the study proceeded to apply an ADL model. The ADL equation for testing the effects of tourism arrivals on human development is

$$\Delta Y_{HDI_t} = \alpha_t + \Delta\beta_0 X_{tour_t} + \beta_2 X_{tour_{t-1}} + \gamma Y_{HDI_{t-1}} + \omega_t$$

To obtain the short-term effects, long-term effects, and the adjustment coefficient, the error correction model can be simplified and written as

$$\Delta Y_{HDI_t} = \alpha_t + \beta_0\, \Delta X_{tour_t} + \gamma[Y_{HDI_{t-1}} - \beta_3 X_{tour_{t-1}}] + \Phi_{dummy} + \omega_t$$

where $\beta_0\, \Delta X_{tour_{t-1}}$ is a first difference operator that represents the short-term impact of tourism on human development, $\beta_3 X_{tour_{t-1}} = \beta_2 X_{tour_{t-1}} / \gamma Y_{HDI_{t-1}}$ and captures the long-term effect of tourism arrivals on human development, $\gamma$ captures the rate at which the model moves toward equilibrium, and $\Phi_{\text{dummy}}$ is a dummy used to capture the effects of dollarization. With this equation, we can estimate the long- and short-term elasticities for tourism and the adjustment speed toward equilibrium.

The results from the ADL error correction model for tourism and human development is[25]

$$\Delta Y_{HDI_t} = -2.11\alpha_t + 0.316\,\Delta X_{tour_t} + 0.23 X_{tour_{t-1}} - 1.3\gamma_{HDI_{t-1}} - 0.11\Phi_{dummy} + \omega_t$$

To obtain the long-term effects and adjustment coefficient, the error correction model can be simplified and written as

$$\Delta Y_{HDI_t} = -2.11\alpha_t + 0.316\,\Delta X_{tour_t} - 1.30\gamma[Y_{Sen_{t-1}} - 0.18 X_{tour_{t-1}}] - 0.11\Phi_{dummy} + \omega_t$$

where the short term effect is equal to 0.316 $\Delta X_{tour_{t-1}}$; the long term effects is $-0.18 X_{tour_{t-1}} = 0.23 X_{tour_{t-1}} / -1.3 Y_{Sen_{t-1}}$; and the rate of adjustment $\gamma$ is equal to −1.30.

The results also demonstrate the long-run relationship between tourism and human development, and both variables have the correct sign. This means that a 1% increase in tourism arrivals improves human development by 0.18% in the long term for the case of Ecuador.[26] It is important to note that the short-term coefficient of tourism is also significant and a 1% increase in $\Delta X_{tour_{t-1}}$ improves human development by 0.316%. Interestingly, the error correction term is also significant but >1, thus implying that in the long run, the long-term effect of tourism on human development increases over unity (overshooting). The overshooting effect of tourism on growth is depicted in Figure 6.6.

Overshooting should not be a surprising result because, as indicated earlier, the economy of Ecuador has a capacity problem with the rapid progress in human development: the economy has not been able to absorb human capital and is characterized by a high incidence of informality. The tourism sector is not isolated from the overall economy and reveals symptoms of lack of sufficient investment to increase the tourist infrastructure in the country. For example, the small hotel inventory in the city of Guayaquil has only grown very slowly over the past ten years. Only two hotels have been added to the room inventory between 2008 and 2012, adding 217 rooms. The growth rate of hotel inventory of 3.2% in the city has been below the economic growth of the country of 4.8%, indicating poor level of performance by the hotel industry in the city of Guayaquil. If the performance had been better, surely more room inventory would have been added to the tourism infrastructure. The reality of the tourism infrastructure has restrained the further growth in international tourism demand.

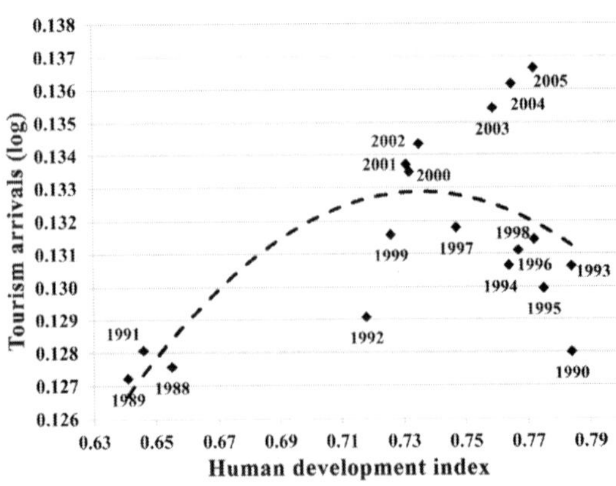


**FIGURE 6.6** Overshooting: Tourism and Human Development.

When we investigated the causality between tourism development and human development, we found that the null hypothesis "tourism does not Granger cause human development" cannot be rejected at any acceptable level of significance. On the other hand, the null hypothesis "human development does not Granger cause tourism" can be rejected at the 1% level, evidencing that human development "Granger causes" tourism.[27] We can therefore conclude that a one-way relationship exists running from human development toward tourism, and not the other way around as expected. This result should not come as a surprise. Tourism basically puts money in people's hands through salaries or vending. Individual incomes, however, can buy health and education, but cannot provide these services. Education and health are typically provided by the government in developing countries. Therefore, money can only buy access, which means that tourism will have an indirect effect on human development. The extent of its indirect effect depends on policies as well as the interaction of personal desires and necessities.

The extent of the indirect effects of tourism also depends on the tourism capacity of a country. We have seen that human development overshoots tourism arrivals, which implies that the tourism sector has capacity constraints. Therefore, for tourism to expand, progress in human development should align itself more effectively with demand in international tourism. Improved market accessibility of a country, an expanded and more profitable hotel sector and better physical infrastructure are needed if the progress of human capital is be put to more productive use. The recent announcement of major investments in the tourism infrastructure by the Minister of Tourism of Ecuador suggests a correction policy of the imbalance between progress in human development and tourism development.

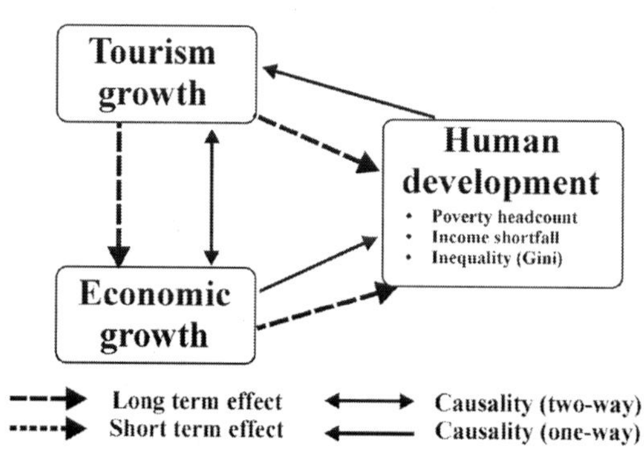


**FIGURE 6.7** Empirical Relationship Between Development and Poverty Obliteration Paradigm (Human Development).

Summarizing, we have explored the relationship between economic growth and tourism arrivals with human development in the case of Ecuador (See Figure 6.7 for summary of results). The findings reveal an interesting fact regarding the role of economic growth and tourism as a development strategy. These findings contradict our initial position, in which we argued that the expansion of tourism promotes human development and could be considered a determining factor in improving the quality of life and capabilities of the people in Ecuador. Instead, the results from our study support the arguments made in the case of Turkey, in which human development promotes tourism. The study of Tosun et al. found that Turkish regions with a higher incidence of HDI also reveal higher tourism figures compared to other regions in the country with lower HDI values.[28]

As for economic growth, this relationship was not only significant, but the magnitude of 1% increase in economic growth results in 0.27% improvement in the human development in the long run. The error correction term was also significant and larger than one, suggesting that the system is restored back to equilibrium immediately. However, in the short term, economic growth does not have the virtue of improving human development. The latter might be due to the fact that any improvement in human development is a prolonged transition. The results from the Granger causality tests indicate that a lopsided HD relationship exists in Ecuador.[29]

The lopsided HD situation in Ecuador reveals capacity constraints in the economy as well as in the tourist sector. The economic sector is growing too slow to integrate the progress in human development, and tourism arrivals are hampered by capacity constraints in the tourism sector. There is room for growth and the country is at a crossroad in terms of aligning supply and demand more effectively. However, by Ranis et al.'s account, Ecuador has the sequencing of the development process right: human development precedes economic expansion. Viewed from this perspective, we could say as well that human development precedes further tourism development.

## TOURISM AND HUMAN DEVELOPMENT IN NICARAGUA AND COSTA RICA

This tenuous relationship between tourism development, economic growth, and human development evidenced in Ecuador was also found in the cases of Nicaragua and Costa Rica. In his work *Assessing Tourism Development from Sen's Capability Approach* (2012), Croes applied a co-integration technique based on the Granger representation theorem to investigate the link tourism development and HDI in the context of Nicaragua and Costa Rica. The study found a mutually reinforcing link in the case of Nicaragua, suggesting that as average tourism receipts increase, the population seems to have greater command over relevant resources (education, health, food, etc.), which lead to better human development performance. The policy implication is that tourism growth accompanied with HD improvements appears to yield a stable relationship over time.

Increased tourism spending means more job opportunities for the poor. A report by Economic Commission for Latin America and the Caribbean (ECLAC) from 2007 suggests that job creation entertains the most potential for tourism in Nicaragua in its search to defeat poverty.[30] Tourism also provides better quality jobs, including healthier, safer, and more pleasant working conditions than other economic sectors in Nicaragua.[31] Tourism receipts are important to the poor in Nicaragua; in other words, the size of the tourism sector in the total economy matters less for the poor, because of the prominence of a large informal economic sector, which is typically where most poor deliver their economic activities. The informal sector of the economy in Nicaragua is strong, limiting the effects of the formal economy on the poor. For example, the Central Bank of Nicaragua estimated that the informal sector in the country accounted for 41% of the total economy. In Nicaragua, self-employment is dominant and there appear to be many unpaid individuals working in family business.[32] Tourism seems to be the key to job generation in the informal sector as well as in providing vending opportunities for poor households.

Additionally, as human development performance improves, tourism services improve, thereby yielding higher tourism revenues. Higher tourism revenues correlate with improvements in health and education, as higher individual incomes and government expenditures focusing on health and education programs have addressed pressing social and human issues in the country. For example, for the last decade, the government of Nicaragua has been providing free and universal access to health and education. Maternal and child health has seen significant improvements over the years, while, according to UNESCO, the illiteracy rate was reduced from 22% to <6%. The Red de Proteccion Social bolstered these programs, thereby promoting HD improvements.

The mutually reinforcing link between tourism development and human development was found missing in the case of Costa Rica, according to Croes. Costa Rica reveals that there is a lack of a long-run relationship running from human development to tourism development. While higher tourism incomes lead to HD improvements, over time these effects tend to diminish. The case of Costa Rica is an interesting one because tourism development created more jobs and the country has high human development. As a matter of fact, Costa Rica, with a HDI of 0.773, is considered by the United Nations' standards as a country with high human development. Tourism development has contributed to this high incidence of human development in Costa Rica. What could be the reason for the lack of impact of human development on tourism development?

Costa Rica, like Nicaragua, has a large informal economy. According to the International Monetary Fund, the informal sector in Costa Rica represents 40% of the total economy.[33] The large size of the informal sector also has its incidence in the significance of large-scale informal employment. By July 2009, for example, Costa Rica had 43.8% of its employees working in the informal sector, which means that these employees lack all basic protection.[34] While a large amount of jobs may have gone to the informal sector, jobs that permeated the formal sector were displaced to immigrants, particularly from Nicaragua. Tourism development in Costa Rica provoked unintended consequences: the poor were excluded from job opportunities and displaced from the job market in the hospitality industry. Higher educated Costa Ricans, foreigners, or immigrants from Nicaragua filled job openings. For example, the poor and local people did not get most direct and indirect jobs in tourism-related business in the Guanacaste area.[35]

The situation of those working in the formal tourism sector may also reflect uncertainty and stress, thereby affecting individual health. This uncertainty may be caused by the job types and characteristics (part time and predominance of women) in tourism in Costa Rica. The escalating crime environment in Costa Rica may also tax health costs affecting especially those at the lower income ladder.[36] Part-time and low-pay female workers tend to spend their income quickly and mainly on food and health items. These low income persons may forego these taxing health costs by not attending health issues, possibly lowering their productivity, which eventually would lower incomes, thereby negatively affecting human development efforts by individuals.

How tourism revenues are shared has a strong impact on poverty reduction in poor households because poor households spend a larger part of their income on food, health, and education. The levels of inequality in Costa Rica have increased since the 1990s and poverty rates have stagnated despite economic growth.[37] At the same time, opportunities for the poor in Costa Rica dwindled, and increased crime assailed the poor.

## TOURISM WITH A HUMAN FACE: DEMOCRATIZATION OF THE DOLLAR?

Deepening the connectivity between tourism and human development can be of great significance where tourism incomes matter to the poor. Tourism growth expands capabilities directly suggesting that as average tourism receipts increase, the population seems to have greater command over relevant resources (education, health, food, etc.), which lead to better human development performance. This connectivity is furthermore mutually reinforcing: as human development performance improves, tourism services improve, thereby yielding higher tourism revenues[38].

But this connectivity does not happen automatically or in all contexts. The cases of Ecuador and Costa Rica illustrate this point. As for human development, tourism only influences the capabilities of the people in Ecuador and Costa Rica indirectly via economic growth. Improvements in human capabilities, no matter how significant, seem easier to accomplish when less complex social issues in human development are concerned. For example, gains in life expectancy through the eradication of preventable diseases are much easier than halting complex diseases, such as cancer. Similarly, lower levels of education are easier to improve (primary education) compared to the diffusion of higher education and higher skills. Providing access to health and schools as a first step is important to improve the quality of life of people, but after reaching a certain threshold of accessibility, the quality of services becomes crucial in further improving the quality of life of the people.[39]

Tourism is powerful when income to the individual is concerned. Because the tourist roams the destination, the tourist dollar can reach everyone. From jobs to street vendors to farmers in rural areas, tourism's arm can touch everyone. Vanegas in his *Poverty Elimination through Tourism Dynamics* called this opportunity process the democratization of the dollar. According to Vanegas, tourism has a strong connectivity with the poor transmission mechanism. The main transmission mechanism is the creation of jobs both for unskilled labor and providing income opportunities for "carpenters, construction workers, gardeners, waiters, security, cleaners, maintenance staff, clerks, drivers, artisans."[40]

The payoff of tourism development may be indicating threshold effects dependent on the fraction of the labor market that has skills. Beyond a threshold other factors may come to play, such as institutional strength, the distribution of income, social expenditure ratios, and the relative position of women. While higher tourism incomes lead to HD improvements, over time these effects tend to diminish. This evidence does not imply, however, that tourism growth is unimportant to broadening human development; rather it is suggesting that the importance of tourism growth is merited in the distribution of its benefits, and the extent to which tourism receipts are allocated to support human development (public health, education, safety, etc.). The larger implication from the evidence of this study is that rising incomes will not necessarily translate into human development performance, thereby rendering support to Sen's contention that well-being should not be measured by its instrumental antecedents (such as income) alone. Figure 6.8 reveals the connectivity between tourism and human development.

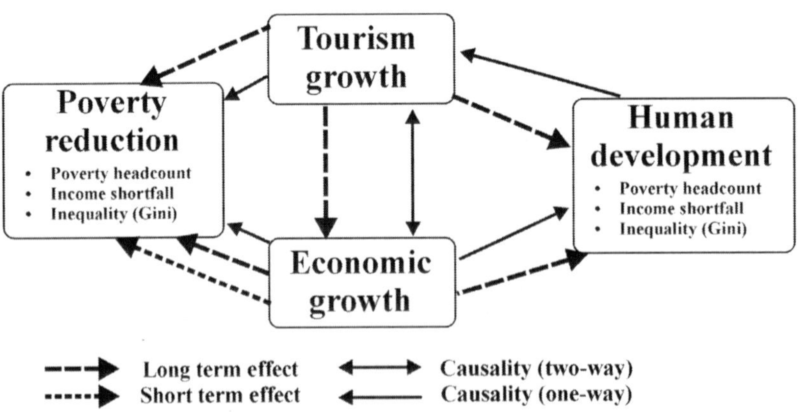


**FIGURE 6.8** Relationship between Development and Poverty Obliteration Paradigm.

We recognize that objective well-being may mask how people really feel about tourism development. For example, someone in Costa Rica who is working in the tourism sector on a part-time job may have been lifted from below the poverty line due to this job. This person may feel stressed because of the insecurity surrounding job uncertainty. This stressed condition could unleash a number of behavioral consequences for the individual, family, and organization, affecting his/her well-being as well as his/her productivity and performance at work. While objectively this person is no longer considered a poor person, this person may feel otherwise: the person may become unhappy.

An increase in income and opportunities for an individual may be perceived differently depending on an individual's cognitive judgment of life satisfaction, moods, emotions, and state of mind. For example, tourism development can influence net population migration, the availability of types of jobs, and the access to and level of education and health. These various types of impact may shape an individual's perception and perspective regarding tourism development, and thereby influence his/her subjective well-being. Different impact on the life experience of each individual may enhance or curb the arm of tourism in reaching to lift people out of poverty. The question is what are the determinants that affect the individual's assessment of subjective well-being? This is the question that we will explore in the next two chapters.

## REFERENCES

Acevedo-Arreguin, L. A. Spatial Temporal Statistical Modeling of Crime Data: The Kernel Convolution Approach. Master's Thesis. University of California Santa Cruz, 2008.

Anand, S.; Ravallion, M. Human development in poor countries: on the role of private incomes and public services. *J. Econ. Perspect.* 1993, 7, 133–150.

Banerjee, A.; Duflo, E. *Poor Economics. A Radical Rethinking of the Way to Fight Global Poverty*; Public Affairs: New York, NY, 2011.

Barros, C.; Barros, V.; Dieke, P. 2012. Tourism and Human Development in Mozambique; An Analysis for Inhambane Province (Working paper no. WP100/2012). http://pascal.iseg.utl.pt/~cesa/files/Doc_trabalho/WP100.pdf.

Budd, E. N. *Democratization, Development, and the Patrimonial State in the Age of Globalization*; Lexington Books: Maryland, 2003.

Chen, C. F.; Chiou-Wei, S. Z. Tourism expansion, tourism uncertainty and economic growth: new evidence from Taiwan and Korea. *Tour. Manage.* 2009, 30(6), 812–818.

Chen, L. L.; Devereux, J. Tourism and welfare in Sub-Saharan Africa: a theoretical analysis. *J. Afr. Econ.* 1999, 8(2), 209–227.

Cortes-Jimenez, I.; Pulina, M. Inbound tourism and long-run economic growth. *Curr. Iss. Tour.* 2010, 13(1), 61–74.

Croes, R.; Rivera, M.; Ramirez, X.; Pizam, A. *Plan Maestro de Desarrollo Turistico: Guayas*; Gobierno Provincial del Guayas y Camara de Turismo: Guayaquil, Ecuador, 2009.

Croes, R.; Vanegas, M. Cointegration and causality between tourism and poverty reduction. *J. Travel Res*. 2008, 47(1), 94–103.

De Soto, H. *The Mystery of Capital*; Basic Books Perseus Books Group: New York, NY, 2000.

Dickey, D. A.; Fuller, W. A. Distribution of the estimators for autoregressive time series with a unit root. *J. Am. Stat. Assoc*. 1979, 74(366), 427–431.

Dickey, D.; Fuller, W. Likelihood ratio statistics for autoregressive time series. *Econometrica*. 1981, 49(4), 1057–1072.

Easterly, W. *The Elusive Quest for Growth: Economists' Adventures and Misadventures in the Tropics*; MIT Press: Cambridge, MA, 2002.

ECLAC. *Economic Growth with Equity. Challenges for Latin America*; United Nations Publications: Santiago de Chile, 2007.

Ferguson, C. Principles of transitional care for young people with longstanding continence problems. *Nurs. Times*. 2010, 106, 47.

Gindling, T. South-south migration: the impact of Nicaraguan immigrants on earnings, inequality and poverty in Costa Rica. *World Dev*. 2009, 37(1), 116–126.

Granger, C. W. J. Investigating causal relations by econometric models and cross-spectral methods. *Econometrica*. 1969, 37(3), 424–438.

Gutierrez, C.; Paci, P.; Ranzani, M. *Making Work Pay in Nicaragua. Employment, Growth, and Poverty Reduction*; World Bank: Washington, DC, 2008.

Hashimoto, A. *Tourism and sociocultural development issues*. In *Tourism and Development: Concepts and Issues*; Sharpley, R., Tefler, D. J., Eds.; Chanel View Publications: London, UK, 2002.

Honey, M.; Vargas, E.; Durham, W. 'Impact of tourism related development on the Pacific coast of Costa Rica', Center for Responsible Travel, Stanford University, 2010. www.responsibletravel.org/resources/documents/Coastal-tourism-documents/Summary%20Report/Summary_Report__Impact_Tourism_Related_Development_Pacific_Coast_Costa_Rica.pdf (accessed Jul 4, 2012).

Joseph, R. A. *Democracy and Prebendal Politics in Nigeria: The Rise and Fall of the Second Republic*; Cambridge University Press: Cambridge, MA, 1987.

Lengefeld, K.; Beyer, M. CSR beyond charity: how the core business of all-inclusive contributes to poverty alleviation and local development in the Caribbean and Central America. Paper presented at the VIth Corporate Social Responsibility for Sustainable Tourism, University of Girona, Spain, 2006.

Mehregan, N.; Kordbacheh, H.; Akbari, A. Foreign Tourism and Human Development in Iran. 2012. International Proceedings of Economics Development & Research, 50.

Mukherjee, C.; White, H.; Wuyts, M. *Econometrics and Data Analysis for Developing Countries*; Routledge: London, UK, 1998.

Ranis, G.; Stewart, F.; Ramirez, A. Economic growth and human development. *World Dev*. 2000, 28(2), 197–219.

Ridderstaat, J.; Croes, R.; Nijkamp, P. Tourism development, quality of life and exogenous shocks: a systemic framework. *Int. J. Soc. Syst. Sci*. 2013, 5(4), 321–336.

Ridderstaat, J.; Croes, R.; Nijkamp, P. The tourism development–quality of life Nexus in a small island destination. *J. Travel Res*. 2014.

Roe, D.; Khanya, P. U. *Pro-Poor Tourism: Harnessing the World's Largest Industry for the World's Poor*; International Institute for Environment and Development (IIED): London, 2001. [Prepared for World Summit on Sustainable Development, Johannesburg].

Romano, S. M.; Falconí, J.; Aguinaga, C. *Una interpretación mesoeconómica del turismo en Ecuador*; Publicaciones Económicas, Banco Central del Ecuador: Quito, Ecuador, 2005.

Sen, A. Commodities and capabilities. Amsterdam New York New York, N.Y. 1985

Torres, R. Linkages between tourism and agriculture in Mexico. *Ann. Tour. Res.* 2003, 30(3), 546–566.

Tosun, C.; Timothy, D. J.; Öztürk, Y. Tourism growth, national development and regional inequality in Turkey. *J. Sustainable Tour.* 2003, 11(2), 133–161.

United Nations Development Program (UNDP). *Report on Human Development in Central America 2009-2010*; Oxford University Press: New York, NY, 2010.

Vanegas, M. *Poverty Elimination through tourism dynamics*. In *Handbook of Tourism and Quality-of-Life Research: Enhancing the Lives of Tourists and Residents of Host Communities*; Uysal, M., Perdue, R., Singy, J., Eds.; Springer Publishers: New York, NY, 2011.

Vuletin, G. *Measuring the Informal Economy in Latin America and the Caribbean*; IMF: Washington, DC, 2008. [Working Paper, WP/08/102].

## ENDNOTES

[1]For more details about Ecuador see Romano et al. (2005)

[2]See, for example, Ranis et al. (2000).

[3]See, for example Anand ad Ravallion (1993)

[4]See, for example Roe and Khanya (2003)

[5]See, for example, the report from the UNDP (2010) about the rampaging effects of crime and violence in Central America.

[6]Data for the HDI was provided by the Oficina Sistema Integrado de Indicadores Sociales del Ecuador (http://www.siise.gob.ec/).

[7]The results of the augmented Dickey–Fuller (ADF) tests indicate that human development is stationary in level form with a constant and a drift. On first differences, the ADF tests indicate that human development is stationary with a drift and a constant. At the same time, the results of the Phillips–Perron (PP) test suggest that human development is stationary in level form with and without a trend. In first differences, the PP tests indicate that human development is also stationary and $I(0)$. The results of the PP test for human development indicate that the variable is stationary in all models.

[8]See UNDP report. The Rise of the South: Human Progress in a Diverse World. Available from: http://hdr.undp.org/sites/default/files/Country-Profiles/ECU.pdf.

[9]See, for example Dickey and Fuller (1979, 1981)

[10]See, for example Granger (1969)

[11]See, for example Mukherjee et al. (2008),

[12]Note:

$$\alpha(t = -1.88,\ P < 0.10,\\ X_{growth\ GDP_{t-1}}(t = 2.05, P < 0.10),\\ \gamma(t = -4.26, P < 0.01), \Delta X_{growth\ GDP_t}\\ (t = 0.75, P > 0.05), \Phi_{dummy}(t = -1.39, P > 0.05),\\ F(4,12) = 4.72, P < 0.05; DW = 2.18 \quad ;$$

$R^2 = 0.61$. adjusted $R^2 = 0.48$.

[13]The diagnostic tests for the ADL model are: Durbin Watson (DW) test (DW = 2.18) and the Breusch–Godfrey (BG) test (BG = 5.097, $P > 0.01$) indicate that the null hypothesis of no serial correlation can be rejected. In addition, the results of the Breusch–Pagan (BP) test for heteroskedasticity indicate that the null hypothesis of no heteroskedasticity is accepted (BP = 0.29, $P < 0.001$).

[14]For example, the underemployment was 44.3% in the City of Guayaquil, according to the Central Bank of Ecuador.

[15]See Ranis et al. (2000). The study of Ranis discover that lopsided human development is a typical situation in Latin America.

[16]Informal employment in developing countries comprises 50%–75% of all non-farm jobs, according to the World Bank.

[17]See Regional Office of Latin America and the Caribbean, International Labor Organization (ILO), recent experiences of formalization in Latin America and the Caribbean. Retrieved October 10, 2014, from http://www.ilo.org/wcmsp5/groups/public/---americas/---ro-lima/documents/publication/wcms_245882.pdf.

[18]Low productivity of the economic activities of the poor is documented and discussed in Banerjee and Duflo (2011).

[19]See De Soto (2000).

[20]For a further discussion, see Torres (2003).

[21]See Croes et al. (2009).

[22]See World Bank, Doing Business. Retrieved August 3, 2014, from http://www.doingbusiness.org/rankings.

[23]$X_{\text{growth GDP}}$ does not Granger cause $Y_{\text{HDI}}$ ($F$-statistic = 0.0800; $P = 0.0800$).

[24]$Y_{\text{HDI}}$ does not Granger cause $X_{\text{growth GDP}}$ ($F$-statistic = 0.0347; $P = 0.8520$).

[25]Note:

$$\alpha_1(t = 2.31,\ P < 0.05),\\ X_{tour\ arrivals_{t-1}}(t = 2.99,\ P < 0.10),\\ \gamma(t = -5.05,\ P < 0.01), \Delta X_{tour\ arrivals_t}\\ (t = 2.19,\ P < 0.05), \Phi_{dummy}(t = 2.65,\ P < 0.05),\\ F(4,12) = 7.81,\ P < 0.05 \quad ;$$

DW = 2.21; $R^2 = 0.72$, adjusted $R^2 = 0.62$.

[26]The diagnostic tests for the ADL model are: DW test (DW=2.21) and the BG test (BG = 1.957 $P > 0.01$) indicate that the null hypothesis of no serial correlation can be rejected. In addition, the results of the BP test for heteroskedasticity indicate that the null hypothesis of no heteroskedasticity is accepted (BP = 0.30, $P < 0.001$).

[27]$Y_{\text{HDI}}$ does not Granger cause $X_{\text{tour}}$ ($F$-statistic = 55.37; $P = 0.0001$); $X_{\text{tour}}$ does not Granger cause $Y_{\text{HDI}}$ ($F$-statistic = 2.13: $P = 0.711$).

[28]See Tosun et al. (2003).

[29]For example, see Ranis et al., (2000).

[30]See ECLAC (2007).

[31]For example, Lengefeld and Beyer (2006) found while the hotel sector may entertain lower wages than, for example, the sugar industry, hotel employees have permanent contracts and have better fringe benefits, such as a bonus and paid leave. Banerjee and Duflo (2011) stressed the importance of job security for the poor.

[32]See, for example, Gutierrez et al. (2008).

[33]See, for example, Vuletin (2008).

[34]See, for example, ILO (2012). Statistical update on Unemployment in the Informal Economy. Retrieved August 3, 2014, from http://laborsta.ilo.org/applv8/data/INFORMAL_ECONOMY/2012-06-Statistical%20update%20-%20v2.pdf.

[35]Honey et al. (2010) reported that employees from other regions of the country and foreigners got these jobs.

[36]Crime is taxing on vulnerable population segments the most by increasing health and other costs significantly (Acevedo-Arreguin, 2008).

[37]See, for example, Gindling (2009).

[38]See, for example Hashimoto (2002)

[39]See, for example, Easterly (2002).

[40]For a further discussion, see Vanegas (2011).

## CHAPTER 7

# TOURISM AND THE SATISFIED BUT UNHAPPY POOR

## CONTENTS

## INTRODUCTION

In the previous chapters we discussed the reach of the tourist dollar to the poor. We saw that through tourism the poor receive more income, thereby lifting them from poverty. We saw that in some cases the poor received more income than other income categories. The distribution of benefits stemming from tourism can provide major resource advantages to the poor. However, having more income does not mean that the poor will spend their money wisely by supporting their own growth and development, or that more money will make the poor happier and more satisfied with life.[1] Objective conditions (e.g., job opportunities) may not necessarily coincide with the life experience of the poor, thereby becoming a hindrance to opportunities to lift the poor out of poverty.

In this chapter, we will listen to the opinions of the poor with regards to how they perceive their quality of life.[2] Quality of life is a multidimensional concept, which includes basic needs, capabilities (as measured by human development index [HDI]), and "livability" of the environment, measured by income per capita and economic growth, and happiness and life satisfaction, measured by subjective well-being surveys. In Chapter 2, we already suggested that metrics are relevant for accountability and policy actions. In this chapter, we will investigate what life domains matter most to the poor, how the poor perceive tourism development, and how this perception shapes their subjective well-being.

## CONCEPTUALIZING QUALITY OF LIFE AND HAPPINESS

Quality of life can be assessed through objective aspects of life such as income, and more specifically, by gross domestic product (GDP), which has been considered for the longest time as the adequate measurement of societal progress. The adequacy of GDP or income as the sole dimension of quality of life has recently received heightened critique for several reasons. Income only captures market-related activities while ignoring non-market activities, such as leisure time and social interactions that frame human condition, and negative externalities such as pollution and security. Furthermore, income-based analyses are narrowly focused on revealed preferences as the yardstick of human behavior, neglecting the role of other factors such as Veblen's conspicuous behavior and low expectations norms.[3] For example, Akerlof and Kranton claim that identity and norms shape consumption and investment choices (behavior), more so than incentives and rationality.[4]

Revealed preferences are also limited in their explanatory power regarding several types of behavior. For example, Banerjee and Duflo found that poor people used their additional income on nonfood items. One expects that poor people suffering from hunger would buy more food when they have additional incomes. In a sample of 18 countries, they found the poor prefer to enjoy life (spending on festivals) instead of increasing their calorie intake.[5] Similarly, Graham and Lora unearthed disquieting findings with regards to health perceptions in Latin America. They reported a lack of association between objective conditions of infant mortality, life expectancy, and health perceptions .

The tourism literature is in its infancy in exploring the association between tourism development and happiness. Table 7.1 provides an overview of selected works in the tourism literature which address this relationship

**TABLE 7.1** Tourism and Happiness

| Authors | Focus | Empirical/ Conceptual | Unit of Analysis | Major Findings |
|---|---|---|---|---|
| Bok (2010) | Tourist and residents | Conceptual | Happiness | Author suggested that happiness should become the core of government policies |
| Corvo (2011) | Tourists | Conceptual | Happiness | The study proposed that the positive effect of tourism on the feeling of happiness could be debilitated by inability of people to separate their leisure time from the daily routines |
| Bimonte and Faralla (2014) | Tourists | Empirical | Happiness | Authors found that the proximity of people to the nature positively affected their emotional and physical well-beings |

Another study also found disquieting results when comparing respondents in Guatemala and Chile regarding health conditions. Respondents in Guatemala reported being more satisfied with the health conditions in their country compared to respondents in Chile. However, an objective evaluation shows that Chile has better health conditions than Guatemala.[6] These examples suggest that choices are shaped by agency, information, and other factors related to poverty or discrimination. In other words, objective indicators may suggest that an individual is poor, while the individual considers himself not poor, or vice versa.

The awareness that life conditions include more than material possessions, like income, prompted the "beyond GDP" debate and query regarding the measurement of societal progress. The notion that more material possessions do not make people happier (the Easterlin paradox) became part of this discussion. Moreover, studies found that people living in extreme poverty convey low levels of happiness with life as a whole, which complicated our discussion of the relationship of happiness and income.[7] Eventually, the answer to the question of what makes people happy shifted from purely income and consumption considerations to a broader conception of happiness, which includes social ties, mindfulness, and opportunities. The happiness literature identifies two important domains: emotion and evaluation (life satisfaction). Emotions are positive or negative feelings toward life experiences. Life satisfaction is the judgment call of an individual on life experiences and regards various life conditions.

Happiness as the ultimate goal of public policy became official through the United Nations' General Assembly resolution of July 2011, which invited UN members to measure happiness as the main guide for public policy. The Organization for Economic Co-operation and Development (OECD) countries also adopted happiness measures as important policy indicators guiding their actions complementing market-oriented yardsticks such as GDP. However, there is literature that claims that happiness is a means and not an end in itself. Happy people tend to be healthier, more productive, creative, and innovative, and engage in better social relations and enjoy more income.[8] Happiness as a multidimensional construct stretches to multiple domains of life such as work, health, environment, education, social connections, security, and political participation.

## THE HAPPY POOR

The subjective well-being approach has been frequently employed to investigate individual perception with regard to life experiences in the economic, social, and health domains.[9] The subjective approach allows for comparing people's perception with the objective evidence. Knowing and understanding the individual perceptions is relevant in the formulation of meaningful policy actions. For example, if absolute poverty does matter little in happiness enhancement, then a policy geared toward economic growth would be of little consequence for poor people. This means that economic growth should not be the primary goal of the government in the effort of poverty reduction.

Previous research on Mexico illustrates and highlights how relevant subjective well-being is in combating poverty. By analyzing the poverty condition in Mexico, a unique dichotomy was found with regard to the objective and subjective realities of the poor. An objective indicator may suggest somebody as not being poor, while a subjective reality indicates that somebody feels poor. In the case of Mexico, it was found that although economically poor, there is a strong presence of "happy poor". The cause of this discrepancy in poor countries may be due to the fact that a large portion of consumption happens outside of the marketplace and is based more on home production and barter (exchange in kind).[10] Indeed, the informal market is a recurrent social and economic arrangement and is sizeable in developing countries.

Latin America is no exception to the informal market arrangements. According to the International Monetary Fund, informal economies account for more than 40% of the GDP in Latin America, Central America, and Africa.[11] In Guatemala, the informal economy dominates the overall economy of the country, supporting 75% of total workers. Ecuador reveals a similar picture where seven out of ten workers toil in the informal economy.[12] In Colombia, the informal sector accounts for 55% of the total economy.[13] Working in the informal economy means lack of legal protection, no pension, no savings, no healthcare, and increased vulnerability. Most of these jobs are odd jobs where millions of tax dollars could have been allocated to healthcare and education, two important capabilities, especially for the poor.

The subjective well-being approach, therefore, considers poverty not as an objectively defined status of deprivation, but views poverty as an individual feeling. Assuming that the poor themselves can reveal their true life satisfaction better than any objective indicator, economic and noneconomic aspects of well-being can be traced. Thus, expressed preferences are gaged in lieu of revealed preferences. Poverty is defined here as a status below a certain degree of life satisfaction. Several studies have gaged poverty lines through the subjective well-being approach, such as those done by Pradhan and Ravallion in the cases of Jamaica and Nepal. They construct "subjective poverty lines", and compare these lines with objective poverty lines. They observed interesting differences such as a greater subjective than objective urban–rural difference in poverty, and greater perceived than actual household scale economies in consumption.[14]

Herrera et al. confirmed the relevance of nonmonetary dimensions (e.g., health, education, family structures, social interactions, and adaptation) in determining well-being in the cases of Peru and Madagascar.[15] Similarly, Guardiola and Garcia-Muñoz found in their study regarding the poor in rural Guatemala that income poverty is not the same as subjective poverty. The latter, according to the study is a better gage of poverty in developing countries because the subjective approach captures all the life domains, including cultural, geographical, and psychological factors.[16] Barros et al. (2012) also found in the case of Mozambique that residents assess positively the contribution of tourism to human development.

The previous studies together with our own observations in several countries we visited in Latin America during a time span of ten years convinced us to consider more carefully the subjective well-being approach. Our multiple conversations with a large number of people in this region taught us that the feelings of poor people may be different than what we have learned through objective though cold aggregate numbers. We learned that by listening to the poor directly, we can better grasp the conditions in which they live (e.g., possessions, needs, livelihoods, aspirations, and the environment) and how this context framed and shaped their conception about their life opportunities.

## PERCEPTIONS AND OBJECTIVE REALITY

Consequently, we investigated the alignment of perceptions and objective evidence in Latin America by looking at poverty, human development, and happiness. Poverty is measured through the head count figures from the world development indicators of the World Bank; human development is measured through the HDI from the United Nations; and happiness is derived from the measurement of positive emotions of people in 138 countries, surveyed by Gallup 2013. On a scale from 0 to 10, positive emotions in 138 countries are canvassed by asking people whether they experienced positive emotions the previous day. Gallup compiles the "yes" results into a Positive Experience Index score for each country. Table 7.2 reveals the results of a selected group of countries in Latin America, displaying poverty, human development, and happiness.

**TABLE 7.2** Poverty, Human Development Index (HDI) and Happiness in Selected Latin American Countries

| Country | Poverty (%) | HDI | Happiness |
|---|---|---|---|
| Nicaragua | 42.5[a] | 0.599 | 83 |
| El Salvador | 40.6 | 0.680 | 81 |
| Guatemala | 53.7 | 0.581 | 83 |
| Honduras | 61.9 | 0.632 | 81 |
| Paraguay | 32.4 | 0.669 | 87 |
| Ecuador | 28.6 | 0.724 | 83 |
| Colombia | 34.1 | 0.719 | 82 |
| Panama | 27.6 | 0.780 | 86 |
| Costa Rica | 21.6 | 0.773 | 82 |
| Mexico | 51.1[b] | 0.775 | 77 |

**Source:** Poverty headcount ratio at national poverty line (% of the population). Data from database World Development Indicators, last updated 07/22/2014. HDI data are from the human development report and happiness data are from Gallup Positive Experience Index. The happiness figure of Mexico is from Ipsos Report 2011. The Ipsos survey was conducted between November 1 and November 15, 2011.
All other data are from 2012.
[a]2009 data.
[b]2010 data.

The discrepancy between poverty, human development, and happiness in a selected group of Latin American countries is clearly revealed in this table. For example, Guatemala and Nicaragua both show high incidences of poverty and a relatively low level of human development as measured by the HDI. Yet, both of these countries' rankings in the happiness index are high. While countries that ranked medium in human development had high poverty head count (e.g., El Salvador, Guatemala, Honduras, Nicaragua, and Paraguay). However, these countries also displayed the highest level ranking in happiness index. For example, Paraguay (a country with high poverty head count and medium human development) scored the highest ranking in the Gallup World Polls as the happiest country on earth for three consecutive years.

The previous table shows that feelings and emotions are not necessarily aligned with the environment. Emotions are a mental appraisal of an objective condition, but not the actual condition itself. The Gallup World Polls also capture this reality as evidenced by the amount of people in Latin America that cannot cover their basic needs for food and/or housing. For example, in Nicaragua and El Salvador, about half of the respondents reported that in the previous twelve months, they could not pay for their homes. There seems to be a clear cognitive dissonance between the objective reality, which is measured by income and human development, and the perception regarding poverty as defined by emotions. An individual may be able to socially adapt to their situation through their level of engagement with others and the environment; however, this may be only a coping strategy of self-denial. In other words, the coping strategy of self-denial enables the individual to endure poverty with regards to their own deprivation.

We were constantly wondering about this possibility of self-denial when we were faced with troubling situations during our multiple visits to Latin America. Just a few months ago, one of the authors faced a situation of despair at the Plaza Juan Rulfo in a village called Pedro Paramo in Comala, Colima, Mexico. The square was named after the famous Mexican writer, Plaza Juan Rulfo, who wrote a novel in 1955 called Pedro Paramo. This novel has exerted a large influence in the subsequent flourishing of the Latin American literature. In that square, we saw a large number of street vendors selling handicrafts, souvenirs, bottled water, or music. Most of these transactions were the result of the presence of tourists. These street vendors were from adjacent regions, such as Oaxaca, Michoacan, Guerrero, and Chiapas. All of these regions are remote and distant from the main tourist areas, which means that the street vendors had to travel several hours by bus to get to the tourist sites, such as the Plaza Juan Rulfo.

Talking to one of the street vendors, we learnt that they sell their merchandise and earn about US$100.00/d. Many of the vendors purchase the handicrafts from others and resell them to tourists, which means that less than a third of the money remains with the street vendor. If the vendor considers all costs included, the remaining amount of money dwindles between 10% and, if lucky, 15%. The vendors toil more than ten hours, sometimes 12 hours, to sell merchandise in order to procure money for their children. We noticed while speaking with them that although their faces were smiling, their eyes strayed from our presence and seemed locked into a place unknown to us. They were polite in our conversations but timid and distrustful. From their account, it became clear that they earned money to feed their children but their posture and eyes did not flash happiness nor did they utter the word happiness. Probably the unhappy eyes may be the result of their awareness that despite hard work, the productivity level of their activities is extremely low as recounted by Banerjee and Duflo.

In the summer of 2008, we braved the rough and high sea of the Jambeli and Morro Channels in the Gulf of Guayaquil to visit the Island of Puna. We were part of an expedition of volunteers to visit the island to clean up the beaches of Puna and to relaunch Puna as an island destination. Getting to the island was an adventure. The island did not have any piers to dock the boat. Thus, if you wanted to reach the shore you had to jump into the ocean some 200 ft away from the shore. Looking at the shore we had to decide to either stay in the boat and head back or jump and swim. We decided to move on, braving the rough sea and momentarily entertaining the notion that perhaps our lives could be in danger. Making the swim to shore in the rough sea meant taking on serious risk to continue our study.

Once we made it safely on shore, we met Tiburon, a local who was proud that we delivered on our promise to help organize the program to visit Puna and to promote and realize the clean-up of the beach project. Tiburon introduced us to Francisco, Julio, and some other community members, all of whom were natives from the island. They all had smiling faces and were very hospitable as hosts. But they emphasized their conditions of poverty, their exclusion from the mainland, and the lack of empowerment to change the direction of the island. They had little or no income at all. Poverty in the fishing village was not only seen through the lens of the filthy little shacks covered by palm trees or zinc and the grimy faces of the little children together with stray dogs but also the smell that came from refuse and defecation, and limited commodities percolated the alleys, the houses, and the beaches.

The locals would flail at every person to try to sell coconut water or *Cebiche de Concha*, the local dish consisting of black clams, lemon, onion and green plantains. They oversold the beauty of the beaches and the island, which in reality were trashed by litter and poverty. All these efforts realized very little money while laboring in the informal sector. In addition, these informal jobs lack the legal protection as enjoyed by those working in the formal sector. The hope of these people was centered on tourism development as a source of income and jobs to escape from poverty. The words well-being or quality of life, or happiness was far from their mouths. Sadly, the only things they aspired for was a job, money, food to feed their children, and wanting to change nonpotable for drinking water. We were not sure what to make out of their recounting of how tourism may influence and help their livelihood.

Poverty literature provides dialog, investigations, and analyses that have seemingly indicated that people in these conditions (such as the locals on the island of Puna) may actually be "happy". The fact that they have little income and nondrinkable water (according to some literature) may actually not serve as predictors to their level of happiness. However, when speaking with them and gazing into their eyes, we did not see signs of happiness – at least not from how we (mainstream society) define happy. This means that income poverty may not necessarily have the same meaning as experienced poverty. If this is a valid and meaningful proposition, then it begs the consideration that the role of tourism development may impact the dissonance in perception and reality of the poor. In order to provide a guided approach that may assess this proposition, we explore next how the subjective well-being approach may frame and shape this link between reality and perception with regards to poverty.

Thus we embark to listening to the voices of the poor.

## POVERTY: WHO ARE THE POOR IN MANZANILLO, PUNTARENAS AND GUAYAQUIL?

We selected three countries in Latin America to investigate perceptions with regard to tourism development on life satisfaction and happiness. Although these three countries do not reflect a representative sample of the region, they are sufficiently diverse to reveal the potential of tourism prowess on poverty reduction. We define happiness as positive emotions, while satisfaction is the evaluation scale of subjective well-being. We canvassed systematically the poor people's opinion in three surveys during the spring of 2014, and were able to collect in total 828 surveys. We collected 257 surveys in Manzanillo, Mexico, 350 surveys in Guayaquil, Ecuador, and 221 in Puntarenas, Costa Rica.[17] Respondents were overwhelmingly from the first and second quintiles of the income ladder of each country, considered as poor by their respective countries. Quite a number of street vendors, hawkers, and PyMEs were involved in shaping the perception regarding tourism development, and their feelings about their life conditions were included in these surveys.[18]

The samples were built through intercept surveys at tourist sites in the respective regions of Manzanillo, Mexico; Guayaquil, Ecuador; and Puntarenas, Costa Rica. All three sites are located in the Pacific coast of their respective countries and are important tourist sites.[19]

On average, respondents were 36.2 years old. Forty-five percent of those surveyed were married, and were predominantly male (56.5%). Nearly 73% of those surveyed had children. The number of children varied greatly from one child to 25 children. Eighty-four percent of the respondents had between one and six children with nearly one-third of the respondents reporting between 2 and 3 children. Two-third of the respondents stated that they were working, while one-third were not working at the time of the data collection. More than 80% (80.7%) had an income below the median of their respective country, while 52.5% reported incomes below the first four deciles of the income ladder. As a matter of comparison, the study of Rojas revealed that close to 55% of the respondents were poor on the basis of their self-reporting income group; actually, 53.5% reported having an income within the first five deciles.[20]

## WHAT IS IMPORTANT IN THE LIVES OF THE POOR?

In order to determine what is important for the poor, we considered a number of items related to the capability approach; covering different combinations of functioning a person should be able to achieve. These are what Sen considers relevant in the lives of the poor. The items used include money, health, live close to family, education, work, food, friends, violence, leisure time, and recognition.[21] We asked the respondents to rank the list of items from 1 being the most important to 10 being the least important. We applied this request only to respondents in Manzanillo (Mexico) and Guayaquil (Ecuador). The ranking gives a good indication of which areas the poor consider relevant in the construction of their subjective well-being. Table 7.2 reveals the results.

The respondents from Manzanillo reported health, money, and living close to family in descending order as the most relevant items in their lives. Education, work, food, and friends were next in order of relevance according to the ranking, while reduction of violence, leisure time, and recognition ranked as the least important items in life. A survey conducted in 50 countries, which is revealed in *Voices of the Poor,* also found health, education, and social connection as relevant social indicators. In the case of the respondents from Guayaquil, the highest rankings were for health, education, and work, followed by living close to family, food, money, and friends. Like Manzanillo, the least important items in life were those related to reduction of violence, recognition, and leisure time.

**TABLE 7.3** Mean Ranking for Important Things in Life for Mexico and Ecuador

| Items | All | | Mexico | | Ecuador | | Significance | Z | Mann–Whitney U |
|---|---|---|---|---|---|---|---|---|---|
| | Mean | Rank | Mean | Rank | Mean | Rank | | | |
| Health | 2.82 | 1 | 3.44 | 1 | 2.37 | 1 | 0.00 | -5.3 | 33,951 |
| Education | 4.15 | 2 | 4.57 | 4 | 3.85 | 2 | 0.00 | -3.8 | 37,013 |
| Close to family | 4.42 | 3 | 4.28 | 3 | 4.52 | 4 | 0.26 | -1.1 | 42,576 |
| Work | 4.59 | 4 | 4.83 | 5 | 4.41 | 3 | 0.02 | -2.3 | 40,174 |
| Money | 5.03 | 5 | 4.02 | 2 | 5.77 | 6 | 0.00 | -7.4 | 29,254 |
| Food | 5.03 | 6 | 5.67 | 6 | 4.56 | 5 | 0.00 | -5.7 | 32,876 |
| Friends | 6.15 | 7 | 5.79 | 7 | 6.41 | 7 | 0.00 | -3.5 | 37,473 |
| Less violence | 6.72 | 8 | 6.77 | 8 | 6.68 | 8 | 0.37 | -0.9 | 43,074 |
| Recognition | 7.88 | 9 | 7.98 | 10 | 7.81 | 9 | 0.02 | -2.3 | 40,222 |
| Leisure time | 8.22 | 10 | 7.65 | 9 | 8.64 | 10 | 0.00 | -7.5 | 29,376 |

Are the respondents different in terms of how they ranked each item according to their perception of what is important in their lives? We applied nonparametric tests to investigate whether differences exist in the distribution of ranks between the respondents of these two regions.[22] The results are revealed in Table 7.3. Only the items living close to family and less violence did not show any statistically significant difference in ranking. Respondents of both countries had the same perception with regard to the relevance of violence and living close to family. While living close to family was ranked high by respondents from both countries, violence was ranked much lower (seven) on the 10-item list. Money, friends, education, health, food, work, leisure time, and recognition were all statistically significant at the 5% level.

Ranking of important conditions in life is contingent upon life purposes. These life purposes are heterogeneous corresponding to personal aspiration, motivations, and opportunities. The implication is that life domains are unequal in importance. For example, the ranking as revealed in the previous table suggests a hierarchy of life conditions. Physical functionings appear as the most important life condition for the respondents. More specifically, health and education dominate the perception of what is the most important condition to enhance life opportunities, according to Sen. Both health and education are considered important pillars, together with the income to comprise the HDI. Health and education are basic capabilities supporting self-development, work, better paid jobs, and enhanced personal enriched opportunities. They are also important pillars together with income comprising the HDI, supporting self-development, work, better paid jobs, and enhanced personal enriched opportunities.

While it is self-evident that health is at the core of all human activities, the poor's lack of interest in getting, for example, clean water and bed nets, despite their potential health benefits, suggests that they are not interested in healthcare. The social science literature contests this impression by providing ample evidence that the poor care about health. For example, health was the most important domain of life in influencing subjective well-being in a study on Yucatan, Mexico.[23] A study in Bangladesh found that ill health was the dominant factor in causing crisis in households, and that on average, 18% of the total household income was allocated to health-related issues.[24] Banerjee and Duflo report that the poor in Nicaragua and Panama spent on average 5% of their income on health-related issues.[25] And so, we recognized the need to explore this issue in greater depth. Education is also identified as an important life domain next to health. Numerous studies have considered health and education as crucial for well-being as we discussed in chapter 2.

The second order of hierarchy is social functioning. Human beings are social animals and being close to family fulfills the need to feel connected as a human being. Family ties are an important aspect of belonging, and belonging is one of the three domains of quality of life including being and becoming. Belonging as revealed in social functionings feeds directly into the first order of hierarchy, because being healthy and educated make individuals more autonomous, capable, and connected. Staying connected through family ties constitutes an important aspect of interpersonal relations that can enhance self-development possibilities. Family ties also could serve as a buffer and nurturing social platform in times of despair and anguish. There is ample evidence regarding the relevance of people's networks of relationships in shaping identity and social status, and an important channel to livelihood strategies in poor countries.[26] The results obtained confirm what we already suggested in Chapter 2 - that some needs are fundamental to human life.

Interestingly, there is an ambiguity in terms of the ranking with regard to money. Money represents the material conditions and opportunities for most people to satisfy their needs. From the Gallup polls, it can be observed that many people in Latin America cannot cover their basic needs. One would expect, therefore, that money would be central in the ranking of important things in life. Money was ranked number two in order of importance of things in life according to respondents in Manzanillo, while in Ecuador, money ranked number six. This ranking suggests that the poor conceive life larger than money (possessions) and value other life domains such as health, education, and family besides material conditions. Some studies found that money as a domain of life did not influence subjective well-being. This result was found in a study in Yucatan, Mexico.[27] However, evidence from Bangladesh indicates that money and income are important life domains for the poor.[28]

## HAPPINESS: ARE THE POOR HAPPY?

We assessed this question by following the two meanings of subjective well-being as identified in the subjective well-being literature. The first dimension of subjective well-being we investigated was the evaluative dimension of subjective well-being, which corresponds to satisfaction with life. Life satisfaction is a measure of how the poor perceive their overall life.

## SATISFACTION WITH LIFE

The scale for satisfaction with life was derived from Diener and colleagues and is considered to be a valid and a reliable measure of life satisfaction, especially suited for use with a wide range of age groups and applications.[29] In addition, it makes possible the savings of interview time and resources compared to other measures of life satisfaction. These scales have high convergence of self-reported measures of subjective well-being. A unique characteristic of the satisfaction with life scale is that it assesses satisfaction with the respondent's life as a whole. The scale refuses to assess satisfaction with life domains such as health or finances and allows subjects to integrate and weigh these domains in whatever way they choose. The statements for the scale were translated into Spanish and the responses were translated back into English. Data collection took place in Costa Rica, Ecuador, and Mexico.

We first aggregated the data from the three countries and computed the mean score from the scores of the five items together. Table 7.4 reveals the descriptive statistics for each item. The overall means for all three countries suggest a moderate level of life satisfaction in the five areas comprising satisfaction with life. The level of expressed satisfaction is aligned with previous studies that investigated subjective well-being in developing countries. In our study, 69.2% reported that they were satisfied with their lives, while only 10.7% disagreed with this statement. The nearly 70% score is closely associated with life satisfaction in developing countries. A study of Gasparini et al. based on the Gallup World Polls found that the overall satisfaction value for Latin America and the Caribbean is 65% compared to 83% in high income OECD countries.[30]

**TABLE 7.4** Descriptive Statistics: Satisfaction with Life: Mexico, Ecuador and Costa Rica

| Satisfaction with Life | Mexico | Ecuador | Costa Rica | All | F |
|---|---|---|---|---|---|
| In most ways my life is close to my ideal | 3.61 | 3.46 | 3.58 | 3.54 | 1.89 |
| The conditions of life are excellent | 3.6[a] | 3.55[a] | 4.06 | 3.70 | 20.09 |
| I am satisfied with life | 3.89 | 3.81 | 3.83 | 3.84 | 0.53 |
| So far I have gotten the important things I want in life | 3.78[a] | 3.7[a] | 3.35 | 3.63 | 10.06 |
| If I could live my life over, would change almost nothing | 3.43[a,b] | 2.86[a] | 4.11 | 3.37 | 68.93 |

[a]Different than Costa Rica.
[b]Different than Ecuador.

It is noteworthy to mention that there were no differences in perception among respondents across countries with regard to life satisfaction and their ideal lives. Where they differ is in their life aspirations, i.e., the realms of life conditions, possession of important things in life, and keeping life as is. Respondents from Costa Rica seem to have the life conditions they prefer, and would not change their lives. Respondents from Ecuador seem to have their life conditions, but would like to have another type of life. Respondents from Mexico seem to have a more balanced perception in their aspirations. Respondents from Costa Rica have the highest aspirations in terms of their lives compared to those from Mexico and Ecuador.

There are no significant differences among respondents with regard to satisfaction with life across Costa Rica, Ecuador, and Mexico. This result is consistent with the economic theory, which asserts that countries enjoying higher levels of income per capita are in general more satisfied with their lives. For example, the income per capita in 2011 purchasing power parity for Mexico was US$15,886, for Costa Rica US$12,693, while the one for Ecuador was US$9,569.

However, if economic growth is taken into account, the link between income and life satisfaction becomes weak. From 2005 to 2011, the annual average economic growth in Mexico was 1.2%; economic growth in Costa Rica was 3.2%; and in Ecuador the annual average growth was 2.5%. Income in Costa Rica is consistent with what one would expect in terms of life satisfaction. However, growth and life satisfaction do not conform to economic theory based on the case of Ecuador. Factors unconnected with income seem key in explaining subjective well-being in poor countries. There are multiple studies of developing countries that attest to the weak link between income and subjective well-being. For example, the study of Kenny provides evidence supporting our findings.[31]

## *SUBJECTIVE HAPPINESS*

We explored next the happiness of the respondents from the three regions mentioned previously. We adopted the four-item happiness scale from Lyubomirsky and Lepper.[32] The uniqueness of the items used is that they consider happiness from the respondent's own perspective. This approach allows individuals to make an overall judgment of the extent to which they are happy or unhappy people. Since our goal is subjective happiness, it seems reasonable for individuals, however they feel inside, to become the ultimate judges of happiness.

We proceeded in the same fashion as we did in the case of satisfaction with life by looking at the descriptive statistics of subjective happiness. These statistics are revealed in Table 7.5. The overall mean (all) of all the items comprising happiness, showcased in Table 7.5, are higher than those from life satisfaction. The level of happiness is different across countries with respondents of Costa Rica reporting the highest level of happiness compared to the other two countries. Figure 7.1 provides an overview of the frequencies for all the respondents together of each one of the items.

**TABLE 7.5** Descriptive Statistics: Subjective Happiness in Mexico, Ecuador and Costa Rica

| Subjective Happiness | Mexico | Ecuador | Costa Rica | All | F |
|---|---|---|---|---|---|
| In general, I consider myself a happy person | 3.72[a] | 3.73[a] | 3.93 | 3.78 | 3.89 |
| Compared to most of my peers, I consider myself (more happy) | 3.84[b] | 3.60 | 3.72 | 3.71 | 4.10 |
| Some people are generally very happy (to a great deal) | 3.66[a] | 3.65[a] | 4.42 | 3.86 | 55.73 |
| Some people are generally not very happy (not at all) | 3.95[b] | 3.57[a] | 3.80 | 3.75 | 12.12 |

[a]Different than Costa Rica.
[b]Different than Ecuador.

Respondents from Costa Rica were significantly happier than those from Ecuador and Mexico. The latter two countries scored almost identical values in terms of happiness. These results are consistent with those obtained in the previous section with regard to satisfaction with life; in other words, respondents from Costa Rica were more satisfied with life and happier compared to those from Mexico and Ecuador. We explored the cognitive and motivational process of happiness, which include specifically social comparison (how individuals compare themselves to others). Social comparison has strong bearing with how individuals regard themselves and has relevance to provide insights into how individuals grasp with well-being.

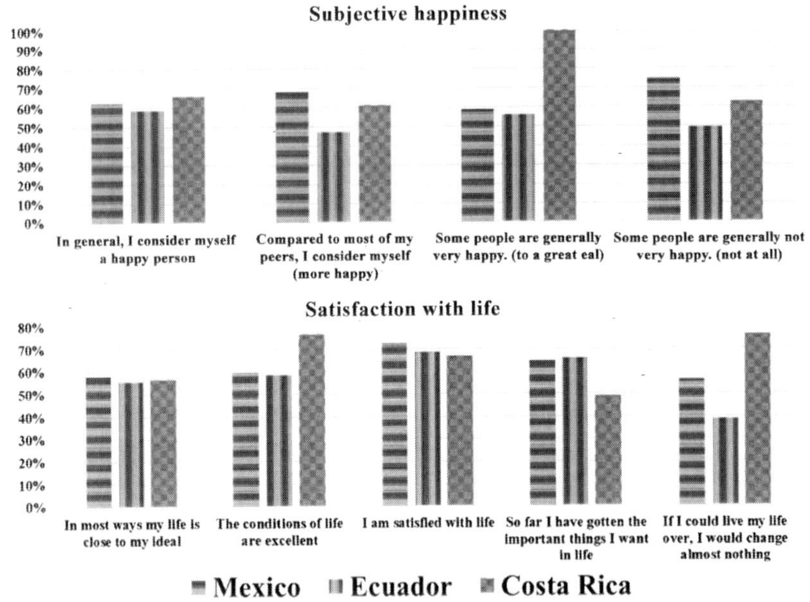


**FIGURE 7.1** Subjective Happiness Frequencies (All Countries).

Social comparison when applied in the context of our study paints a curious picture. Social comparison impacts differently the happiness profile of the respondents. Respondents from Mexico are relatively happier when they compared themselves to peers than when considering themselves as a happy person. The level of happiness increased with social comparison, which is contrary to what happens in Ecuador and Costa Rica. Respondents from Ecuador and Costa Rica perceive social comparison differently than Mexico. In their cases, social comparison prompts stronger unhappiness when they compared themselves as a happy person.

The results imply that poverty may not be completely related to possession of goods, but to social status. Studies of poverty in developing countries corroborate this assertion about the meaning of poverty as an element of social status.[33] In his book *The Wealth of Nations*, Adam Smith dwelled on this notion of poverty associated with social status when he asserted that poverty impacted happiness because it prompts social embarrassment. He recounted the social embarrassment that poor experienced when they walked without shoes during the mid-eighteenth century in England. Sen used a same concept borrowing from Smith by referencing a "linen shirt" as the threshold for social inclusion in village activities in the eighteenth century England.[34] The lack of social inclusion is associated to a structural lack of opportunities either caused by race or ethnic discrimination, or lack of required skill set to get a decent job, or simply being born from poor parents. In Sen's perspective, poor people simply lack the set of broad capabilities to socially catch up.[35]

## INCOME DEFINING HAPPINESS AND SATISFACTION WITH LIFE

Income, happiness, and satisfaction are interconnected in a positive way. Figure 7.2 showcases the positive relationship among income, happiness, and life satisfaction, implying increasing rate of happiness with rising personal income. On average, respondents with higher income or grouped in higher quintiles are happier and satisfied with their life. Table 7.6 reveals that happiness and satisfaction with life tend to move together with income. More income thus has positive effects on happiness and satisfaction. This result is consistent with what is generally found in the happiness literature. For example, the first quintile is significantly less satisfied with life compare to quintiles 4 and 5 (see Table 7.5). The first quintile includes the people with the lowest income, while the fifth quintile includes the people with the highest income.

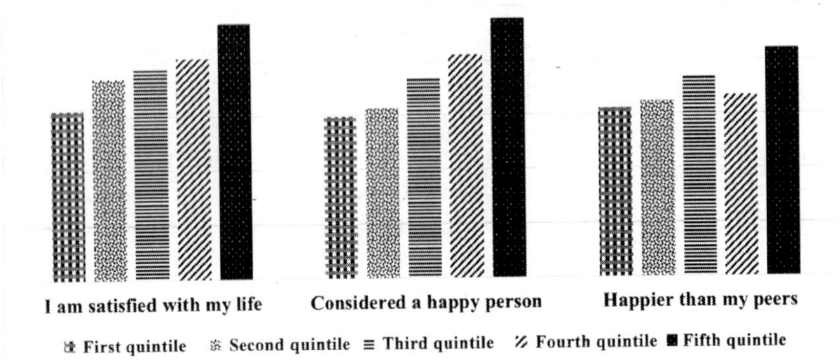


**FIGURE 7.2** Happiness and Satisfaction by Income Group.

However, being income poor as defined by the UNDP does not align with subjective well-being poor. For example, while 52.5% of the respondents are income poor by standard objective definitions, only 8.5% stated that they were unhappy. This result implies that needs of the poor are absolute rather than relative and may resonate with the theory of basic needs. Some needs seem fundamental to human existence such as subsistence, protection, and affection. Additionally, the poor seem more satisfied with life than being happy, as revealed by Table 7.6. The perceptions of satisfaction run higher than happiness till right before reaching the fourth quintile. The previous results regarding the relationship between income, happiness, and satisfaction is of a far more complex nature than originally anticipated.

Table 7.6 also reveals significant differences in satisfaction and happiness across the income groups. Quintile 1 is less satisfied with life compared to all the other four income groups, while quintile 5 is more satisfied with life only compared with quintile 1. Quintiles 2–4 are more satisfied than 1, while only quintile 2 is less satisfied than quintile 5. Quintiles 3–5 seem to enjoy the same level of life satisfaction.[36] In terms of happiness, quintiles 1 and 2 consider themselves less happy than the other quintiles, while quintiles 4 and 5 consider themselves happier than the other quintiles.[37] Finally, when comparison with others is concerned, two trends are observable. The first one refers to the lowest two quintiles: the poor are more satisfied than happy compared to how happy they are (happy person), and they seem even less happy when compared to others. Quintile 4 is miserable when compared to others, while quintile 5 is the happiest of all, even when comparing to others.[38]

**TABLE 7.6** Differences in Satisfaction and Happiness by Quintiles

| Income Group | I Am Satisfied with My Life | I Consider Myself a Happy Person | Compared to Most of My Peers, I Consider Myself More Happy |
|---|---|---|---|
| First quintile | 3.56 | 3.49 | 3.37 |
| Second quintile | 3.85 | 3.56 | 3.55 |
| Third quintile | 3.95 | 3.85 | 3.77 |
| Fourth quintile | 4.04 | 4.05 | 3.93 |
| Fifth quintile | 4.35 | 4.39 | 4.55 |
| *F*-statistic | 7.198 | 11.555 | 11.814 |
| Significance | 0.000 | 0.000 | 0.000 |

Our study detects from our respondents that while the poor are satisfied with their lives, they seem less happy. We did not find the "happy poor", which has been touted in the literature. Studies in Mexico, Bangladesh, Guatemala, and in Calcutta, India, found a happy poor despite living in dismal conditions. The suggestion of a "happy poor" seems counterintuitive, because it is unthinkable that a person who has to walk long distances to search for opportunity, get access to health, education, and drinking water is happy with this kind of life.

The perception exposed by quintile 3 suggests a threshold or baseline for social comparison in our case. The results reveal that quintile 1 seems resigned to its situation, while quintile 2 has aspirations to move up the ladder. However, there is much less difference among quintiles 3–5. Those who considered themselves rich (quintile 5) or average (quintiles 3 and 4) are not happy when they compare themselves to others. These observations suggest that the poor are more concerned with meeting their basic needs and realizing that goals make them happy. In contrast, the rich and average seem to face a threshold that separates basic needs from relational needs. When someone arrives in the social space beyond basic needs returns from more income result in diminishing returns. The results reveal that the first quintile seems resigned to its situation and shows no differences between the various well-being dimensions, while other quintiles have aspirations to move up the ladder.

The study by Graham and Lora indicates that as people move beyond a certain baseline, what others do, or have, becomes relevant in their lives. Rojas identified the baseline as those respondents who are neither unsatisfied nor satisfied; people who considered themselves as unsatisfied would be regarded as experienced poor. Thus, individuals experience poverty from a subjective well-being perspective if they experience low satisfaction. The latter definition of poverty is a departure from the conventional definition of poverty as income or consumption poor. Subjective poverty and income poverty may therefore have different poverty lines.

Applying the Rojas criteria to our sample implies that 11% of the respondents would be considered as being in experienced poverty. This number is very close to what Rojas found in his study, which was 14% were in experienced poverty. The 11% of our study means that the subjective poor is much less than the income poor if compared to the official poverty numbers revealed in Table 7.1. The relative income effects are smaller in subjective well-being at low income levels. Either income is not a good proxy of subjective well-being or the poor in our three countries have resigned themselves to their objective conditions and believe that no matter what they do, they will just give up hope for a better life and adjust to the condition that they are in. The literature identifies several coping strategies of the poor in adapting to their situations, such as denial of the misery, downward comparisons, and optimistic bias.

We exercised next an exploration of differences within each quintile. We applied a within-subjects analysis of variance (ANOVA) to explore the effects of happiness and life satisfaction on the subjects in each quintile. The results show that only quintiles 2 and 4 reveal differences from within when considering the three variables: satisfied with life; considered a happy person; and happier than my peers. Respondents in quintile 2 are significantly more satisfied than they were happy.

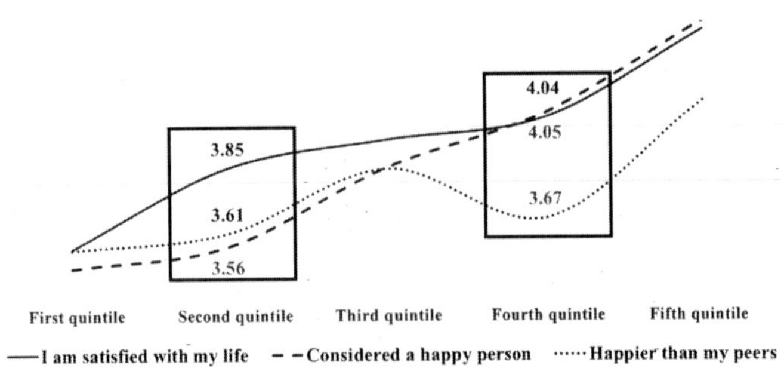


**FIGURE 7.3** Satisfaction and Happiness within Quintiles.

**Notes:** Significant mean differences between satisfaction with life and considered a happy person and happier than my peers within quintile 2; significant mean differences between satisfaction with life and happier than my peers within quintile 4.

A comparison of the three dimensions of well-being previously discussed (i.e., mainly satisfaction with life, considered a happy person, and happier than my peers) shows that every quintile group has a distinct and evolving view for each dimension (see Figure 7.3). The results from a within group comparison show that only two groups, the second and fourth quintiles, reveal differences from within when considering three dimensions of well-being. Respondents in the second quintile are significantly more satisfied with their life than they were happy. Similarly, the poor in the second quintile perceived a higher degree of satisfaction with life but they are less happy than their peers. On the other hand, those in the fourth quintile demonstrate a similar degree of happiness and satisfaction with life. However, this group seems less happy when they compare themselves to their peers. The possibility of achieving higher incomes or being in proximity to individuals with higher incomes might seduce them to look up the income ladder for a sense of achievement or happiness.

We also investigated the potential role of age in influencing subjective well-being. Figure 7.4 reveals the results. We did not find any difference across age cohorts, but we found significant differences within two age cohorts, i.e., generation Y and baby boomers. Both age cohorts comport in a similar fashion, in the sense that social comparison weighs on their perception of happiness. When those in these cohorts look at their peers, they feel significantly less happy.

The implications of Figures 7.2–7.4 are that all individuals assess their subjective well-being in the same way. Past experience, future expectations, and comparing to others certainly impact the assessment that individuals make regarding their lives. However, context and circumstances also impinge upon subjective well-being, which is consistent with evidence from the literature. For example, the case of Guatemala reveals that a set of economic, social, and livelihood related aspects have a bearing on the lives of the poor.[39]

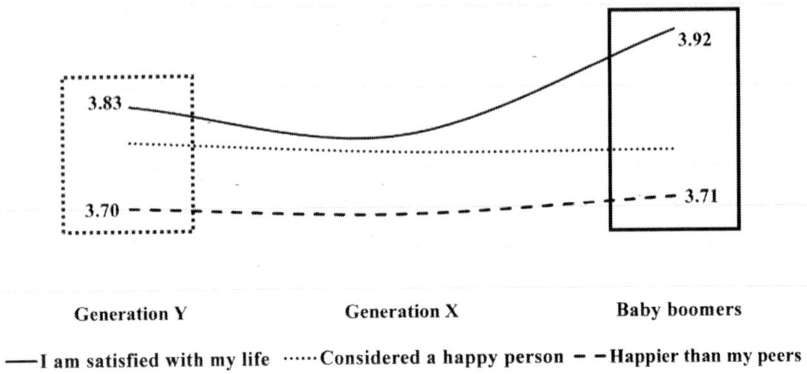


**FIGURE 7.4** Satisfaction and Happiness Within Age Cohorts.
**Notes:** Significant mean differences between satisfaction with life and happier than my peers within generation Y; significant mean differences between satisfaction with life and happier than my peers within baby boomers.

In summary, perceptions of the poor differ from their objective reality. They rank health, education, family, and work in descending order as their priority life domains and as their most important motivation in life. There is a clear hierarchy in life conditions; physical functioning is followed by social functioning (connections). The role of money in determining the priority in life domains, while important, is ambiguous. The perception of the poor regarding subjective well-being is more complex than the one derived from the literature. The poor are satisfied with life but they are less happy. We did not find "happy poor". Those in quintile 2 seem to drive this paradox of being satisfied with their lives, while at the same time, not feeling happy. In the next chapter we will investigate what are the conditions that drive this paradox in Mexico, Costa Rica, and Ecuador, and the role of tourism development in feeding this paradox.

## REFERENCES

Akerlof, G.; Kranton, R. *Identity Economics. How Our Identities Shape Our Work, Wages, and Well-being*; Princeton University Press: New Jersey, 2010.

Banerjee, A.; Duflo, E. *Poor Economics. A Radical Rethinking of the Way to Fight Global Poverty*; Public Affairs: New York, NY, 2011.

Barros, C.; Barros, V.; Dieke, P. Tourism and Human Development in Mozambique: An Analysis for Inhambane Province, 2012. http://pascal.iseg.utl.pt/~cesa/files/Doc_trabalho/WP100.pdf (retrieved Sep 12, 2014).

Bimonte, S.; Faralla, V. Happiness and nature-based vacations. *Ann. Tour. Res*. 2014, 46, 176–178.

Bok, S. The Politics of Happiness. 2010. Princeton University Press: Princeton, NJ.

Bourguignon, F. *Comment to 'Multidimensioned Approaches to Welfare Analysis' by Maasoumi, E.* In *Handbook of Income Inequality Measurement*; Silber, J., Ed.; Kluwer Academic: Dordrecht, The Netherlands, 1999; pp 477–484.

Camfield, L.; Choudhury, K.; Devine, J. *Relationships, Happiness and Well-being: Insights from Bangladesh*; Economic and Social Research Council: Bath, UK, 2006. [WeD Working Paper 14].

Conde, E.; Amaya, C.; Gonzalez, E. Factores que influyen en el comportamiento del consumidor turista: el case de Manzanillo, Mexico. *Teoria y Praxis*. 2013, 14, 109–139.

Corvo, P. The pursuit of happiness and the globalized tourist. *Soc. Indic. Res*. 2011, 102(1), 93–97.

Croes, R.; Semrad, K. *Forward Progress: A Time to Act. Working together for the Future Success of Tourism Development in Guayaquil. The Dick Pope Sr*; Institute for Tourism Studies: Orlando, FL, 2012.

Cummins, R. The domains of life satisfaction: an attempt to order chaos. *Soc. Indic. Res*. 1996, 38, 303–328.

Davis, P. Power-resources and Social Policy in Bangladesh: A Life-History Perspective. Doctoral Dissertation, University of Bath, Bath, UK, 2005.

De Neve, J.; Diener, E.; Tay, L.; Xuereb, C. The objective benefits of subjective well-being [CEP Discussion Paper No. 1236], 2013

Diener, E. The satisfaction with life scale. *J. Pers. Assess*. 1985, 49(1), 71–75.

Easterlin, R. A.; Angelescu, L. *Modern Economic Growth and Quality of Life: Cross-sectional and Time Series Evidence*. In *Handbook of Social Indicators and Quality of Life Research*; Land, K. C., Michalos, A. C., Sirgy, M. J., Eds.; Springer: Dordrecht, The Netherlands, 2012; pp 113–136.

Gasparini, L.; Escudero, W.; Marchionni, M.; Olivieri, S. *Objective and Subjective Deprivation*. In *Paradox and Perceptions. Measuring Quality of Life in Latin America*; Graham, C., Lora, E., Eds.; The Brookings Institution: Washington, DC, 2009, 22-56.

Graham, C.; Lora, E.; Eds. *Paradox and Perceptions. Measuring Quality of Life in Latin America*; The Brookings Institution: Washington, DC, 2009a.

Graham, C.; Lora, E. *Health Perceptions and Quality of Life in Latin America*. In *Paradox and Perceptions. Measuring Quality of Life in Latin America*; Graham, C., Lora, E., Eds.; The Brookings Institution: Washington, DC, 2009b, 158-191.

Guardiola, J.; Garcia-Muñoz, T. Subjective Well-being and Basic Needs: Evidence From Rural Guatemala, 2009. http://www.ugr.es/~teoriahe/RePEc/gra/wpaper/thepapers09_03.pdf (retrieved Sep 8, 2014).

Guardiola, J.; Gonzalez-Gomez, F.; Grajales, A. The influence of water access in subjective well-being. Some evidence in Yucatan, Mexico. *Soc. Indic. Res*. 2011, doi: 10.1007/s11205-011-9925-3.

Heltberg, R.; Hossain, N.; Reva, A. *Living through Crises: How the Food, Fuel, and Financial Shocks Affect the Poor*; World Bank: Washington, DC, 2012.

Herrera, J.; Razafindrakoto, M.; Roubaud, F. *The Determinants of Subjective Poverty: A Comparative Analysis in Madagascar and Peru. (Working paper DT/2006-01)*; DIAL: Paris, 2006.

Kenny, C. Does development make you happy? Subjective wellbeing and economic growth in developing countries. *Soc. Indic. Res*. 2005, 73, 199–219.

Layard, R. *Happiness: Lessons from A New Science*; Penguin: New York, NY, 2005.

Lora, E.; Chaparro, J. *The Conflictive Relationship between Satisfaction and Income*. In *Paradox and Perceptions. Measuring Quality of Life in Latin America*; Graham, C., Lora, E., Eds.; The Brookings Institution: Washington, DC, 2009, 57-95.

Lora, E.; Chaparro, J.; Rodriguez, M. *Satisfaction beyond Income*. In *Paradox and Perceptions. Measuring Quality of Life in Latin America*; Graham, C., Lora, E., Eds.; The Brookings Institution: Washington, DC, 2009, 96-117.

Lyubomirsky, S.; Lepper, H. A measure of subjective happiness: preliminary reliability and construct validation. *Soc. Indic. Res*. 1999, 46, 137–155.

Peña, X. *The Formal and Informal Sectors in Colombia. (Country Case Study on Labor Market Segmentation)*; ILO: Geneva, 2013.

Pradhan, M.; Ravallion, M. Measuring poverty using qualitative perceptions of consumption adequacy. *Rev. Econ. Stat*. 2000, 82, 462–471.

Rojas, M. Experienced poverty and income poverty in Mexico: a subjective well-being approach. *World Dev*. 2008, 6, 1078–1093.

Schneider, F.; Buehn, A.; Montenegro, C. New estimates for the shadow economies all over the world. *Int. Econ. J*. 2010, 24(4), 443–461.

Semrad, K.; Bartels, J. An inward look using backward economic linkages in a developing country: the case of Puntarenas, Costa Rica. *Worldwide Hospital. Tour. Theme J*. 2014, 6(3), 244–260.

Sen, A. *Poverty and Famines: An Essay on Entitlements and Deprivation*; Clarendon Press: Oxford, UK, 1982.

Tasci, A.; Croes, R.; Bartels, J. Rise and fall of community-based tourism: facilitators, inhibitors and outcomes. *Worldwide Hospital. Tour. Theme J*. 2014, 6(3), 293–300.

Veblen, T. *The Theory of the Leisure Class*; Penguin: New York, NY, 1987.

## ENDNOTES

[1]For a discussion about the relationship between income and happiness, see, for example, Lora and Chaparro (2009).

[2]We followed the footsteps of "Voices of Poor" alluded to in Chapter 2 and the work of Heltberg et al. (2012) which recounted the coping strategies of the poor in eight countries by listening to the poor.

[3]For example, Veblen (1987) stated that: "… a satiation of the average or general desire for wealth is out of the question … no general increase of the community's wealth can make any approach to satiating this need, the ground of which is the desire of every one to excel every one else in the accumulation of goods."

[4]See Akerlof and Kranton (2010).

[5]For further discussion, see Banerjee and Duflo (2011).

[6]See Graham and Lora (2009a,b).

[7]See, for example, Graham and Lora (2009a,b).

[8]See, for example, De Neve et al. (2013).

[9]For a discussion about the differences between objective and subjective approaches of quality of life, see, for example, Easterlin and Angelescu (2012).

[10]See Rojas (2008).

[11]See http://www.imf.org/external/pubs/ft/fandd/2012/06/singh.htm, retrieved September 10, 2014. For an estimation of shadow economies, see, for example, Schneider et al. (2010).

[12]See, for example, Informal economy swallows Latin American workers. Retrieved August 1, 2014, from http://www.globalpost.com/dispatch/news/regions/americas/120702/informal-economy-swallows-latin-american-workers.

[13]See, for example, Peña (2013).

[14]See Pradhan and Ravallion (2000)

[15]See Herrera et al. (2006).

[16]See Guardiola and Garcia-Muñoz (2009).

[17]The authors are very appreciative of the assistance they received in the survey design and data collection from Dr. Carlos Amaya of the University of Colima, Mexico, for Dr. Jorge Macchiavelo from the University ECOTEC in Guayaquil, Ecuador, and from Dr. Jorge Bartels from the University of Costa Rica, the Pacific Campus. For a discussion on Manzanillo, see, for example, Conde et al (2013).

[18]PyME is the Spanish acronym for small and medium enterprises.

[19]Manzanillo is located in the state of Colima, Mexico. Its location at the Pacific Coast of Mexico prompted the site as an important trade and logistic hub of Mexico, while its natural resources (beaches) are converting the site also into a tourist destination. The state of Colima has experienced dwindling activities in the tourist sector and is looking for pathways to re-energize the sector. For further discussion, see for example Perez et al. (2013). Puntarenas is one of the most popular tourism regions in Costa Rica given its islands, inlets, beaches and access to beautiful natural sites. Costa Rica is a well-known eco destination in the world and the government is currently trying to recalibrate the tourism activities in order to bring more benefits to the local populations. For further discussion, see, for example, Tasci et al. (2014) and Semrad and Bartels (2014). Guayaquil is the most important economic and financial hub of Ecuador. Guayaquil has intermittently paid attention to spawning tourism as an important engine of growth since the last decade in order to diversify its local economy and to create more jobs due to high unemployment. For further discussion, see for example, Croes and Semrad (2012).

[20]See Rojas (2008).

[21]For a discussion of the items, see, for example, Graham and Lora (2009).

[22]The reason for applying the Mann–Whitney *U* test is because we did not assume any normal distribution of the data and the aim was to rank each one of the life domains.

[23]See Guardiola et al. (2011).

[24]See, for example, Davis (2005).

[25]See Banerjee and Duflo (2011).

[26]See, for example, Camfield et al. (2006).

[27]See, for example, Guardiola et al. (2011), Lora and Chaparro (2009), and Lora et al. (2009).

[28]See, for example, Camfield et al. (2006).

[29]See Diener (1985). See also Cummins (1996) for a discussion on the topic.

[30]See Gasparini et al. (2009).

[31]See Kenny (2005).

[32]See Lyubomirsky and Lepper (1999). For a critical view on the factors influencing happiness, see also Layard (2005).

[33]See, for example, Kenny (2005).

[34]See Sen (1982).

[35]Bourguignon (1999) examines in depth the consequences of relative poverty and social exclusion.

[36]ANOVA results for "satisfaction with life": Levene statistic = 0.6, *df1* = 4, *df2* = 593, sig. = 0.66, sum of squares = 26.29, *df* = 4, mean square = 6.57, *F* = 7.2, sig. = 0.000. (1) Quintile 1: is significantly lower that all others; (2) quintile 2: is only different than quintiles 1 and 5; (3) quintile 3: is only different than quintile 1; (4) quintile 4: is only different than quintile 1; and (5) quintile 5: is only different than quintile 1.

[37]ANOVA results for "I consider myself a happy person": Levene statistic = 1.92, *df1* = 4, *df2* = 594, sig. = 0.11, sum of squares = 36.32, *df* = 4, mean square = 9.08, *F* = 11.56, sig. = 0.000. (1) Quintile 1: is only different than quintiles 3–5; (2) quintile 2: is only different than quintiles 3–5; (3) quintile 3: is only different than quintiles 1 and 5; (4) quintile 4: is only different than quintiles 1 and 2; and (5) quintile 5: is only different than quintiles 1–3.

[38]ANOVA results for "compared to most of my peers, I consider myself more happy": Levene statistic = 2.25, *df1* = 4, *df2* = 595, sig. = 0.06, sum of squares = 47.45, *df* = 4, mean square = 11.86, *F* = 11.81, sig. = 0. (1) Quintile 1: is only different than quintiles 4 and 5; (2) quintile 2: is only different than quintile 5; (3) quintile 3: is only different than quintiles 4 and 5; (4) quintile 4: is only different than quintiles 1 and 5; and (5) quintile 5: is only different than all quintiles.

[39]See Guardiola and Garcia-Muñoz (2009).

**CHAPTER 8**

# THROUGH THE LOOKING GLASS: TOURISM DEVELOPMENT AND THE POVERTY PARADOX

## CONTENTS

## INTRODUCTION

The poor perceive tourism development differently when thinking in terms of happiness or life satisfaction. Contrary to studies that discovered "happy poor", our findings provide a more nuanced.picture of the poor.[1] We found a satisfied, but unhappy poor. Life satisfaction is about meaning in life, while happiness is about emotions, and emotions are fleeting. When the poor reflect on life and on tourism development, they perceive tourism as positive. The channel through which this positive perception is articulated is opportunities. But, interestingly, when they consider happiness, those same opportunities prompt a negative perception. Tourism development, channeled through opportunities, does not seem to overcome the everyday struggles of the poor.

The phrase "satisfied but unhappy poor" is a paradox. We saw that the relationship of happiness and satisfaction is mutually reinforcing, but when tourism development is introduced in the dynamic relationship, the perception regarding tourism development changes. Is this paradox a result of how the poor perceive satisfaction as what they possibly can achieve in life (adaptation) different from happiness as what they desire for in life? A case can be made that tourism jobs in, for example, Costa Rica are of a part-time or seasonal nature, affecting advancement opportunities of the poor. Lack of job security is devastating to the psyche of the poor. Job insecurity is demotivating and spawns much distress. The poor work long hours, in most cases more than 48 hours a week, trying to make ends meet.[2]

Although tourism can increase the income of the poor, thereby lifting them out of poverty, the way the poor experience the impact of tourism (e.g., displacement, job insecurity, unpredictable income flow) shapes the power of tourism in combating poverty.[3] In this chapter, we will investigate why the poor entertain this juxtaposed reality of tourism development, which is being satisfied with life but unhappy?

## THE MEANING OF TOURISM DEVELOPMENT FOR THE POOR

Tourism development is a broad concept that reveals multiple meanings depending on the person and context. In general, tourism development is conceived as a means to advance human development. This activity creates jobs, spawns income and opportunities, and provides government taxes to pay for other relevant societal needs as well as an activity that spreads personal and social malaise, such as distressed behavior, addiction, family fragmentation, cultural infringement, social disruption, and anxiety.[4] How the poor perceive these tourism externalities as they impact their lives has been under researched in the tourism literature.[5] The reason for this omission is surprising since poverty has received heightened attention from social sciences, academe, and the international community.

The sample for the upcoming discussion considers only two regions to investigate how the poor perceive tourism development, namely, the city of Guayaquil in Ecuador and the city of Manzanillo in Mexico. Understanding whether tourism is perceived as opportunity or harm is important for policy and planning purposes. A total of ten different items about tourism development were identified as part of our investigation.[6] The tourism development items were originally scanned from the tourism literature and canvassed from conversations with a number of experts and academics from each region. Respondents rated the ten tourism development items on a five-point Likert scale to indicate their level of agreement. Table 8.1 lists the descriptive statistics for the items.

**TABLE 8.1** Tourism Items

| Tourism Factors | Mean | Standard Deviation |
|---|---|---|
| Satisfied with the tourism planning and development that is taking place | 3.72 | 1.03 |
| The development of tourism has improved the image and cleaning of my region | 3.93 | 0.95 |
| The development of tourism protects the environment my region | 3.79 | 0.99 |
| Tourism promotes an increase in the welfare of the residents | 3.95 | 0.88 |
| Tourism improves the infrastructure and public utilities | 3.63 | 1.17 |
| Tourism increases the pride of the residents in the local culture | 3.90 | 1.01 |
| Tourism helps preserve the cultural identity and heritage of my region | 3.89 | 1.05 |
| Tourism promotes the participation and the enjoyment of local arts and culture | 3.96 | 0.96 |
| Local entrepreneurs benefit the majority of the tourists | 3.98 | 1.01 |
| Tourism creates a variety of jobs for residents in the community | 4.01 | 0.91 |

Table 8.2 reveals the list of items valued by respondents. All items valued by the poor are positive, suggesting that respondents identify tourism as an opportunity and not an imposition. Positive perception regarding tourism development indicates that according to respondents, the poor would be interested in engaging in tourism activities. We encountered this feeling in the multiple fieldwork visits that we undertook in countries in Latin America. Tourism seems a lifeline for the poor to escape poverty.

For example, a beach vendor in the Montañita Commune in Ecuador talked about what tourism and what the tourist represents for him in terms of sustenance for his family:

> *"tourists are the only asset that we have ...... we are interested in knowing how to bring them to our beaches ...... is the only way we can subsist and provide to our families"; "as it was said earlier ...... we are poor ...... we are very poor ...... our work only ...... whatever we make ...... simply helps to feed the family day by day ...... we subsist day by day."*

The implication is that the poor see benefits in being involved with tourism. Therefore, a positive perception about tourism represents an important first economic step if the poor are willing to seize opportunities stemming from tourism development. Several studies document similar results with regards to the support of people for tourism development. For example, residents in the very economic limited developed area of the *Flowers Route* in El Salvador expressed their support for tourism development from a community-based perspective. That area in question is a relatively poor area in that country.[7]

**TABLE 8.2** Analysis of Variance Results for Tourism Items by Country

| Tourism Factors | Mexico | Ecuador | Mean Difference | F-statistic | Significance |
|---|---|---|---|---|---|
| Tourism increases the pride of the residents in the local culture | 3.57 | 4.13 | 0.56 | 45.70 | 0.000 |
| The development of tourism has improved the image and cleaning of my region | 3.71 | 4.09 | 0.38 | 24.52 | 0.000 |
| Tourism promotes an increase in the welfare of the residents | 3.66 | 4.17 | 0.51 | 53.66 | 0.000 |
| Tourism creates a variety of jobs for residents in the community | 3.78 | 4.18 | 0.39 | 28.83 | 0.000 |

**TABLE 8.2** *(Continued)*

| Tourism Factors | Mexico | Ecuador | Mean Difference | F-statistic | Significance |
|---|---|---|---|---|---|
| Tourism improves the infrastructure and public utilities | 3.71 | 3.56 | -0.15 | 2.55 | 0.111 |
| Tourism promotes the participation and the enjoyment of local arts and culture | 3.54 | 4.16 | 0.62 | 61.06 | 0.000 |
| Satisfied with the tourism planning and development that is taking place. | 3.46 | 3.92 | 0.46 | 30.52 | 0.000 |
| Local entrepreneurs benefit the majority of the tourists | 3.63 | 4.23 | 0.60 | 56.14 | 0.000 |
| Tourism increases the pride of the residents in the local culture | 3.61 | 4.21 | 0.60 | 62.88 | 0.000 |
| The development of tourism protects the environment my region | 3.69 | 3.85 | 0.16 | 4.00 | 0.046 |

We explored whether respondents from Mexico and Ecuador differ in terms of how they value each one of the items identified as components of tourism development. Table 8.2 indicates that significant differences in perception among respondents from Mexico and Ecuador respondents exist regarding the value of tourism development. Respondents from Ecuador have a higher perception of tourism development when compared to those from Mexico. The only not significant difference is in terms of infrastructure. The highlighted contrast between Mexico and Ecuador may stem from the position of the product life cycle. Respondents from Guayaquil (Ecuador) have been involved with tourism longer than those from Manzanillo (Mexico), and may therefore be aware of the benefits emanating from tourism development.

## PERCEPTION ON THE TOURISM PRODUCT, HERITAGE, AND OPPORTUNITIES

The ten items labeled previously loaded in three unique factors. These three factors were identified on the basis of factorial analysis. These factors are tourism product, heritage, and economic opportunities. The factor tourism product consists of tourism planning, image, environment, social welfare, and infrastructure. The second factor – heritage – involves arts, strong tradition, and cultural growth, while the third factor, opportunities, entails local businesses and jobs. Together, these factors explain 63.73% of the perception of tourism development. Table 8.3 showcases the components of each factor. Overall, product was the most significant component of tourism development, explaining 34.07% of the variance, followed by heritage (18.05%) and opportunities (11.61%).

**TABLE 8.3** Perception of Tourism Development in Mexico and Ecuador

| Tourism Factors | Factor Loading | Variance Explained (%) | Cronbach Alpha |
|---|---|---|---|
| Factor #1: tourism product | | | |
| Satisfied with the tourism planning and development that is taking place | 0.790 | 34.07 | 0.77 |
| The development of tourism has improved the image and cleaning of my region | 0.778 | | |
| The development of tourism protects the environment my region | 0.761 | | |
| Tourism promotes an increase in the welfare of the residents | 0.649 | | |
| Tourism improves the infrastructure and public utilities | 0.580 | | |
| Factor #2: heritage | | | |
| Tourism increases the pride of the residents in the local culture | 0.837 | 18.05 | 0.76 |
| Tourism helps preserve the cultural identity and heritage of my region | 0.798 | | |
| Tourism promotes the participation and the enjoyment of local arts and culture | 0.602 | | |
| Factor #3: opportunities | | | |
| Local entrepreneurs benefit the majority of the tourists | 0.884 | 11.61 | 0.71 |
| Tourism creates a variety of jobs for residents in the community | 0.831 | | |

The first factor – product – reveals why respondents would like to get involved with tourism. The tourism product provides more than income opportunities (e.g., jobs and vending). It provides opportunities of accessibility to services and infrastructure (access to health, training, water); to natural resources (e.g., land); to social connection. Access to a wider web of social connection is an important source for opportunities: opportunities for landing a job, for support during crisis, and to raise their quality of life.[8] Indeed, the lack of all these resources defines poverty, and the poor are aware of the necessity to get involved in order to keep hope alive to overcome the stressful daily conditions.

We noticed firsthand this clamor of the poor to participate in tourism development when we visited a poor village in the coastal area of Ecuador. We attended a meeting in a church in the Venus de Valdivia commune to discuss a tourism project with the villagers. The villagers were initially suspicious, reluctant to talk to us, and outright hostile. The attendees displayed resentment and animosity toward us, showing suspicion and mistrust. After explaining the purpose of our visit, the attendees were more at ease and keen to participate. For example, one of the "cabildos" (council man), very motivated and emotional, indicated:

> *the importance of having you here is the project potential ....... these people are simple, people definitely want to progress ...... thank you and excuse us ...... you're here at home, you can get to any of our homes any them ....... and you will be greeted with great affection, we are a big family.*
>
> *Immediately after, the "presidente" (the highest authority in the commune) of the Manglarito Commune declared how important it was that they were included in the meeting and given a voice that could help them by saying:*
>
> *all our people have inspiration and want our projects to become a reality ...... we want to dazzle everyone ...... excuse me my friend but ....... we are tired of projects, and hopefully with you ...... dear friends ...... our words do not remain in your heart but in projects, thank you very much.*

They showed hope, optimism, and anticipation. Very emotionally, a "comunero" from Manglarito that works as a mason by trade said:

> *I hope you take something of what you hear here today and let people in the United States know ....... hopefully with time we will have something, hopefully God can pay handsomely. Thank you.*

The lack of voice and power of the poor is more apparent when the poor try to communicate their ideas and find possible financing for growing their farms or small businesses. A farmer from the Santa Elena Commune expressed his frustration by recounting his experiences with various financial institutions. While revealing his challenges he mentioned:

*The bank manager is someone who doesn't even like the "comuneros" ...... any documentation we provide he literally throws in the garbage ...... they cannot help us because we are "cholitos"[slur to depict indigenous people] ... but yes ... we are intelligent ... we know what we are doing...what happens is that Ecuador politics is like that ...... the big society and the people on the top only need to pick up the phone and get whatever ... and us ... we can't even get a five hundred dollar "quirografario"[Unsecured loan]*

Tourism development affects the livelihood of the poor more than any other groups. The benefits accruing from tourism to individuals and households has the power to transform the lives of the poor for the better. In a recent study in Puntarenas (Costa Rica), one of the participants in the study narrated the relevance of tourism for their livelihood: "Tourism that is affiliated with the sea is the main source of Puntarenas (Costa Rica) employment and livelihood for locals. It is important that we protect this industry for the economic welfare of the people who live here" (p. 252).[9] Similarly, Shakya asserts in her study regarding tourism in Nepal that the poor in remote areas of the country want to be involved with tourism, because they understand the potential of tourism. But they want to be treated as "rational decision makers" who pursue their best economic option within limited opportunities.[10]

The study of Semrad and Bartels narrated how the poor wanted participation in tourism planning in Puntarenas and how the pitfalls of participation are marring opportunities for the poor.[11] Mitigating vulnerabilities that are imminent in tourism development requires involvement with the tourism product, and therefore, considering involvement in tourism planning is a reasonable and sensible desire.[12] Health hazards, natural disasters, economic downturns, or man-made disasters can have lasting negative impact on the tourism industry. The poor seem aware of tourism vulnerability and desire participation in the evolvement of the tourism product.

The concern for defining and redefining the tourism product is also directly related to the concern for heritage. Place plays an important role in product development and the attraction of many countries in Latin America and other developing countries resides in their past. Bringing the past to the present, and thereby providing opportunities to the poor is an awareness that is slowly getting traction with the poor. The poor are interested in economic opportunities as well as keeping the tourism product "real" or authentic.[13] They seem to have a sense of tourism self-image and feel pride in being part of a vital industry.[14] During our field research in the province of Guayas in 2008 we found that cultural identity, culture, and community pride help alleviate the psychological stress caused by poverty. For instance, poor communities in the cities of Venus de Valdivia and San Antonio in Ecuador maintain their cultural identity through celebrations and festivals. For the poor, the substance of participating in these types of activities cannot be overstated. It is one of the most important assets. Even if financial sacrifices have to be made, the poor will divest themselves to participate.

One of the comuneros from Cadeate made reference to a festival that took place the week before our visit and indicated:

> *last night we were celebrating 15 years of making bread … this is a great opportunity to be united by savoring these delicious flavors of the bread they make … sales were not good … but it was a great feeling.*

On the other hand, the lack of opportunities to get involved can suppress the poor and they will berate any organization that overlook or neglect them. This was the case in Venus de Valdivia, were the comuneros expressed their disappointment with the Central Bank for not recognizing or promoting the archeological and cultural pieces of their region during a major museum exhibition in the city of Guayaquil.

Indeed, most regions where poor people live are rich in heritage and cultural sites. For example, the North coast of Peru is a site that harbors a wealth of Pre-Inca cultural heritage. People living in those areas are poor and they understand that spotlighting the past through tourism development could be a pathway to enhance their quality of life.[15] In the Central American region, there are 17 cultural properties declared patrimony of humanity by United Nations Educational, Scientific, and Cultural Organization (UNESCO).[16] The poor are also aware that living in area designated as heritage has its pitfalls. Heritage can be a double-edged sword; heritage can be an opportunity but also a blight.[17] For example, several Latin American cities are faced with the tension between gentrification, city branding, and the regeneration of their cities (creation of livable cities) equally accessible by users and visitors. Street vendors have been displaced from their livelihood in cities such as Quito, Cuenca, and Cuzco to infested neighborhoods with crime, poverty, and urban decay.[18]

These cities are popular tourist sites and listed as UNESCO World Heritage Sites. The displacement process neglected voices of the poor and inflicted a stressful situation for these people living in these cities who are at economic and social disadvantages. A recent publication of the World Bank talked about the historic and economic relevance of heritage sites in developing countries but spent few or no words about the consequences of displacement. A chapter in that publication from Rojas specifically refers to stakeholders, the expanding of their use values of heritage buildings, and discusses the experience of the applied structure of the use values of these stakeholders in several heritage projects in Latin America such as Oaxaca, Quito, Salvador de Bahia, and Valparaiso. However, this chapter about Latin American heritage experiences did not utter one word about the displacement hardships imposed on the poor due to these projects.[19]

Displacement hardships have been document in several studies about heritage sites in Latin America. For example, Cuenca, Ecuador, listed as UNESCO World Heritage Site since 1999, experienced the displacement of low-status groups from the city center, *El Ejido*, to be replaced by commercial buildings or other functional use to cater to more affluent users.[20] A similar situation of displacement happened in the historic center of *San Felipe* in Panama City. San Felipe was designated by the UNESCO as world heritage site in 1997. Subsequently, the street vendors, renters, and squatters were displaced by affluent newcomers and the site lost its colorfulness, diversity, and attractiveness.[21]

Opportunities are the final factor. Tourism brings opportunities for the poor to overcome the barriers that keep them in poverty. Getting a job is one of the most powerful opportunities for escaping poverty.[22] Tourism jobs in many occasions are more attractive than subsistence agricultural jobs, because the latter is hard work, low paying, and dependent on the vagaries of the weather. Tourism spawns multiple job opportunities for women in developing countries thereby empowering them to direct more resources to children. Several studies pointed out that when women have more resources, their children eat more.[23] For example, the PROGRESA program in Mexico puts more money in women's hands. Because tourism provides so many job opportunities for women, tourism is a powerful vehicle to improve the quality of life situation in the households. According to the International Labor Organization, women represent between 60% and 70% of the tourism and hospitality labor force.[24]

But tourism is also helpful in other ways: tourism provides opportunities for the poor to engage in selling their products and services to the tourists, thereby providing them with a source of income. Mitchell and Ashley report how tourism in the Gambia has generated a large number of jobs in the informal sector through the creation of entrepreneurial ventures.[25] Tourism is a powerful vehicle to reach the poor through multiple channels such as vending, tour guiding, transportation, food, and employment. As we already recounted, these opportunities can better the life conditions and subjective well-being of the poor. But the poor seem to realize that their participation in the protection of the tourism product and their heritage is required if tourism is to serve as a platform for them to escape poverty. We already referred to some heritage projects in Chapter 2, such as the inscription of the Ichapeken Piesta Moxos onto the 2012 UNESCO Representative List of Intangible Cultural Heritage of Humanity and the Museo Yacuma in the Bolivian Amazon and the North Coast of Peru.[26]

## THE IMPACT OF TOURISM DEVELOPMENT ON HAPPINESS

We already noted that income poverty may not necessarily have the same meaning as experienced poverty. Tourism development may impact the dissonance in perception and reality of the poor. Therefore, it is important to explore how the perception of tourism development affects happiness of the poor. In other words, what is the impact of tourism development on happiness? To answer these questions, we regressed the three factors – tourism product, heritage, and opportunities – on happiness. The results are revealed in Table 8.4. Only two factors indicate statistically significance level at the 5%, namely, heritage and opportunities. Opportunities and heritage have an almost identical impact on happiness; happiness has the largest impact on happiness, followed by heritage. The low $R^2$ of 0.054 implies that the determination of tourism make it harder to predict happiness.

**TABLE 8.4** Tourism Im\pact on Happiness

| | B | t | Significance |
|---|---|---|---|
| Constant | -0.003 | -0.065 | 0.948 |
| Factor #1 tourism product | 0.070 | 1.331 | 0.184 |
| Factor #2 tourism heritage | 0.156 | 2.968 | 0.003 |
| Factor #3 tourism opportunities | 0.158 | 3.013 | 0.003 |

Dependent variable: happiness *F*-statistic = 6.55 ($P < 0.001$); $R^2 = 0.046$.

We delved deeper in the dataset to discover which other influences are at play in defining happiness. We included next satisfaction with life as control variable together with the three factors. We assumed that satisfaction with life has a bearing on happiness of individuals. This assumption stems from the social literature regarding subjective well-being.[27] As mentioned in the beginning of this chapter, happiness and life satisfaction overlap, but they are not the same. Life satisfaction is about meaning in life while happiness is about emotions, and emotions are fleeting. Life satisfaction may therefore make someone happy or unhappy. The relationship can bear either a positive or negative sign. The results are presented in Table 8.5.

Controlling for satisfaction with life renders heritage insignificant, but reduces the effect of factor #3 opportunities significantly compared to the previous model in Table 8.5. However, satisfaction with life substantially increased the explanatory power of the model. The determination power is 26% (increased from 0.054). In this model, factor #3 opportunities remained statistically significant and had the positive sign. Satisfaction with life has a strong impact on happiness.

**TABLE 8.5** Tourism Impact on Happiness: Controlling for Satisfaction with Life

| | B | t | Significance |
|---|---|---|---|
| Constant | -0.003 | -0.057 | 0.955 |
| Factor #1 tourism product | 0.008 | 0.168 | 0.866 |
| Factor #2 tourism heritage | 0.076 | 1.603 | 0.110 |
| Factor #3 tourism opportunities | 0.163 | 3.470 | 0.001 |
| Satisfaction w/life | 0.465 | 9.730 | 0.000 |

Dependent variable: happiness *F*-statistic = 29.91 ($P < 0.001$); $R^2 = 0.260$.

We conducted a final analysis that was to include sociodemographic control variables to the model. More specifically, we added as control variables education, gender, income, and work. We conducted a stepwise regression technique in order to discern the change of impact of tourism development on happiness. The results are revealed in Table 8.6. Age and gender were not significant and this result is consistent with similar findings in a study conducted in Guatemala.[28] Only education and income turned out to be significant predictors. Clearly education has a larger bearing on happiness compared to income, which implies that happiness is conceived by respondents as being larger than income.

That education bears larger than income on happiness is surprising. Banerjee and Duflo found that 14%–50% of children do not go to school despite education being free in most developing countries.[29] This may be an indication of parental resistance for sending their children to school. When considering education, parents invest in their children in the present while hoping that their children will bear the fruits later in life. The poor are poor precisely because they lack the resources, like jobs, health, and connections to support their capability to be educated. Because they lack resources, it is hard for them to think about or invest in education. These constraints would give the impression that the poor do not care about education.

However, evidence suggests that the poor do care about education.[30] In our encounters with the poor in several Latin American countries we got the impression that they are aware of the importance of education in providing opportunities for a better life. During the multiple conversations that we had with the "comuneros" in Guayas, Ecuador, we discovered this desire for education. For example, a comunero from Esmeraldas stressed the relevance of education to better their lives and lamented the lack of support to get an education:

> *they have no mercy on us, we have the intelligence, we have hands, we have everything to work, unfortunately our parents could not educate us, they could not give us an education that will make us business men, but thanks to tourism we can develop we can say we have opportunities.*

Education prompts better job opportunities in the future, because education leads to lower fertility and reduced family size. Education spawned other opportunities as well both as an end and means toward realizing more income, equity, and personal self-fulfillment. Sen (1999) considers education an important capability in prompting reading, communicating, and making more informed decisions. Banerjee and Duflo recount how an educational program in the Dominican Republic tied income gains to education and was able to incentivize parents and students to pay more attention to education.[31] Our results testify that education matters to the poor and defines their happiness.

The effect of tourism, through factor #3 opportunity, is the only factor that is directly related to tourism development that was significant. In Chapter 3, we discussed the economic channels that convert opportunities into better subjective well-being. These channels include jobs, connections, business, and income transfer through government intervention. However, the impact of opportunities differs depending on context and capabilities. The impact of sociodemographic variables on opportunities seems to influence the perception of well-being. The inclusion of the sociodemographic control variables prompted opportunities to switch sign from positive to negative while remaining significant. Satisfaction with life remains with the highest impact on happiness, similar to the previous model (see Table 8.6).

**TABLE 8.6** Tourism Impact on Happiness: Controlling for Sociodemographics

| | B | t | Significance |
|---|---|---|---|
| Constant | -0.579 | -3.412 | 0.001 |
| Factor #1 tourism product | 0.050 | 1.363 | 0.173 |
| Factor #2 tourism heritage | 0.035 | 0.997 | 0.319 |
| Factor #3 tourism opportunities | -0.073 | -2.084 | 0.038 |
| Satisfaction | 0.485 | 13.412 | 0.000 |
| Education | 0.122 | 4.218 | 0.000 |
| Income | 0.041 | 2.384 | 0.017 |
| Age | -0.001 | -.376 | 0.707 |

Dependent variable: happiness; *F*-statistic = 39.43 ($P < 0.001$); $R^2 = 0.327$.

## THE IMPACT OF TOURISM DEVELOPMENT ON SATISFACTION WITH LIFE

The second component comprising subjective well-being is long-term satisfaction with life. As we discussed previously, satisfaction with life is an evaluative practice of the individual. We regressed the three factors – tourism product, heritage, and opportunities – on satisfaction with life. The results are revealed in Table 8.7. Unlike the case with the happiness model, tourism product and heritage turned out to have a significant impact, while opportunities was insignificant. Heritage had the highest impact on satisfaction followed by tourism planning. The $R^2$ was 0.049, indicating low explanatory power of the three factors on satisfaction with life.

**TABLE 8.7** Tourism Impact on Satisfaction with Life

| | B | t | Significance |
|---|---|---|---|
| Constant | -0.004 | -0.069 | 0.945 |
| Factor #1 tourism product | 0.135 | 2.553 | 0.011 |
| Factor #2 heritage | 0.176 | 3.329 | 0.001 |
| Factor #3 opportunities | -0.014 | -0.259 | 0.796 |

Dependent variable: satisfaction with life; *F*-statistic = 5.86 ($P < 0.01$); $R^2 = 0.049$.

Next, we included happiness as a control variable, together with the other three factors. We assume that happiness has an important bearing on satisfaction with life. Our expectation was that happy individuals will be satisfied people, thus expecting a positive sign in the relationship. The results are in Table 8.8. By considering happiness, the explanatory power of the model shows a fivefold increase ($R^2$ increase from 0.049 to 0.255). All independent variables were significant at the 5% level, except opportunities that were significant at the 10% level. The strongest effect on satisfaction was from happiness, followed by almost identical weight from tourism product and heritage. However, the effect of Factor #3 opportunities is now negative.

We did a final analysis by including the sociodemographic control variables in the model. Similar to the case of the happiness model, we added as control variables, education, gender, income, and work. We conducted a stepwise regression technique in order to discern the change of impact of tourism development on satisfaction with life. The results are revealed in Table 8.9 and indicate that three variables are significantly impacting satisfaction with life. Happiness has a significant positive impact on satisfaction, while factor #3, opportunities, also had a significant positive impact on satisfaction. Only education as one of the control variables was significant at the 5% level. The explanatory power revealed in the $R^2$ increased to

0.309 from 0.255. A comparison of the two models shows that the explanatory power of satisfaction with life model (which includes happiness and opportunities) is almost as strong as the happiness model (which includes satisfaction with life, opportunities, education, and income).

**TABLE 8.8** Tourism Impact on Satisfaction with Life: Controlling for Happiness

| | B | t | Significance |
|---|---|---|---|
| Constant | -0.002 | -0.042 | 0.966 |
| Factor #1 tourism product | 0.102 | 2.168 | 0.031 |
| Factor #2 tourism heritage | 0.102 | 2.141 | 0.033 |
| Factor #3 tourism opportunities | -0.087 | -1.827 | 0.069 |
| Happiness | 0.468 | 9.730 | 0.000 |

Dependent variable: satisfaction with life; *F*-statistic = 29.25 ($P < 0.001$); $R^2 = 0.255$.

**TABLE 8.9** Tourism Impact on Satisfaction with Life: Controlling for Socio Demographics

| | B | T | Significance |
|---|---|---|---|
| Constant | -0.446 | -2.595 | 0.010 |
| Factor #1 tourism product | -0.010 | -0.267 | 0.789 |
| Factor #2 tourism heritage | 0.016 | 0.460 | 0.646 |
| Factor #3 tourism opportunities | 0.170 | 4.866 | 0.000 |
| Happiness | 0.495 | 13.412 | 0.000 |
| Education | 0.059 | 2.016 | 0.044 |
| Income | 0.009 | 0.542 | 0.588 |
| Age | 0.003 | 1.164 | 0.245 |

Dependent variable: satisfaction with life: *F*-statistic = 36.27 ($P < 0.001$); $R^2 = 0.309$.

The $R^2$ of the happiness as well as the life satisfaction model are remarkably similar. These values are similar to those found in several studies as reported by Blanchflower and Oswald, Rojas, and Guardiola, Gonzalez-Gomez and Grajales.[32] These values of the $R^2$ (explaining about one-third) imply that there are other factors impacting happiness and life satisfaction. The subjective well-being literature claims that the DNA configuration and luck substantially matter in defining a person's happiness.[33] Other studies claim that societal factors such as freedom, security, equality, and solidarity play a role in shaping happiness.[34]

## TOURISM OPPORTUNITIES AND THE POVERTY PARADOX

The switching of signs from positive to negative in the case of opportunity prompted by the happiness and life satisfaction models is puzzling. Why is it that the poor perceive opportunities as negative in the happiness model, while perceiving the same opportunities as positive in the life satisfaction model? In the previous chapter, we already noticed that we were facing wholly satisfied but unhappy poor. The poor are satisfied with life, but they seem unhappy. This is inconsistent with the study in Mexico conducted by Rojas who suggested that the poor are happy.[35] Is it that opportunity was pulling and hauling the poor in directions that make them satisfied with life but unhappy? In other words, are opportunities intervening between happiness and satisfaction with life? One could assume that to be happy one must be satisfied with life. In this particular case, satisfaction with life is an antecedent of happiness. That is exactly what we have been told by the subjective well-being literature. Indeed, the life satisfaction view of happiness pervaded these studies.

But happiness could influence life satisfaction as well. In other words, instead of being an end, happiness can be a means to realize life satisfaction. De Neve, Diener, Tay, and Xuereb support this proposition of happiness causing life satisfaction. Happy people tend to be healthier, more productive, creative, and innovative, and engage in better social relations and enjoy more income. Other studies also support this contention that happiness precedes and predicts positive outcome in life.[36] Some international organizations have also adhered to this position that happiness is a means toward life satisfaction.

Our results put the meaning of happiness and life satisfaction and their relationship as central focus in trying to explain the puzzling results we found in the previous chapter of a satisfied but unhappy poor, and the negative perception of opportunities when viewed from a happiness perspective or a positive perception of opportunities when viewed from a life satisfaction perspective. To uncover this puzzle we first assume that opportunities could be an intervening variable shaping and defining the nature of the relationship between happiness and life satisfaction. Our previous analysis showed that happiness and life satisfaction have a feedback relationship: happiness causes life satisfaction, while life satisfaction also causes happiness.

We considered the intervening nature of opportunity first as a mediating variable. For example, an impoverished person may encounter a tourist and the tourist requires this person's services as a guide to the heritage sites of a destination. After providing the service, she/he gets an income that provides food, medicine, and some sweet for her/his two children. That opportunity brought joy to the person and the family and explains why the person is happy and experienced an enhanced perspective of life satisfaction. To consider that possibility of mediation of opportunity, we applied the following procedure: (1) life satisfaction predicts happiness; (2) life satisfaction predicts opportunities; and (3) opportunities predict happiness.

The results indicate that life satisfaction has a significant impact on happiness as well as on opportunities. However, factor #3, tourism opportunities, did not have a significant impact on happiness.[37] We did a similar exercise for life satisfaction, and the results revealed that while happiness had a significant impact on life satisfaction, happiness did not have a significant impact on opportunities.[38] Therefore, we conclude that opportunities were not a mediating variable between happiness and life satisfaction.

An intervening condition can also be revealed through moderation effects. The same job opportunity may be seized differently by men or women, and may be very short-lived. The poor who get a job may assume that the job may make them permanently better off, but the benefits may quickly wear off, because to be permanently better off means a long life of ceaseless work and seizing opportunities. Additionally, gender can make a difference for a family. Men tend to use the additional income to indulge, while women would bring more food to the table for the children. Banerjee and Duflo documented this occurrence in their study of poverty in developing countries. Similarly, Chant referenced the mounting responsibilities of household survival of women in poor households in The Gambia, the Philippines, and Costa Rica.[39]

Consequently, we examined whether opportunities could play the role of moderator in relation to happiness and life satisfaction. We created an interaction between opportunities and happiness, and we regressed on life satisfaction together with the three tourism development and sociodemographic variables. These results indicate that the interaction value has no significant bearing on happiness.[40] However, the interaction modified the direction of the sign, thereby making the relationship opportunities and happiness positive. A similar result was revealed when we applied the moderation effect of tourism and life satisfaction on happiness; thus, the moderating effect makes the relationship with opportunities a negative one. Therefore, we conclude that there are moderating effects impinging on the relationship between happiness and life satisfaction, making the poor happy but dissatisfied with life.[41]

So how do the poor perceive opportunities in relation to their happiness and life satisfaction? Our qualitative exploration in several Latin American countries documents that the poor yearn for opportunities. Overall, we did not detect any differences when looking across countries or within countries such as in Ecuador, Mexico, Nicaragua, Colombia, or Costa Rica, regarding this powerful thirst for opportunities. Our quantitative approach also confirms this desire for opportunity. Tourism development seems an opportune vehicle to satiate the peoples' longing for opportunity.

However, we also uncovered a flip-flopping of the perception that the poor have about opportunity. This flip-flopping depends upon the lens that the poor observe tourism development through. In other words, it seems that poor people look at tourism development from two different perspective lens that are filtered by either life satisfaction or happiness. When looking at tourism development through the life satisfaction lens, the people seemed to perceive tourism opportunities as negative through the moderation effect. However, the opposite occurred for the same people when looking at tourism opportunities through the happiness lens where those opportunities were perceived as positive through moderation effects.

## THE MEANING OF OPPORTUNITY FOR THE POOR

How do we explain this paradox? The social science literature seems to insinuate that life satisfaction and happiness move together in the same direction. This is a logical assumption to follow. If an individual is happy, then her life satisfaction level should be higher and vice versa. But, why are the poor telling us a different story? One plausible explanation for this puzzle may be in the poor's perception that nothing good for a poor man lasts forever. We found this perception seems to be ingrained as a mainstream societal acceptance for those that are born to, exist within, and somehow find a way to function with poverty conditions.

The poor are accustomed to setbacks and broken promises. They know all too well how vulnerable they really are to the daily livelihood risks they face every day. Their existence is never a measurement of only one day, but, is instead a measurement of an entire life that will require toiling about how they will manage to get through every day that is to come. Their living conditions are besieged by risks that make them vulnerable. Banerjee and Duflo (2011, p. 136) describe the situation as follows: "For the poor, risk is not limited to income or food: Health is one major source of risk. There is also political violence, crime and corruption,"

The impoverished live with the relentless agony of having nothing or having something they may quickly lose. The poor are aware that tourism will bring growth potential. However, the poor are also aware that the growth potential tourism brings may mostly be absorbed by those who were fortunate to be educated, by those who have the right connections to get a job, and simply good luck. This is exactly what happened in the case of Costa Rica, which was narrated in Chapter 4. Countless broken promises experienced by the poor have resulted in a veil of apathy. The poor know that these individuals are the ones that have the greatest likelihood of earning more money through tourism. Life experience has taught them to have modest or no life expectations at all.

The poor also know that tourism demand is sensitive to natural disasters and economic shocks. A study in Mexico found a significant decrease of human development indicators at the municipal level due to flooding and droughts. The natural disasters affected in particular poor households.[42] According to the Economic Commission for Latin American and the Caribbean, natural disasters impose substantial material damages to these countries. By the account of the Economic Commission, Latin American countries suffer nearly US$7 billion in material damages annually, and the poor people suffer the most from the consequences of these disasters.[43]

They understand that if they embrace the opportunities that tourism may provide to them that they, as marginalized and poor people, will be the ones that suffer the most in downturn economic situations, and their consequences will be far reaching with the most irreversible hardships. Tourism-related households are more exposed to external shocks than nontourism-related households. This is because the jobs are part-time, exposed to seasonality, and are the most likely jobs that will disappear because of the low content of skills required to work such positions.

The growth effects that stem from tourism benefiting the poor's livelihood may only be short-lived. Those who have a tourism job may live with the anxiety of losing that job. This is because tourism growth may only provide ephemeral gains – and the poor are all too familiar with this notion that nothing good lasts forever. They already live with the stress of job insecurity, of losing everything after having only tasted the benefits of a better life for a short while. It is a generational hardship circle that has happened so many times in the past. The poor may consider that an industry that depends upon the health and wealth of people abroad (i.e., tourists) may not be a sure footing to provide them any long-term economic relief. In other words, any slight sign of economic downturn, and the labor provided by the poor will be the first to be cut. We have seen this situation in Costa Rica spawning so much struggle, disappointment, and anger.

There will also be those people who are left behind and were not fortunate enough to acquire a position in the tourism industry. Therefore, they may live with the daily frustration of seeing the benefits of tourism development in the local areas lifting their peers out of poverty while they are stuck in poverty. The effect of being left behind by their peers could create a sentiment of envy, working against satisfaction and happiness. Evidence exists in Latin America that when the poor compare themselves to others in relation to buying and doing, envy can rise to dangerous levels. We also found traces of envy in the younger age cohort in Costa Rica, Ecuador, and Mexico.

The poor also know that the benefits from tourism may be hijacked by criminal organizations and corruption. This growing reality in Latin America is captured in the acclaimed novel by the Latin American novelist and Nobel Prize winner, Mario Vargas Llosa. He narrates in *The Discreet Hero* how the benefits accompanying development in Peru have been slowly syphoned by criminal organizations. He continues that the few who are fortunate to receive economic relief leave the others behind resulting in frustration and hostility by those who just were not lucky enough to be fortunate. The exclusion of the poor from development is also recounted in the book by Acemoglu and Robinson *Why Nations Fail*. The premise of these two books is that for the poor, exclusion is the source of failure because the vast majority are left behind, which is revealed by the lack of investment in people to discover talents and nurture skills.[44] We detected the pernicious effects of exclusion in many conversations we had with the poor throughout our journey in Latin America.

## THE HAPPY-BUT-DISSATISFIED-WITH-LIFE POOR

This "unhappy growth" paradox may have a deeper implication if we revisit the meaning of life satisfaction and happiness. Why would the poor say that they are happy even in view of the harsh reality that tourism development may leave them behind? The poor may be telling us that the meaning they attach to happiness is that tourism development is okay, that tourism development is not bad compared to other toils they must confront in their lives such as working the farms.

There may even exist the notion that in such dire and stressful situations, the poor compare downward to their peers as a coping strategy to release the daily stress; and, therefore, may consider their lives as happy. However, believing that their lives are in better shape than their peers will not make them feel good in the long-term, and will drive consideration for what they do as meaningful. They surely don't "feel good" (the emotional component of happiness); and, their needs are not be fulfilled by living under conditions with lack of security, exclusion, lack of control of their lives, and lack of meaningful activities (all of which are the fulfillment components of happiness). The hardships that the poor endure are certainly not a happy occurrence.

While the poor consider tourism development as a potential positive for their communities – tourism development does not seem to facilitate a perception among the poor that it can alleviate the subjective well-being of poverty. In other words, tourism development may satisfy the needs of the poor by providing potential opportunities; but tourism development does not seem to satisfy the aspirations of the poor. This means that just like everybody else, the poor may have "wants" that may adjust overtime due to the development of higher aspirations and expectations. When happiness is related to the gratification of wants as revealed in life satisfaction, then happiness is relative and tourism development seems to decrease the subjective well-being of poverty.

From the poor's perspective, opportunities are related to access and steadiness. Having access to jobs is necessary but not enough. Their experience taught them that jobs may be short-lived. Access to steady opportunities are considered the tiebreaker for the poor. This means that unless opportunities stemming from tourism development bring long lasting tangible benefits to the poor in the betterment of their lives, for example, through steady jobs, tourism development may be ephemeral in alleviating subjective well-being of the poor.

This chapter investigated the poverty paradox uncovered in the previous chapter by considering the role of tourism development. The poverty paradox consists of a poor person who is satisfied with life while feeling unhappy. The poor conceive tourism development as revealed in three components: product, heritage, and opportunities. Opportunities seem to be the key to unlock the paradox. In other words, tourism opportunities with benefits for the poor that are long lasting will increase the subjective well-being of the poor. How to put the results of the previous four chapters to work for the poor is the focus of our last chapter.

## REFERENCES

Acemoglu, D.; Robinson, J. *Why Nations Fail. The Origins of Power, Prosperity, and Poverty*; Crown Publishing: New York, NY, 2012.

Afridi, A. *Social Networks: Their Role in Addressing Poverty*; Joseph Rowntree Foundation: York, UK, 2011.

Arezki, R.; Cherif, R.; Piotrowski, J. *Tourism Specialization and Economic Development: Evidence from the UNESCO World Heritage List*; IMF: Washington, DC, 2009. [Working Paper].

Banerjee, A.; Duflo, E. *Poor Economics. A Radical Rethinking of the Way to Fight Global Poverty*; Public Affairs: New York, NY, 2011.

Baud, M.; Ipeij, A.; Eds. *Cultural tourism in Latin America. The Politics of Space and Imagery*; Koninklijke Brill N.V: Leiden, The Netherlands, 2009.

Blanchflower, D.; Oswald, A. *International Happiness. A New View on the Measure of Performance*; Academy of Management Perspectives: Briarcliff Manor, NY, 2011; pp 6–22.

Boehm, J. K.; Lyubomirsky, S. Does happiness lead to career success? *J. Career Assess*. 2008, 16, 101–116.

Chant, S. The feminization of poverty and the feminization of ant poverty programs: room for revision? *J. Dev. Stud.* 2006, 44(2), 165–197.

Cohn, M.; Fredickson, B.; Brown, S.; Mikels, J.; Conway, A. Happiness unpacked: positive emotions increase life satisfaction by building resilience. *Emotion*. 2011, 9(3), 361–368.

De Neve, J.; Diener, E.; Tay, L.; Xuereb, C. *The Objective Benefits of Subjective Well-Being*; CEP: London, 2013. [Discussion Paper No. 1236].

Guardiola, J.; Gonzalez-Gomez, F.; Grajales, A. The influence of water access in subjective well-being. Some evidence in Yucatan, Mexico. *Soc. Indic. Res*. 2011, 110, 207–218.

Guardiola, J.; Garcia-Muñoz, T. Subjective well-being and basic needs: evidence from rural Guatemala. 2009. http://www.ugr.es/~teoriahe/RePEc/gra/wpaper/thepapers09_03.pdf (accessed Sep 8, 2014).

Heltberg, R.; Hossain, N.; Reva, A. *Living through Crises: How the Food, Fuel, and Financial Shocks Affect the Poor*; World Bank: Washington, DC, 2012a.

Heltberg, R.; Hossain, N.; Reva, A.; Turk, C. *Anatomy of coping: evidence from people living through the crises of 2008-11*. In *Living through Crises: How the Food, Fuel, and Financial*

*Shocks Affect the Poor*; Heltberg, R., Hossain, N., Reva, A., Eds.; World Bank: Washington, DC, 2012b, 23-60.

Lopez-Guzman, T.; Sanchez-Cañizares, S.; Pavon, V. Community-based tourism in developing countries: a case study. *Tourismos*. 2011, 6(1), 69–84.

Lora, E.; Chaparro, J. *The conflictive relationship between satisfaction and income*. In *Paradox and Perceptions. Measuring Quality of Life in Latin America*; Graham, C., Lora, E., Eds.; The Brookings Institution: Washington, DC, 2009.

Mitchell, J.; Ashley, C. *Tourism and Poverty Reduction: Pathways to Prosperity*; The Cromwell Press Group: London, UK, 2010.

Ridderstaat, J.; Croes, R.; Nijkamp, P. The force field of tourism. A conceptual framework on tourism development in relation to quality of life, external events and future challenges. *Rev. Econ. Anal.* 2012, 5, 1–24.

Rodriguez-Oreggia, E.; Fuente, A.; Torre, R.; Moreno, H.; Rodriguez, C. *The impact of Natural Disasters on Human Development and Poverty at the Municipal Level in Mexico*; UNDP: New York, NY, 2008.

Rojas, E. *Governance in historic city core regeneration projects*. In *The Economics of Uniqueness. Investing in Historic City Cores and Cultural HERITAGE Assets for sustainable Development*; Licciardi, G., Amirtahmasebi, R., Eds.; World Bank: Washington, DC, 2012,143-182.

Rojas, M. Experienced poverty and income poverty in Mexico: a subjective well-being approach. *World Dev*. 2008, 6, 1078–1093.

Schatan, C.; Montiel, M.; Romero, I. *Climate Change and Challenges for Tourism in Central America*; ECLAC: Mexico, 2010.

Semrad, K.; Bartels, J. An inward look using backward economic linkages in a developing country: the case of Puntarenas, Costa Rica. *Worldwide Hospital. Tour. Theme J.* 2014, 6(3), 244–260.

Sen, A. Development as Freedom; Anchor Books: New York, NY, 1999.

Shakya, M. Local perceptions of risk and tourism: a case from rural Nepal. *Rasaala*. 2011, 1(2), 1–25.

Steel, G. Local encounters with globetrotters. Tourism's potential for street vendors in Cusco, Peru. *Ann. Tour. Res*. 2012, 39(2), 601–619.

Steel, G.; Klaufus, C. Displacement by/for development in two Andean cities. Paper presented at the 2010 Congress of the Latin American Studies Association, Toronto, Canada, 2010.

Suman, D. Tamales & Bollos- Patrimonio de la humanidad-world heritage: challenges faced by restoration efforts in Panama City's San Felipe historic District. *Tenn. J. Law Policy*. 2014, 4(2), 403–466.

Underberg-Goode, N. Cultural heritage tourism on Peru's North Coast. *Worldwide Hospital. Tour. Theme J.* 2014, 6(3), 200–214.

Vargas Llosa, M. *The Discreet Hero: A Novel*; Macmillan: London, 2015.

Veenhoven, R. *Measures of Gross National Happiness. Measuring Happiness and Making Policy*. Roundtable conducted, In OECD World Forum on Statistics, Knowledge and Policy, Istanbul, Turkey, 2007.

Walker, J. Reflections on archeology, poverty and tourism in the Bolivian Amazon. *Worldwide Hospital. Tour Theme J.* 2014, 6(3), 215–228.

## ENDNOTES

[1]See, for example, Rojas (2008).

[2]See, for example, Banerjee and Duflo (2011).

[3]For a discussion between the relationship income and satisfaction, see for example, Lora and Chaparro (2009).

[4]For further discussion, see, for example, Ridderstaat et al. (2012).

[5]There is a growing literature in tourism studies which investigate the impact of tourism development on the quality of life of residents, but poor people as a separate group are not specifically considered as a special group to be researched. See, for example, Guardiola and Garcia-Muñoz (2009) and Shakya (2011).

[6]For a discussion how social connections can help the poor cope or move out of poverty, see, for example, Afridi (2011) and Banerjee and Duflo (2011).

[7]For further discussion, see the study of Lopez-Guzman et al. (2011).

[8]Social connection has been identified in social sciences as a good predictor of an enhanced quality of life. See, for example, note 4.

[9]See Semrad and Bartels (2014).

[10]See Shakya (2011).

[11]See Semrad and Bartels (2014).

[12]For a discussion on tourism vulnerabilities, see, for example, Shakya (2011).

[13]See, for example, Underberg-Goode (2014), Walker (2014), Shakya (2011).

[14]See, for example, the studies of Underberg-Goode (2014) in Peru, Walker (2014) in Bolivia, Semrad and Bartels (2014) in Costa Rica, and Tasci, Croes and Bartels (2014) in Costa Rica.

[15]For a discussion on tourism heritage and quality of life of local people, see, for example, Underberg-Goode (2014).

[16]See UNESCO World Heritage List at http://whc.unesco.org/en/list/

[17]See, for example, the study from, Arezki et al. (2009) for a discussion on the role of heritage sites in attracting international tourists.

[18]See, for example, Baud and Ipeij (2009), Steel (2012).

[19]See Rojas (2012).

[20]For further discussion on displacement in Latin America, see for example, Steel and Klaufus (2010) and Baud and Ipeij (2009).

[21]See, for example, Suman (2014).

[22]See, for example, Banerjee and Duflo (2011).

[23]See, for example, Banerjee and Duflo (2011).

[24]See ILO. (2010). *Development and Challenges in the Hospitality and Tourism Sector*. ILO: Geneva.

[25]See Mitchell and Ashely (2010).

[26]See Walker (2014) and Underberg-Goode (2014) for further discussion on this topic.

[27]See, for example, De Neve et al. (2013).

[28]See Guardiola and Garcia-Muñoz (2009).

[29]See Banerjee and Duflo (2011).

[30]See Banerjee and Duflo (2011).

[31]See Banerjee and Duflo (2011).

[32]See Blanchflower and Oswald (2011), Guardiola et al. (2011), Rojas (2008).

[33]See, for example, Boehm and Lyubomirsky (2008).

[34]See, for example, Veenhoven (2007).

[35]See Rojas (2008).

[36]See, for example, Cohn et al. (2011).

[37]The Regression results for the mediator effect of tourism on happiness are: (1) Dependent Variable = Happiness; $R^2 = 0.281$; $F$-statistic = 235.26 ($P < 0.001$); Beta Coefficient for Satisfaction with Life = 0.531 ($P < 0.001$); (2) Dependent Variable = Happiness; $R^2 = 0.012$; $F$-statistic = 0.088 ($P > 0.10$); Beta Coefficient for Factor #3 Tourism Opportunities = -0.12 ($P > 0.10$); (3) Dependent Variable = Factor #3 Tourism Opportunities; $R^2 = 0.025$; $F$-statistic = 15.23 ($P < 0.001$); Beta Coefficient for Satisfaction with Life = 0.158 ($P < 0.001$).

[38]The Regression results for the mediator effect of tourism on satisfaction are: (1) Dependent Variable = Satisfaction; $R^2 = 0.282$; $F$-statistic = 235.26 ($P < 0.001$); Beta Coefficient for Happiness = 0.530 ($P < 0.001$); (2) Dependent Variable = Factor #3 Opportunities; $R^2 = 0.000$; $F$-statistic = 0.088 ($P > .10$); Beta Coefficient for Happiness = -0.12 ($P > 0.10$); (3) Dependent Variable = Satisfaction with Life; $R^2 = 0.025$; $F$-statistic = 15.23 ($P < 0.001$); Beta Coefficient for Factor #3 Tourism Opportunities = 0.15($P < 0.001$).

[39]Banerjee and Duflo (2011) claim that gender plays a role in defining the use of income in a poor household. See Banerjee and Duflo (2011). See also Chant (2006).

[40]The statistics for the moderation effect of happiness and tourism on life satisfaction are: $R^2 = 0.308$; $F$-statistic = 27.91 ($P < 0.001$); Beta Coefficient for Happiness ′ Factor #3 Tourism Opportunities = -0.23 ($P > 0.10$). However, the Beta Coefficient for Opportunities is now 0.183 ($t = 0.000$).

[41]The statistics for the moderation effect of satisfaction with life and tourism on happiness are: $R^2 = 0.329$; $F$-statistic = 30.74 ($P < 0.001$); Beta Coefficient for Satisfaction ′ Factor #3 Tourism Opportunities = 0.02($P > 0.10$). However, the Beta Coefficient for Opportunities is now -0.080 ($t = 0.029$).

[42]See Rodriguez-Oreggia et al. (2008).

[43]See Schatan et al. (2010).

[44]See Acemoglu and Robinson (2012).

## CHAPTER 9

# A CRAZY ENOUGH IDEA: A DEMAND-PULL APPROACH

## CONTENTS

## INTRODUCTION

In the *The White Man's Burden*, Easterly challenged those who are interested in helping the poor to come up with "crazy ideas." We accept and address Easterly's challenge in this chapter. We argued at the beginning of the book that the poor should be helped out of self-interest and that tourism can help the poor. Tourism did not disappoint. The previous chapters demonstrated that tourism can reduce poverty. We looked at several countries in Latin America, examining in depth how tourism development reaches the poor. We provided insights on the dynamic relationship between tourism and poverty reduction. We explored poverty and its impact upon development at the macro and micro levels through multiple research techniques. While the promise is clear and embedded in strong empirical evidence, we also account for potential pitfalls. After multiple conversations with the poor, we conclude tourism development has the seeds of promise and hope for a better future.

Tourism's prowess can reach the poor in any corner of a country. Developing tourism can provide income directly to poor households either through jobs or through vending. Private income can provide relief to the consumption of private goods (food, shelter, and clothing). In addition, the benefits of tourism development are channeled through economic growth, which may impact capabilities such as education and health. We already saw in Chapter 7 that health and education are considered by the poor as the most important functionings in their life conditions. We also noticed that direct grants to poor households through financial support can have significant positive effects in lifting the poor from under the poverty line. Finally, we observed that once the poor are lifted from below the poverty line, it is difficult to revert to a situation below the poverty line. Thus, there is a clear persistence of income shocks benefits to the poor.

However, tourism's prowess is constrained by the dynamics and configuration of social forces. The first force is inequality. Our empirical results show inequality can cancel out potential benefits tourism would bring to the poor in the short term. Tourism may have a significant effect in reducing inequality only in the long run. The second force is related to the willingness and ability of governments to put social programs in place to benefit the poor. The effects of private incomes may stall on access and consumption of collective goods such as education and health. Especially in rural areas, the poor are at a great disadvantage in gaining access to these collective goods.[1] For tourism to help the poor, it should have a double impact on private as well as on collective goods. The relationship between tourism development and poverty reduction is, therefore, a complex social issue, contingent on a number of factors, such as personal motivation and aspirations, opportunities, institutional strength, the level of inequality, the strength of wealth creation, and a clear focus on helping the poor.

In this chapter, we will propose a pathway for strengthening the link between tourism development and poverty reduction.

## EXPERIMENTING WITH POVERTY REDUCTION STRATEGIES: THE TROIKA OF MORE AID, FAIRER TRADE AND LABOR MOBILITY

How best to help the poor escape from poverty has been debated for the past fifty years without providing clear answers. The main premise in the developing literature is the poor should be helped. Reasons range from moral imperatives to the urgency to prevent wasting lives, talents, and capital. The debate concerns the most effective ways to remedy poverty. For example, freedom seems a powerful concept that defines and shapes choices, aligns private and social interest through the market mechanism, and provides access to private property rights to the poor. The premise that freedom and empowerment may be antecedents for escaping poverty is shared in the literature, albeit under the condition of well-functioning institutions. Other scholars posit that only the poor can decide if they will escape the poverty trap, thereby insisting that investigating why the poor make certain choices will enhance the understanding of why some people are and remain poor. Others reject the notion that the poor can escape from poverty without help. Still others, such as Sachs, argue that only foreign aid will enable the poor to escape from poverty. Despite these perspectives and their corresponding remedies, poverty persists.

In *The White Man's Burden*, Easterly criticizes international organizations for their misplaced assistance to the poor. "The status quo—large international bureaucracies giving aid to large national government bureaucracies—is not getting money to the poor."[2] He posits official aid has the wrong focus, centering on government instead of individuals. By focusing on governments, aid got wasted in large inept and corrupt bureaucracies. While international organizations are aware of this predicament, they continued pumping money into these governments because of arrogance, internal bureaucratic politics, and lack of accountability. The intrusive and ineffective international aid underlines Easterly's pessimistic account of the role of international aid and his account leaves a sour taste of whether international organizations are able to help the poor. .

If not more international aid, what about better preferential market access to help the poor? Mainstream literature has asserted that trade will make every country and their citizens better off. However, the experience of poor countries has been unfair trade and deteriorating terms-of-trade. Raul Prebisch was the champion of this ideal in Latin America and had a large impact on subsequent assessment of trade opportunities for helping the poor.[3] However, some commentators claim that if only poor countries can be provided with better market access for their products, they would sell their products to more affluent countries, thereby getting much needed foreign exchange to pay for their imports of critical goods to create and sustain economic wealth. For example, if poor countries can get their agricultural products in rich countries and rich countries can get rid of their agricultural subsidies and protectionism, poverty reduction in these poor countries would take place. This is exactly what the World Bank and Oxfam have been arguing. But does liberalizing agricultural trade help the poor in poor countries? Nancy Birdsall from the Center for Global Development and Dani Rodrik from Harvard claim that the impact of agricultural liberalization would not be significant to the poor.[4] The effects of agricultural liberalization are ephemeral and small to the poor's condition by their account. If not better market access, what about temporary freedom of labor mobility across borders, particularly of low-skilled labor?

This is the core suggestion of Birdsall and Rodrik to alleviate poverty in poor countries. The main premise of this suggestion is that the temporary migration of low-skilled labor to more affluent countries would generate money to poor countries through remittances. Moreover, when residents from poor countries return to their country of birth, they will bring with them new ideas, new ways of doings, and money to invest. Their experience in the rich recipient countries will provide them with a new lens of discovering opportunities in their country of origin, and if provided with the opportunity to invest in their country, they will thereby lift the whole country, including the poor. Indeed, the World Bank estimated that the proportion of poor people would be reduced by 0.4 when remittances increased by one percentage point in the share of gross domestic product.[5]

Lant Pritchett from the World Bank argues in his book *Let their People Come* that it is in the self-interest of rich countries to allow for free movement of labor. A cost and benefit take of the free movement of low-skilled people will result in net economic gain for rich countries, according to Pritchett. In addition, his example of substituting aid for free movement of labor will generate more than four times the financial resources to poor countries.[6]

However, the suggestion for labor mobility of unskilled labor reveals a number of pitfalls. First, Pritchett explains that the movement of goods eventually will equalize wages, removing the comparative advantage of differences in wages between poor and rich countries. Mainstream economics calls the erosion of differences factor "price equalization." Second, providing more labor to economies may curb the need for innovation. Scarcity, which is the increase in labor costs, is the father of innovation. The lack of scarcity may retard technological progress and productivity growth in the rich country. Third, for years, the United States has implemented the Bracero program allowing Mexican farm workers to temporarily work in the United States. However, the Mexican poor have not seen their standard of living increase due to this program. And fourth, there is little support in the rich countries for this type of labor mobility for unskilled workers. Actually, popular resistance has increased over the past decade against this type of program. While the focus of free mobility of unskilled labor is on the individual and not on the government, a different approach than preferential trade and more aid, it is highly improbable that the political situation in rich countries will change any time soon for this idea to become feasible and effective in helping the poor.

All the previous programs to reduce poverty depend to a considerable extent on the will and ability of governments. More aid and fairer trade depends on institutional prowess in poor countries, a hallmark typically lacking in poor countries. Actually, a large number of poor countries are considered failed states because of their institutional weaknesses. In *Why Nations Fail* Acemoglu and Robinson attribute poverty to social exclusion, inequality, and failing institutions. They eschew geography, culture, and weather as defining factors of poverty. They illustrated their argument with the case of the region of Nogales. One Nogales is located in Arizona (USA) and the other Nogales is in Sonora, Mexico. The average household income in Nogales Arizona is US$30,000 a year, while this level of income in Nogales in Sonora (Mexico) is only one-third of that of Nogales in Arizona. The same people, the same geography, the same weather, yet with essentially significant differences in standard of living.[7] Arguably, other factors are at work.

We showed poor countries are entrenched with weak institutions, which exhibit significant coordination problems. Coordination problems typically occur when the market cannot coordinate the needs of development, such as harnessing inclusive markets, encouraging technological innovation, investing in people, and discovering and mobilizing talents. But markets typically fail in developing countries spawning distortions in prices and behavior. Coordination failures may cause perverse consequences for everyone. A coordination failure is a typical situation in which choices of either sellers or buyers, or a combination of both, leave everybody worse off. For example, people may not have the incentive to put technology to work even if they know that technology could enhance productivity.[8] For example, the overabundance of low-skilled labor may generate low productivity in economic activities. These low productivity activities may influence the behavior of the poor by not investing in the future.

## CASH DIRECTLY IN THE HANDS OF THE POOR

But perhaps the major predicaments of programs aimed at reducing poverty are related to the presumption that governments and international organizations know what is best for the poor. Programs such as building schools, roads, and health facilities, training teachers and doctors are aimed at helping the poor. And yet, the poor are not attending these schools or are not visiting the health facilities as expected and assumed. These programs ignored demand barriers confronted by the poor when accessing these services. Not that the poor do not want to enroll their children in schools or send them to do regular checkups at health facilities. They know as they have manifested to us that education is key for more income and to attain better jobs. But the effective use of time for the poor is essential for their survival. Sending their children to school may mean less income for the family. They may know that education is a good investment in the future, as indeed the poor in Costa Rica, Ecuador, and Mexico told us, but foregoing income in the present may mean that some of them will no longer live in the short term. In other words, education in the long term may be a good investment, but in the long run they may not exist.

Alternately, the poor may suffer from an aspiration gap. We noted in Chapter 7 that respondents from Costa Rica, Ecuador, and Mexico entertain different levels of aspirations. Respondents from Costa Rica had the highest aspirations in life compared to Ecuador and Mexico, with Ecuador having the lowest aspiration level. Poor people tend to be conservative and pessimistic about what they might achieve in life, thereby perpetuating their living conditions. Low aspirations can lead to underachievement, and underachievement may become a social barrier for the affluent and less affluent to interact with each other, creating a distance between the two groups and a feeling among the poor that they cannot achieve what the affluent have attained. Financial constraints and low aspiration may prevent the poor from effectively making use of what governments and international organizations may offer, thereby foregoing any help that can assist them in escaping from poverty.

A response to the significant costs incurred in second guessing the needs and aspirations of the poor and the corresponding requirements to escape poverty prompted the design and the rolling out of new programs. These programs provide cash directly to the poor. The premise is that the poor know best what they need and how to escape from poverty, and therefore, the programs should squarely focus on the poor. The extension of this premise is that the poor should be trusted with direct cash. Consequently, governments initiated programs of giving poor households small cash amounts to do as they want. These cash transfers were either with or without conditions. The conditional cash transfers (CCTs) aimed for parents to send their children to school or to visit health facilities on a regular basis for checkups. The cash programs started in Mexico with the Programa Nacional de Educacion, Salud y Alimentacion, now renamed *Oportunidades*, and quickly spread to other Latin American and developing countries. These programs supported individual households in particular, helping women directly. Management of these programs was cost-effective.

CCTs are premised on two relevant considerations. First, the individual need of the poor household is respected by allowing the poor to exercise the actions that best fit their individual preferences. The poor know better what benefit them. Second, CCTs also recognize the existence of demand barriers to consumption of services that are crucial to human development, such as health and education. We already alluded to the opportunity costs involved in consuming education and lost income from child labor. Once these barriers are accounted for and removed, the poor are active in lifting themselves from below the poverty line. For example, the CCTs have been very successful as attested by the *Oportunidades* in Mexico where 30% of those who received the cash transfer experienced a decline in income poverty. Similarly, beneficiaries from the *Red de Proteccion Social* in Nicaragua were able to sustain their consumption level compared to the nonbeneficiaries of the program even in stark challenging situations such as the coffee crisis. *Bolsa Familia*, the largest program in the world with 11.1 million beneficiaries in Brazil, also demonstrated its positive impact on reducing poverty and inequality in Brazil.[9]

Another program with a high level of success is Ecuador's *Bono de Desarrollo Humano* (BDH) program. The BDH is a cash transfer program for poor households with US$35 monthly transfer in 2009. Schady and Araujo from the World Bank estimated that the impact of the BDH on school enrollment was four times larger when poor households believe enrollments were linked to cash transfers.[10] Another study found that money matters in improving child health conditions in rural Ecuador. Households receiving cash transfers had substantial improvements in their children's nutritional intake, made greater use of health care, and demonstrated better parenting, especially for the poorest children.[11] In general, these CCT programs have been very successful in Latin America, demonstrating significant positive impact in nutritional intake, providing greater accessibility to education and health services, and reducing poverty and inequality.

Cash transfers have shown to be a powerful tool to reduce poverty in the short term. However, cash transfers are limited in the sense that they depend on the budget of governments or rely on international donors. Financial constraints of governments can be a major hurdle for their sustainability. The cash program sustainability is also linked to political support both in the poor country and the donor country. The poor lack political mobility capacity, which means that any political program depends on the support of other groups. Some in society may perceive these programs as creating dependency and undermining incentives to work. Another impediment to this cash program is the definitive obliteration of poverty is associated with strong and sustained economic growth. The CCTs do not have the economic power to lift the poor permanently from below the poverty line. In other words, the link between the CCTs and economic growth is tenuous.

We have observed throughout this book how tourism can achieve a double effect on obliterating poverty: by putting money directly in the hands of the poor and by provoking economic growth, tourism development can promote social programs that help the poor move up the economic and social ladder. Thus, tourism development delivers a structural blow to poverty. The question is: how can we render the double barrel blow of tourism stronger on poverty reduction?

## AN IDEA CRAZY ENOUGH TO ENACT CHANGE: THE DEMAND PULL APPROACH

Easterly challenged those of us who think about the poor and who are in constant search of how to defeat poverty to come up with crazy enough ideas. We are heeding this challenge. Our demand pull approach (DPA) is premised on the promotion of tourism by a variety of means, and centers on the poor as an individual and not as the government or society.[12] The DPA eschews the supply push approach advocated and implemented by the majority of international donors and favored by developing countries governments. In addition, the demand-pull approach bypasses the coordination problem that is so pervasive in developing countries. Tourism seems to exert an autonomous impact on aggregate growth beyond the influence induced by institutional quality.[13]The DPA promotes tourism by suggesting rich countries provide incentives to their citizens to travel to poor countries. The DPA is illustrated in Figure 9.1.

More arrivals in poor countries will create jobs, which are desperately needed and valued, as confirmed by our conversations with the poor. We have seen that in Ecuador, for example, for every twelve additional arrivals, one new job will be created. These jobs may be permanent if there is enough spread of arrivals during the year. Tourists at a destination would visit natural attractions and heritage sites that are populated by poor people as indicated in the case of many places in Latin America. The roaming of tourists in these areas provides the opportunity to the poor to directly earn money and have more income to satisfy their needs as they see fit and consume goods according to their preferences. This may be one of the reasons that tourist areas reveal less poor people than in other regions within a destination. For example, in Mexico, poverty in tourist's towns are lower than the national average level, according to the Mexican Government.[14]

This suggestion focuses on market forces where the tourist uses his/her free will to choose a developing country of preference and spends money in accordance with individual needs and wants. On the receiving end is another person who sell goods and services, and who will use the money according to needs and wants.

The market relationship functions without disruption from a third party government or bureaucracy working in between. There is no distortion imposed by graft, corruption, or inequality. The tourism money will flow through these economies and will be distributed according to market forces. The money will go where individual entrepreneurs and consumers have decided the money can be invested and spent productively. The money will go to local entrepreneurs who know the local economy and know where the best opportunity for growth lies. That opportunity may be providing laundry and tour services, or perhaps souvenirs, handicrafts, and music, or it might involve providing basic goods needed by the tourism industry such as agricultural products. These individuals will know better than a foreign aid bureaucrat thousands of miles away where to invest and what is likely to succeed in their own economies. We have seen that the poor is eager to take up opportunities, to look more intensively and extensively for a job and find ways to earn an income. This demand-pull approach will also take care of the stigma of dependency that the poor may carry through the cash transfer programs.

Consider the US$70 billion that rich countries provide to developing countries in aid. We already alluded to the heightened critique to conventional ways of providing aid to poor countries. There is much evidence that the current system of providing economic aid to poor countries does not work, and that merely upping the ante will, in the long term, do little to make poor countries better off. Suppose that a portion of the US$70 billion of aid is allocated to provide incentives for residents from a rich country to travel to poor countries. The traveler will decide which country is of his/her preference. Let us say that half of the US$70 billion would go for compensating travel to poor countries via tax incentives. In other words, travel to any poor country of a traveler's choice will be tax deductible in the rich country. We are not advocating to increase the amount of aid; on the contrary, what we are saying is that rich countries should be smarter at using their money.

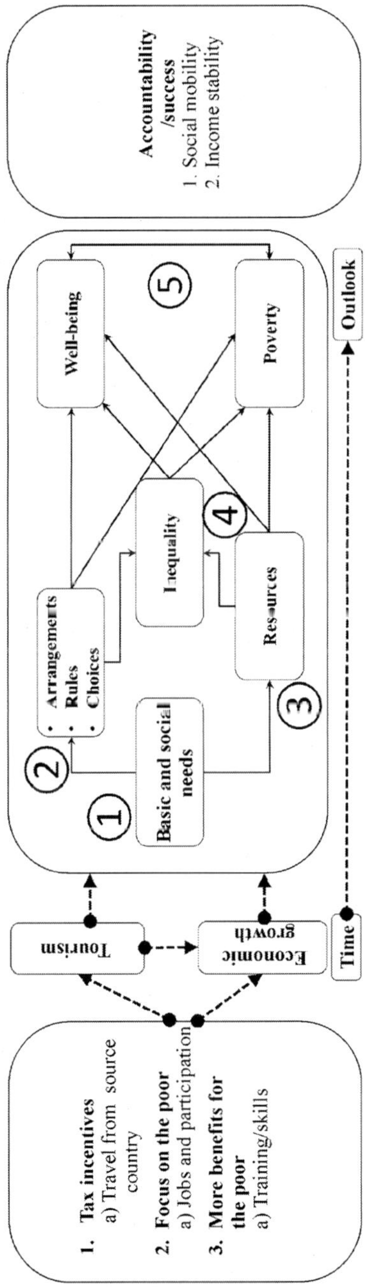


FIGURE 9.1 Demand Pull Approach (DPA) to Poverty Obliteration Paradigm.

What would the economic effects of those US$35 billion be for poor countries? For discussion sake, a region such as Latin America would receive an amount in travel incentives equivalent to its proportion of poor people on a global scale. For example, the amount of poor in Latin America is 68 million people, which is equivalent to 6% of the world's poor. Based on that proportion, consider that the region receives US$2.1 billion in additional travel due to tax breaks from rich countries. In 2013, Latin America and the Caribbean benefited from US$72 billion in international receipts. The additional flow of tourist money will have an impact of US$4 billion with an additional 2.9 million arrivals. The result is a significant impact on the local economies spreading well beyond what tourists pay directly to businesses and individuals because the money is respent in the local economy. New money creates jobs and income in the community, especially benefiting the poor, in addition to expanding the tax base for the government. New money harnesses and hones economic growth.

If we take Ecuador's ratio of arrivals to jobs, the additional 2.9 million arrivals would mean 240,674 new jobs in the region. Ecuador's minimum wage is US$390 per month, which is equivalent to US$13 per day. Per year, this amount means an income stream of US$4,680 per person. This amount will immediately lift the poor from below the poverty line. A recent report of the World Bank asserts that US$4 per day implies moderate poverty and exceeding US$10 per day means incurring a lower risk to fall back into poverty.[15] For a typical poor family consisting of 4.6 persons, it would mean an income of US$2.82 per capita.[16] The amount of US$2.82 is an amount similar to that found by the World Bank for those who recently escaped from poverty in Latin America. The upward mobility is a real opportunity for the poor and empirical evidence from Latin America demonstrates strong persistence of this upward mobility, a situation also unearthed in our analysis of Ecuador.

Successfully implementing the DPA could have a significant impact in terms of lifting the poor from below the poverty line. However, these individuals and families will remain vulnerable. Actually, this type of family is the largest social group in Latin America and has become the most prominent social class in the region. The report of the World Bank just referenced describes this group as "the vulnerable". However, there is also another reality in Latin America: once the poor escape the poverty trap, the likelihood of reverting to their previous situation is slim as we unearthed in the case of Ecuador and corroborated by the recent study of the Inter-American Development Bank.[17]

Rich countries have the ability to provide incentives to their citizens. For example, the United States through the Caribbean Basin Initiative had a limited tax break program compensating American companies for selecting a Caribbean country as the venue for their business and convention meetings, the so-called Caribbean Basin Economic Recovery Act 1989. Rich countries and international organizations are aware that much of the official aid provided to poor countries goes wasted and that preferential market access has had limited success because of the lack of market intelligence and other types of barriers.

Any political resistance in rich countries to the DPA would be less than what is suggested by other commentators or applied by international organizations. We already mentioned the tenuous viability of the cash transfer programs supported by donor countries. The issue of creating dependency or takers is strongly debated in the Unites States and might negatively impact any possibility of CCTs. Providing travel incentives may receive popular support because it directly benefits citizens from rich countries. Citizens from these countries have a strong tradition in travel and they understand the benefits of traveling to their well-being. Moreover, this program is based on the notion of zero additional costs to rich countries: it simply means a reallocation of resources to a more rational use. On the other end, recipient countries will be incentivized to build effective and efficient efforts and activities in order to convince travelers from rich countries to visit their destinations. Besides, this demand-pull program will not create any dependency: poor people have to hustle to get the money from travelers or have to acquire the skills in order to fill jobs that are being created. The demand-pull program should be conditioned to make sure that the poor clearly receive the most benefits. The monitoring of this program is based on annual assessment from feedback based on the opinions and views from the poor about the direct benefits of tourism to them.

Tourism has proven to be an effective economic vehicle that seems to be working in poor countries and benefiting the poor because it does not include barriers that are embedded in the trade of goods and services. The presence of tourists in a destination enables quick and cost-effective learning of local entrepreneurs regarding tastes and preferences of tourists. These tastes and preferences according to Lejarraja and Walkenhorst are of two types: preferences that resemble those in the home country of the tourists (sophisticated and higher value demand) and preferences entailing local cultural and exotic goods. These preferences are catered to directly by the tourist sector (e.g., accommodation, restaurants, entertainment), and also street vendors, tour guides, and craftsmen.[18] Depending on the capacity of the tourist sector to align itself with other sectors within the local economy, linkages are created that expand the economy.

To enable the poor to seize opportunities that tourism can spawn, it is important that the poor understand their own financial needs, the use of money, the role of teamwork, organization, and other resources, and the financial realities of entrepreneurship. The poor seem very active as entrepreneurs. For example, in Ecuador, the sheer number of business owners among the poor is staggering. For example, 44% of the rural extremely poor in Ecuador own a business.[19] We have seen in the redevelopment project in the Serro Santa Ana in Guayaquil that while the project enhanced the quality of life of the poor, business activities supporting the livelihood of the poor were waning. These businesses are too small and undifferentiated from the many around them with almost negligible profits. Does it at all make sense for the poor to engage in business activities while profits are so negligible? Surely, only if opportunities, as we have learned from the poor, do not depend on a specific situation or person. In other words, opportunities as a means should exist, recognized, and valued by everybody (education will be valued only if it is shared by all members of society). In addition, the consequences of the use of opportunities should realizes multiple goals and should be construed as a trade-off. For example, getting more education realizes a variety of goals, such as higher income, enhanced health, prestige, etc.

Discovery, assessment, and exploitation of opportunities are promoted by training and education. For example, the Entrepreneurial Development Training Centre advocates for alternative education and training as a way to hone the entrepreneurial spirit of the poor. This important educational and training program for the poor is practiced in Papua New Guinea, aiming to increase the business knowledge for the poor. The center provides practical training to marginalized people (youth) regarding how to come up with a business proposition, how to calculate risk within their own context, and how to implement a business project in an economically sustainable manner. The program is certified by the Global University for Lifelong Learning.[20] The key principles of this alternative educational practice are revealed in the book *Lifelong Action Learning for Community*

*Development* by Zuber-Skerritt and Teare and focus on how the poor can seize business opportunities in a web of stakeholders, typical of the tourism sector.[21]

While the poor consider education as an important functioning for their lifelong opportunities, as reported in previous chapters, starting, engaging, and managing business enterprises is stressful, and even a dreadful proposition, especially when results and perspectives are bleak. The poor are stuck in the present, living in a context that prevents the poor from having a sense of the future. If the poor can have a perspective of the future, their behavior may change toward making reasonable short-term sacrifices to invest in the future. If the poor perceive that they have opportunities to realize their aspirations in the future, they may entertain the reasoning to sacrifice today for the sake of the future. The onus is to generate opportunities. We learnt in the previous chapter that from the poor's perspective they want steadiness. However, as Banerjee and Duflo commented, "It is hard to stay motivated when everything you want looks impossibly far away".[22]

## WORKING FOR THE FUTURE

Tourism development may be impossibly far away from the poor unless it brings them long lasting tangible benefits in the betterment of their lives, for example through steady jobs. Tourism can provide the stability of income so desperately needed by the poor, as recounted by Banerjee and Duflo. For example, Banerjee and Duflo found that the stable flow of income that is apportioned to the household influences the poor's behavior. Stability of income is associated with perspectives toward the future, which seem lacking in a poor household. The report of the World Bank referred to in the previous paragraphs attest the changing behavior of the poor in terms, for example, of increased enrollment in schools. Therefore, externalities stemming from coping strategies may play an important role in aligning private and social returns from various activities.

Our suggested crazy idea focuses on the poor as a separate group and the identification of contextual forces as shaping the behavior of the poor. The focus on the poor as a separate group means eschewing the premise of trickle-down economics. Tourism needs to directly connect to the poor for it to be an effective vehicle of poverty reduction as indicated in our poverty obliteration paradigm framework. However, we understand that giving the poor the opportunity to earn income and use that income based on their individual choice (empowerment) by itself cannot solve the poverty issue. We know that a compelling force of tourism is its power to provoke economic growth. Economic growth is an undeniable lever to hone poverty reduction efforts. It can create more stable jobs with more stable income. In addition, economic growth will provide the resources that, if governments are willing, could be used to create social programs that can help lift people out of poverty and reduce inequality. The increase in individual income can handle such items as food, shelter, and clothing. However, other capabilities such as education and health would require programs directed and promoted by the government.

Recipient governments will stay in the program as long as the poor are lifted from below the poverty line, and become less vulnerable to external shocks such as a recession. The premise here is one of economic security, which means in practice a stable income. And, second, the poor should get more benefits from this program compared to other groups in the poor countries. Our study indicates that tourism has the potential to provide more benefits to the poor compared to other groups in a country. These two conditions reveal an important distinguishing aspect compared to the CCTs: the focus on output or achievements. Arguably, tourism alone cannot sustain upward mobility of the poor. Other supply side policies need to be in place such as increasing the quality of education and providing more job security as well as engaging in deliberate efforts to reduce poverty .

The question is whether governments will be able to comply with this task when there are strong indications of institutional weaknesses in Latin America provoked by corruption and crime.[23] To be successful, a destination must solve a large amount of complex problems to spawn memorable experiences as discussed previously. The only way for tourism to be an effective tool in poverty alleviation is to resolve all complex problems, such as promoting and coordinating collaborative processes among multiple stakeholders, embedded in the tourism system. However, focusing on solving all these complex problems related to tourism development and poverty simultaneously may be misplaced. The institutional weakness pervasive in so many Latin American countries stifles any comprehensive approach to resolve the poverty problem. Additionally, the lack of trust among the poor due to empty and broken promises may stifle any good intention of a Latin American government to effectively intervene to help the poor. In other words, this dreadful context may provoke pessimism and inertia.

For tourism to work, we suggest a shift from grand solutions to small but powerful solutions with immediate and tangible results to the masses of the poor, i.e., jobs. Jobs not only provide income but lead to increasing self-confidence, motivation, and recovery. Connecting individuals with self-confidence will reinforce hope and promise among individuals, thereby prompting a culture of antipoverty. Governments could take the following actions to battle poverty:[24]

- Governments should focus on the creation of jobs. There is nothing more empowering than a steady job for the poor.
- Governments should require from any new tourist project a specific plan regarding how many jobs are created for the poor, especially for those poor in rural areas.
- Governments should align the increase in hotel room inventory with jobs for the poor. For example, each hotel room should generate one job for the poor.
- Any tourism project that generates a certain amount of jobs for the poor will receive tax incentives.
- An aggressive information program should be launched informing all stakeholders about the main objectives of breaking the cycle of poverty through the tourism program. For example, the government could announce that the program will halve the number of poor people within three years.
- By making the objectives clear and transparent, the government will also increase accountability.
- Share and celebrate any progress with all stakeholders, including the poor.
- Work with donor organizations, universities, and nongovernmental organizations to partner to develop campaigns, educational and training programs for human and social capital development.
- Any finally, work together with social scientists to understand the motivations and constraints of all stakeholders, including the poor, for collaborating in creating memorable tourist experiences.

Surely, tourism is not the sole answer to obliterate poverty in poor countries, but it is proven to have the greatest potential, in particular, when initiatives geared to alleviate poverty take into account market forces and individual choice to direct any help to its most valuable objective: lift the poor from below the poverty line. While market forces are a compelling vehicle to align individual rewards with societal contribution, it is crucial that the physical and social functionings of the poor, as revealed in Chapter 7, are provided with as much support as possible for the poor to take advantage of opportunities. We cannot make the poor take advantage of opportunities; all we can do is come up with ideas to spawn opportunities, provide information about those opportunities, and insist on encouraging an economic and political environment supporting the physical and social functionings of the poor. Finally, the feedback from any of these actions should come directly from the poor as the ultimate judge about their self-efficacy and well-being.

As the famous, Nobel laureate Chilean poet, Pablo Neruda, once said in his poem *Poverty* in the *Captain' Verses*:

Ah you don't want to,
you're scared
of poverty,
you don't want
to go to the market with worn-out shoes
and come back with the same old dress.
My love, we are not fond
as the rich would like us to be,
of misery. We
shall extract it like an evil tooth
that up to now has bitten the heart of man.

We developed a crazy enough solution – using tourism and the demand-pull approach – to join in the work of extracting people from the grips of poverty. Along with Pablo Neruda, we are putting our hope in the future. We have faith in the ability of the poor to climb the social ladder and reach a better life as long as opportunities are provided to them.

## REFERENCES

Acemoglu, D.; Robinson, J. *Why Nations Fail. The Origins of Power, Prosperity, and Poverty*; Crown Publishing: New York, 2012.

Alaimo, V.; Fajnzylber, P.; Guasch, L.; López, H.; Oviedo, A. Behind the investment climate: back to basics – determinants of corruption. In Does the Investment Climate Matter? Microeconomic Foundations of Growth in Latin America; Pablo Fajnzylber, P., Guasch, L., Humberto López, J., Eds.; World Bank: Washington, DC, 2009; pp 139–178.

Banerjee, A.; Duflo, E. *Poor Economics. A Radical Rethinking of the Way to Fight Global Poverty*; Public Affairs: New York, 2011.

Batista Pereira, F. Political Knowledge Levels across the Urban-Rural Divide in Latin America and the Caribbean. *Americas Barometer Insights.* 2011, 68, 1-7.

Birdsall, N.; Rodrik, D. How to help poor countries. *Foreign Aff.* 2005, 84(4), 136–152.

Blattman, C.; Fiala, N.; Martinez, S. Generating Skilled Self-Employment in Developing Countries: Experimental Evidence from Uganda. 2013. http://papers.ssrn.com/sol3/papers.cfm?abstract_id=2268552## (accessed October 23, 2014).

Brau, R., Di Liberto, A., and Pigliary, F. Tourism and Development: A Recent Phenomenon Built on Old (Institutional) Roots? Fondazione Eni Enrico Mattei 2010, http://www.econstor.eu/bitstream/10419/43558/1/640267807.pdf, retrieved September 10, 2014.

Britto, T. Brazil's Bolsa familia: understanding its origins and challenges. *Poverty Focus.* 2008, 15, 6–8.

Croes, R. Tourism and poverty reduction in Latin America: where does the region stand? *Worldwide Hospital. Tour. Theme J.* 2014, 6(3), 261–276.

Croes, R.; Schmidt, P. Promoting tourism as U.S. foreign aid: building on the promise of the Caribbean basin initiative. *J. Multidiscip. Res.* 2007, 1(1), 1–15.

Croes, R.; Tesone, D. Small firms embracing technology and tourism development: evidence from two nations in Central America. *Int. J. Hospital. Manage.* 2004, 23(1), 557–564.

Easterly, W. *The White Man's Burden: Why the West's Efforts to Aid the Rest Have Done So Much Ill and So Little Good*; Penguin Press: New York, 2006.

Ferreira, F.; Messina, J.; Rigolini, J.; López-Calva, L.; Lugo, M.; Vakis, R. *Economic Mobility and the Rise of the Latin American Middle Class*; World Bank: Washington, DC, 2013.

Gobierno de La Republica. Plan Nacional de Desarrollo. Mexico 2013. http://pnd.gob.mx/. Retrieved August 2015.

Lejárraga, I.; Walkenhorst, P. Diversification by Deepening Linkages through Tourism. Paper presented at the World Bank workshop on 'Export Growth and Diversification: Pro-active Policies in the Export Cycle', The World Bank, Washington, DC, 2007.

Paxton, C.; Schady, N. *Does Money Matter? The Effects of Cash Transfers on Child Health and Development in Rural Ecuador*; World Bank: Washington, DC, 2007. [World Bank Policy Research Working Paper 4226].

Pritchett, L. *Let their People Come: Breaking the Gridlock on International Labor Mobility*; Center for Global Development: Washington, DC, 2006.

Schady, N.; Araujo, M. *Cash Transfers, Conditions, School Enrollment, and Child Work: Evidence from a Randomized Experiment in Ecuador*; World Bank: Washington, DC, 2006.

Sprout, R. The Ideas of Prebisch. *CEPAL Review*, 1992, 46, 177-192.

Stampini, M., Robles, M., Sáenz, M., Ibarrarán, P. and Medellín, N. *Poverty, Vulnerability and the Middle Class in Latin America.* Inter-American Development Bank. Washington DC. 2015.

Walker, J. Reflections on archeology, poverty and tourism in the Bolivian Amazon. *Worldwide Hospital. Tour. Theme J.* 2014, 6(3), 215–228.

Zuber-Skerritt, O.; Teare, R. *Lifelong Action Learning for Community Development: Learning and Development for a Better World*; Sense Publishers: Rotterdam, 2013.

## ENDNOTES

[1]See, for example, Batista Pereira (2011).

[2]See Easterly (2006).

[3]For a discussion on the core ideas of Prebisch, see, for example, Sprout (1992).

[4]See Birdsall and Rodrik (2005).

[5]See World Bank. *Global Economic Prospects 2006: Economic Implications of Remittances and Migrations*; World Bank: Washington, DC, 2006.

[6]See Pritchett (2006).

[7]See Acemoglu and Robinson (2012).

[8]Croes and Tesone (2004) illustrate this technological gap in the hospitality industry in Costa Rica and Nicaragua

[9]See, for example, Britto (2008).

[10]See Schady and Araujo (2006).

[11]See Paxton and Schady (2007).Other studies show that the poor do not misuse the cash received and that the cash assisted in substantial and persistent increases in investment, work and income. See, for example, the case of the self-employed program in Uganda examined by Blattman et al. (2013).

[12]We expand the idea proffered by Croes and Schmidt (2007) of the DPA in applying this framework to the solution of poverty.

[13]See, for example, the study by Brau et al (2010).

[14]See, for example, Gobierno de La Republica (2013).

[15]See Ferreira et al. (2013).

[16]The 4.6 persons per poor family is derived from a typical poor family in El Salvador. See, for example, Ferreira et al. (2013).

[17]See Stampini et al (2015).

[18]See Lejarraja and Walkenhorst (2007).

[19]See Banerjee and Duflo (2011).

[20]For further details about EDTC's work, please visit: www.edtc.ac.pg; for details about GULL's work, please visit www.gullonline.org.

[21]See Zuber-Skerritt and Teare (2013).

[22]See Banerjee and Duflo (2011), page 204.

[23]For a discussion on corruption in Latin America, see, for example, Alaimo et al. (2009).

[24]These recommendations are adopted from Croes (2014).

# INDEX

## H



## I



## K



## L



## M